Supporting Parents

Supporting Parents

Series edited by David Quinton, Professor of Psychosocial Development,
University of Bristol
Consultant editors: Carolyn Davies and Caroline Thomas, Department for Education
and Skills and Department of Health

This important series is the result of an extensive government-funded research initiative into how we can best support parents and carers as part of an integrated service for children. Underpinning current policy directives including the Children's National Service Framework, the titles in the series are essential reading for practitioners, policy makers and academics working in child care.

other titles in the series:

Parenting in Poor Environments
Stress, Support and Coping
Deborah Ghate and Neal Hazel
ISBN 1 84310 069 X

Supporting South Asian Families with a Child with Severe Disabilities
Chris Hatton, Yasmeen Akram, Robina Shah, Janet Robertson and Eric Emerson
ISBN 1 84310 161 0

Fostering Adolescents
Research Messages on Placement Success
Elaine Farmer, Sue Moyers and Jo Lipscombe
ISBN 1 84310 227 7

Foster Carers
Why They Stay and Why They Leave
Ian Sinclair, Ian Gibbs and Kate Wilson
ISBN 1 84310 172 6

Foster Placements
Why They Succeed and Why They Fail
Ian Sinclair, Kate Wilson and Ian Gibbs
ISBN 1 84310 173 4

Foster Children
Where They Go and How They Get On
Ian Sinclair, Clair Butler, Kate Wilson and Ian Gibbs
ISBN 1 84310 278 1

Imprisoned Fathers and their Children
Gwyneth Boswell and Peter Wedge
ISBN 1 85302 972 6

Supporting Parents

Messages from Research

David Quinton

Foreword by the Right Honourable Margaret Hodge,
Minister for Children, Young People and Families

Jessica Kingsley Publishers
London and New York

First published in the United Kingdom in 2004
by Jessica Kingsley Publishers Ltd
116 Pentonville Road
London N1 9JB, England
and
29 West 35th Street, 10th fl.
New York, NY 10001-2299, USA

www.jkp.com

Copyright © David Quinton 2004
Foreword copyright © Margaret Hodge 2004

Library of Congress Cataloging in Publication Data
A CIP catalog record for this book is available from the Library of Congress

British Library Cataloguing in Publication Data
A CIP catalogue record for this book is available from the British Library

ISBN 1 84310 210 2

Printed and bound in the United Kingdom by The Alden Group, Oxford

Contents

FOREWORD   7
Margaret Hodge

THE OVERVIEW PROCESS   9

Part 1 Background and Concepts

Chapter 1   The Supporting Parents Research Initiative   13

Chapter 2   Support and Parenting   21

Chapter 3   The Policy Context   33

Part 2 Parenting and its Supports

Chapter 4   Studies in the General Population   57

Chapter 5   Studies of Foster Care   85

Chapter 6   Parenting and Support in the Context of Disability   107

Chapter 7   Supporting Parents who may be Hard to Help   133

Part 3 Cross-Cutting Themes

Chapter 8   Summary and Cross-Cutting Themes   177

APPENDIX A: THE RESEARCHERS' SUMMARIES OF THEIR STUDIES   207

APPENDIX B: LIST OF READERS   259

APPENDIX C: MEMBERS OF THE OVERVIEW GROUP   261

SUBJECT INDEX   263

AUTHOR INDEX   271

Foreword

In the years since the Government took office there has been a major policy focus on the quality and organisation of support for parents and children. This commitment to better co-ordinated services has now been given a major impetus through the creation of the Children and Families Directorate within the DfES, which brings together the good work that has already been done to support families by the Departments of Education, Health, the Home Office Family Policy Unit, the Children and Young Persons Unit and the Sure Start Unit.

From the beginning the Government's commitment to improve services has included a firm understanding that changes had to be based on sound evidence, evidence that came not only from researchers looking at the how well services helped families but also from the views of parents and young people themselves.

The research in the Supporting Parents initiative, which is summarised in this book, amply demonstrates the need for reform as well as the part that research can play in showing what is needed. We see how services can succeed in meeting families' needs and how they can fail to do so, especially through not working together. We also hear clearly the voices of parents and children telling us what would help them and how they would like that help delivered.

The research ranges widely from the lives of families parenting in poverty or under other stresses, through the needs of foster parents and children, of families dealing with disability, to the lives of imprisoned fathers, teenage parents and parents who cannot accept some of their children. Across all these different circumstances the messages are the same. Parents want services to work together to help them and they want services to listen to them and treat them as experts in their own problems.

All those working with children and families need to reflect on these findings and draw the lessons for their own practice. The Government, for its part, will continue to strive to reform services so that they address family needs in a holistic way.

Margaret Hodge,
Minister for Children, Young People and Families

The Overview Process

For many years non-technical summaries of research programmes and initiatives funded by the Department of Health's Children's Social Care section have been produced. The intention is to make the messages from the research useful and intelligible to policy makers, service providers and practitioners. Each overview has a distinctive process through which the overview is produced. Each is written by an academic expert and each incorporates the comments of policy makers and practitioners on the projects and on the overview text. Each overview also tries to ensure that the researchers are happy with the synthesis produced, although the writer of the overview has the responsibility of drawing out the messages that she or he think are warranted by the research.

The Supporting Parents initiative is unusual within this tradition in that it included such a diversity of projects. For this reason it was not possible to convene a group to comment on the projects and on drafts of the overview text. Such a group would have run the danger of being too diverse for discussions to be productive. The following procedure was used instead:

- During the years in which the projects were under way, meetings between the researchers and the policy customers from the Department of Health (DH) were held in order to discuss the emerging findings and their connection with the policy-making process. These meetings were essential to our understanding of different research perspectives and of the research–policy links.

- When the studies were nearly completed, each team was asked to nominate two non-academic professionals knowledgeable in the topic with which their study dealt and involved in delivering services in one way or another. These readers were asked to read the project and comment on its importance to their area of professional expertise. A list of the readers who were able to respond in this way is given in Appendix B. This was an onerous task and we are very grateful to them for the time they gave and the wisdom they imparted.

- A smaller 'overview group' of policy makers and members drawn from the independent and voluntary sectors read and commented on the text of the overview as it developed. Again we are very grateful for the help we received from this group. The members of the overview group are given in Appendix C.

- When the text was sufficiently advanced relevant sections were sent back to the researchers for comments on their accuracy and on whether the important messages had been drawn out.

This programme of research was coordinated by Dr Carolyn Davies of the Children's Social Care Research and Development Division and the academic coordinator, Professor David Quinton from the School for Policy Studies at Bristol University, who compiled this overview.

Part 1
Background and Concepts

Chapter 1

The Supporting Parents Research Initiative

Background and aims

The Supporting Parents research initiative was the first themed research initiative funded by the Department of Health (DH). Although studies around related issues had often been undertaken prior to this, this was the first time that a prospectus for a research programme was set out ahead of time and researchers invited to compete to be included in it. One innovative element from the previous pattern of research funding was retained: the overview of the findings. These 'Messages from Research' are intended to summarize the findings for practitioners and policy makers in non-technical language. The most recent overviews have dealt with child protection, residential care and adoption. This one on the Supporting Parents initiative is the latest in this line of influential research summaries.

This initiative was first thought of in 1994 during the International Year of the Child. The idea behind it was to broaden research in children's social care to consider how all parents might be helped to look after their children well and to move away from an emphasis on more marked family and parenting problems. One idea was that there might be many family and community supports that could be 'mobilized' to this end. Another was that the research programme should be opened up to a wider range of issues and researchers.

This new approach certainly caught the attention of the research community. The prospectus encouraged applications on a wide range of parenting issues. This attracted over 450 outline proposals on diverse topics, from parenting in poverty, to studies of disabled parents and children, step-families, foster carers, teenage parents, imprisoned fathers and parents who reject their children, as well as studies of services and the relationships between them. This was by far the largest set of initial proposals for any research programme funded under the themed initiative approach to date.

This very large number of proposals was whittled down to a shortlist of 32 studies and then to 11 funded projects. To these were added three already commissioned studies on parenting. The selection process involved independent academic refereeing of the methodological quality of the studies and internal and external assessments by policy makers and practitioners on the importance of the proposed studies to policy generally and to the themes of the initiative in particular. Both requirements had to be satisfied.

The diversity in the proposals is reflected in the 14 studies within the initiative. Inevitably, many still involved parenting problems that need support from services, such as those of parents and children with disabilities, foster carers or fathers in prison. On the other hand, the intention to widen the focus of research was successfully addressed through studies of parenting in poor environments, of children's behaviour problems in the community and of patterns of normal childhood injuries and step-parenting. The issue of breadth was taken further by the expectation that all the studies would look at the relationship between formal and informal support – that is, at the whole 'ecology' of support and not just at what services did.

One important consequence of this change in thinking was the shifting of the discussion away from one in which services were seen as *interventions* to one in which services are seen as part of a range of *supports* that parents might draw on to help them cope with and look after their children in their own way.

The overall aims of the initiative were:

- to explore the range of supports that parents find effective
- to discover what parents who are having difficulties lack in the way of support
- to see how support might be better mobilized.

History

The first study in the programme began in the autumn of 1996 and the last one reported in the autumn of 2002. The period between these dates has been marked by a great deal of activity in policy and practice around parenting and parenting support. These policy changes have ranged from those affecting parenting and parents' resources generally – such as tax credits or changes in benefits – to initiatives intended to change parents' and children's behaviour – such as parenting orders or parent training – to specific policies and guidance around helping and supporting parents with specific problems – such as children's disabilities.

Many of the studies in this initiative were under way before these policy changes were implemented and many fed into the reshaping of policy. Do studies done before these new policies were introduced have new messages to deliver on supporting parents? Well, of course they do. Not only because they have things to say on whether policies will be effective and on where there are gaps but also because of the breadth of the programme of work. What is innovative and important about this is that it highlights issues that are common for parents with a wide variety of parenting concerns and circumstances. For this reason the studies have a great deal to say about how we think about support and thus frame the policies that will be helpful to parents.

Of course, not all parenting problems or ways of supporting parents are included in the initiative. There were, for example, no studies that looked at the effects of changes in taxation, benefits or incentives on parents' ability to cope. Nevertheless, the studies still have implications for these policies because they begin to tease out the extent to which parenting difficulties arise through hardship, rather than through family or personal problems that need a service response.

The scope of this overview

The expansion of policy and practice initiatives around parenting has been paralleled by a spectacular increase in the amount of debate and discussion in the academic literature on parenting and the effects of support upon it. For example, between 1996 and 2002, when this initiative started and finished, there were 403 academic papers on the Bath Information and Data Services (BIDS) database concerning parenting and support, not to mention many books and reports. Luckily, Messages from Research overviews are not intended to be reviews of the literature, even in those areas directly addressed by particular studies. The purpose of the overview is to draw out practical messages from the funded studies. References made to research outside the initiative will be selective and intended to illuminate particular issues rather than to weigh evidence.

A second restriction in this overview is that the presentation and discussion is confined to what the studies have to say about support. By its nature, as well as because of the researchers' academic and theoretical interests, research in these areas produces a large number of findings and speculations. Readers interested in the whole gamut of these will need to track down the researchers' publications. Publications known about at the time of writing are listed along with the researchers' own accounts of their studies in Appendix A.

Chapters 4 to 7 discuss the studies in four related groups. These are outlined below in order to give the flavour of the initiative. Each chapter is intended to draw out issues for readers interested in particular areas. Chapter 8 is concerned with themes and issues that go across the studies. In our view it is important to read this chapter as well the chapters on specific studies if the insights on support that the initiative can provide are to be appreciated. Because of the diversity of the studies a brief profile of each is given below, to give readers an idea of how varied they are. A fuller account of each study and its authorship, prepared by the researchers, is given in Appendix A.

A brief overview of the studies

Studies in the general population

This first group of studies is important because they all involve families recruited from parents in general, not from those coming to services for one reason or another. For this reason they tell us a lot about how common parenting stresses and problems are and how problems and family circumstances link together. This 'general population' information is essential if we are to understand the lives and needs of families who have problems that need more help from services. These studies are also the key to knowing whether the hope that there are resources in the family and community that might help parents could be realized.

The first three studies are concerned with particular kinds of family circumstances or events: poor environments, step-parenting and children's injuries. The other two, while still taken from the 'general population', were recruited because parents were finding it hard to deal with their children's behaviour.

1. STUDIES OF FAMILY CIRCUMSTANCES AND EVENTS

Parenting in poor environments (Policy Research Bureau)

This was a large-scale study of a representative sample of 1754 parents in Great Britain living in areas with many disadvantages that are known to be associated with parenting difficulties. The statistical findings from this large sample were illuminated by a qualitative study of 40 families who faced many adversities. Parents were asked about what help they were able to draw on from their families and friends, what services they used and what they thought of them, and what strategies they used to help them cope with caring for their children in these very poor circumstances.

Step-children and step-parenting (Thomas Coram Research Unit)

In this study a representative community sample of step-families was studied by questionnaires to parents and by interviews. A sample of step-families that had been established from one to four years was identified from 9776 questionnaires completed by parents through primary schools. Parents, step-parents and children were interviewed in 184 new step-families. The study dealt with children's and parents' experiences and adaptations to their new families. It was one of the three DH-funded studies added to the initiative.

A normative study of children's injuries (Thomas Coram Research Unit)

We know surprisingly little about the pattern of day-to-day injuries in children. This study documented these through diaries and interviews with a community sample of 671 mothers of children aged eight or under. The interest was in the social context of injuries as well as the relationship between the frequency of minor injuries and of more serious ones. Understanding the patterning of injuries is important information for service providers trying to understand how injuries arise and what the meaning of different patterns may be. This was also a study added to the initiative.

2. STUDIES OF PARENTS WHO FIND THEIR CHILDREN'S BEHAVIOUR DIFFICULT

Strategies with young children with behaviour problems (University of Southampton)

This was a follow-up study of families in the New Forest/Southampton area. They had been surveyed when the children were three and again when they were eight to assess emotional and behavioural problems. Four groups of 30–40 children were followed up when the children were 11: those with no problems previously, those with problems at three but not at eight, those whose problems began after they were three and those with problems at both earlier points. The study focused on the parenting approaches, family circumstances and family and service supports associated with the onset, cessation and persistence of problems.

A community-based programme for parents of children with behaviour problems (Institute of Psychiatry and University of Oxford)

This study uniquely combined well-established approaches to helping parents with two factors known to be associated with behaviour problems: parent training using the Webster-Stratton method and work to support the development of literacy. The intention was to develop a programme that could be taken forward in community initiatives. Fifty-eight families with difficult children were identified from parents' and teachers' questionnaires and randomly assigned to the intervention, and 46 to support through a telephone helpline. Measures on the children's behaviour, adjustment and reading were collected at the start of the intervention and again at the end of the intervention, which spanned three school terms.

Studies of foster care

Supporting foster placements (University of York)

This was a major questionnaire-based study of 944 carers and of approximately 596 placements. A follow-up of both sets of data looked at the factors predicting whether carers continued or gave up fostering and factors associated with stability and change in the children's lives. The second element of the study is discussed in this overview. The analysis of the impact of support focused mostly on the inputs from social services to both kinds of outcome, although family and other stresses were also taken into account.

Fostering adolescents (University of Bristol)

This study looked at the relationship between foster carers' skills and placement stability by the end of one year for 68 young people aged 11–17 in placements intended to be medium to long term. The first aim was to investigate whether carers in placements that lasted 'parented' the children differently from those where breakdowns occurred. A second focus was on the supports that foster carers use and need, and on assessing the part played by support in placement stability. Carers, young people and social workers were interviewed at three months into the placement and again nine months later.

Parenting and support in the context of disability

Caring for a technology-dependent child (University of Manchester)

Medical advances have increased the numbers of children dependent on technology for their survival. This study examined, through in-depth interviews, the needs of 24 parents caring for such children at home and the quality of the services they got. Interviews were also conducted with 44 professionals providing services to the families, and four children. The important issue of the transfer of the children from hospital to home was also studied.

Asian families with a child with severe disabilities (University of Manchester)

Severe learning difficulties are more common in children of South Asian origin than in any other ethnic group in the UK. Quantitative data were collected from 136 families from India, Pakistan and Bangladesh. These data were supplemented by 26 qualitative interviews. This study looked at the process of the identification of the problem and how parents were told about it, and at the relationship between stress, support, positive parenting and child outcomes.

Formal and informal support for parents with disabilities (University of Leicester)

A central aim of this study was to shift the focus of recent discussions away from 'young carers' to the supports their parents need in order to allow them to continue parenting successfully. It examined support for 67 parents with physical and mental impairments recruited through a variety of agencies through interviews with the disabled person, their spouses and some of the children.

Supporting parents who may be hard to help

Preparation and support for parenthood for looked-after teenagers (National Children's Bureau)

This study was concerned with looked-after teenagers who have children or who are pregnant. The intention was to help in the development of intervention strategies through understanding young people's perspectives. There were interviews with 30 looked-after teenagers who were or who were about to become parents and with some of their social workers and carers. In the second part of the study a comparison was made between questionnaires completed by 67 looked-after young people and a school-based comparison sample to explore attitudes to sex education and views about early pregnancy and its consequence.

The parenting role of imprisoned fathers (University of East Anglia)

Sentencing men to prison also 'sentences' their children to very restricted contact with their fathers and problems in coming to terms with what has happened. This study focused explicitly on the effectiveness of fatherhood courses and visiting schemes in maintaining and supporting the father's role when he was in prison, through interviews with 181 inmates – including young offenders – their partners and some of the children. Particular attention was paid to parents' experiences of visiting and of contact arrangements, reactions to parenthood, links with agencies and views on how the fathering role could be better supported. Staff/agency views were also included.

Parents who single out and reject one of their children (Institute of Psychiatry)

This study set out to understand why and how often some parents reject one of their children – a topic that has received little systematic study. Although the researchers found it impossible to identify potentially rejecting parents in the community they were able to get questionnaire data from 107 health visitors and talk to eight parents. Fifty-three mental health professionals were interviewed about their experience and understanding of the phenomenon. Finally, a study of the identification and management of emotional abuse was done in two social services departments.

The role of family centres in coordinating formal and informal support services (Royal Holloway College)

This study was concerned with the extent to which family centres could, would, should or did have a linking and coordinating role for services for their users. The study was conducted in three phases: first, an extensive questionnaire survey of 559 centres that were part of the family centre network at the beginning of 1999;

second, an intensive study of 40 centres purposively sampled from the questionnaire returns to cover a variety of types and locations of centres. This part of the study included interviews with managers and parents and a postal questionnaire to workers linked to the centres. In the third phase postal questionnaires were collected from 344 centres from amongst the 408 still known to be operating in order to look at changes and to check the conclusions from the earlier sweep.

Chapter 2

Support and Parenting

Support

What do we mean by 'support'?

Before discussing the findings of the studies we need to think what we mean by 'support' and to outline some of the key questions posed by the ideas behind the initiative. 'Support' is a very general term. It's easy to respond to a problem by saying that we should put in more support without being at all clear on what we mean by that or what we want to achieve. The word carries with it implications about its effectiveness, so that the discussion can go round in circles. If we stay at this level of generality the word itself becomes of little use and the idea of support becomes devalued. It becomes a vague umbrella term that can mean little beyond something we do when we can't think of anything more specific.

The problem is that the term implies an action that makes a difference for the better or is at least benign. If we receive support we should enjoy what we are doing more and feel more confident about it. If we find something difficult or stressful we should be able to cope with it better. We may even be able to do something that we thought impossible before the support was given. The idea of support reflects the positive side of social life and social integration. We expect to feel and act better for it and to enable others to feel and act better if we give it to them.

But it is more complicated than that, because support involves both a giver and a receiver. Their views on what is needed may not be the same. A brief personal reflection will remind us that support is sometimes not there when we want it, is not what we want or is even inappropriate or intrusive. We may blame what goes wrong on a lack of support even if this is not justified. We may claim that we did something without the help of others, even if this is not so. If we offer support we may be rebuffed. We may feel ambivalent about what to do because what we think should be done runs counter to the views of the person we are trying to help. We may even decide that something needs to be done against one person's wishes in order to support the needs of another.

Support, even as a good piece of ordinary social action, is complex to assess, to get right and to deliver. This is especially apparent when it comes to supporting parenting, because of the balance required between the neglect of family problems and intrusion into family life, not to mention differences in individual and cultural ideas of what satisfactory parenting is, how and when this needs support and who should decide that.

Mobilizing support to enable better parenting

Those participating in this initiative on 'Supporting Parents' wanted to learn how to help parents parent better and less stressfully. The intention was to explore how this might be done, not only by identifying unmet needs of a fairly obvious sort or by looking at the ways in which services work and are organized, but also by seeing if support from family, friends and the community could be mobilized to help parents.

In the academic jargon services are usually referred to as 'formal' support and support from the family or friends as 'informal' support. Not surprisingly, community groups or organizations often sit in the middle of this classification and their support is called 'semi-formal'. This is a useful way of dividing up support: by whom it is delivered and where parents might look for it.

It is also common for these different sources of support to be seen as having different characteristics and supporting somewhat different things. For example, formal services are generally seen to provide a kind of specialist help beyond the skills and resources of the informal 'network' – another piece of jargon meaning relatives, friends and neighbours – which is seen to give the comfort and emotional support that is not generally expected from formal services.

There is, of course, a large assumption behind all of this. That assumption is that support actually does make a difference to parenting; that it reduces problems or makes it easier for parents to cope. This may seem rather obviously true when the support involves, say, providing practical help for disability in a parent or child. In this case assessing the needs, providing the support and judging its effectiveness may be *relatively* straightforward. But it may be less obvious what kind of help would best make a difference to problems with children's behaviour or social development, because it may be harder to decide what the root of the problem actually is and what should be provided in an attempt to help with it. Moreover, even with disabilities, the impact on parenting often spreads far beyond the immediate issues and inconveniences caused by the specific impairment to an impact on social relationships, education, income and resources, all of which may affect parenting in an indirect way.

There was an additional idea behind the initiative that might or might not be true. This was that policy and practice could find ways of drawing on or 'mobilizing' informal and community sources of support in the quest for better parenting. This idea still has much currency, as reflected, for example, in proposals to draw on the services and expertise of grandparents to help with child-rearing tasks or the recommendation that the kin network should be the first place to look for foster carers.

Finally, there is the equally big question of what we mean by 'parenting'. If we are to support it and intervene in it, it is as well to be clear what we think it is. Otherwise we shall not be able to be clear about what we are trying to support and to know whether our support has had the desired effect or not. A discussion of the concept of parenting is given later in this chapter. First we outline how the researchers conceptualized support.

How the studies conceptualized support

A useful discussion of the notion of support is given by Ghate and Hazel in their study on parenting in poor environments. They distinguish the *sources* of support (who gives it) from their *content* (what they give). They divide the sources of support into the three types discussed above: informal, semi-formal and formal. Variations on this way of classifying the sources of support are used in all the studies, although many concentrate their investigations on the provision and effectiveness of formal services of one kind or another. It is worth getting used to the ways in which these terms are used because so much of the academic literature on the topic follows them. Ghate and Hazel describe the kinds of support in the following way.

SOURCES OF SUPPORT

Informal

Informal support is the support given by people's relatives, friends and neighbours. This support is based on two strong principles: first, that we feel it right to help each other as a key part of our relationship (a sense of *responsibility*) and, second, that we do this in a reasonably balanced way (often referred to as the principle of *reciprocity*). These things are part of what a personal relationship is. So we give the comfort and advice and do the practical day-to-day things that help each other get by. Informal supporters are able to anticipate and adapt to needs in a very flexible and responsive way. We know how our families and friends feel and what is on their minds or is making life difficult for them at the moment. Of course, this is rather a rosy picture. Families and friends are not necessarily supportive. They themselves can be what is on our minds or giving us trouble.

The studies bring out one aspect of this grouping of family, friends and neighbours under 'informal support' that is not always reflected in the analyses. It will become clear that support from partners and children themselves is very important to parenting. This 'within household' support is not always separated out in analyses but should be so in future. It is discussed separately in this report wherever possible.

Semi-formal

Semi-formal sources of support include all those community and self-help organizations that are set up to help with particular needs or to give support and advice for specific problems. They include both community-based organizations, such as baby and toddler groups and toy libraries, as well as groups serving more specialized needs, such as those supporting lone parents or people with mental health problems. Some groups may be organized by formal support organizations but run by their members. Foster carer groups are an example of this.

Formal

Formal support is usually provided by larger organizations in response to needs on which service users expect them to have expertise. They usually have a referral and filtering system. The principal formal organizations relevant to parenting issues are those providing health care, social services and education. However, a number of specialist independent service providers offering parent training and family support should also be included.

KINDS OF SUPPORT

Alongside the categorization of sources of support runs a second classification organized according to the kind of support provided. Again, researchers divide the *content* of support into different 'types'. Usually this involves something like:

- emotional support or comfort
- advice
- practical help (usually involving child care in one form or another)
- resources (borrowing or lending things or financial help)
- specialist services.

Not surprisingly, informal sources are seen as providing most in the way of day-to-day 'emotional' support and advice and formal sources as providing mostly support of a specialist sort. Of course, as a generalization this is true but, as we shall see later, it is also a dangerous over-simplification. This is because, as Ghate and Hazel argue, *relationships between individuals lie at the heart of support.* This relationship aspect will become clear as we discuss what parents say about what they especially value in the ways they are treated by those providing support.

This emphasizes the point that understanding 'support' includes understanding how being given support makes people feel. Of course, support may be effective

even if it is not given in a friendly and respectful way. We might try to decide empir-
ically whether the manner of delivery makes a difference to 'outcomes'. However,
even if the way in which support was delivered made no difference, this would be
no justification for ignoring these 'relationship' aspects. As Sinclair and Gibbs
point out, there is a proper and respectful way to treat people, regardless of whether
this makes an intervention more effective. Put the other way round, it makes
nonsense of the everyday meaning of 'support' if we think of services and interventions as supports when they do not fulfil the normal notion of 'supportive behaviour'.

Deciding if support makes a difference to parenting

In order to know how better to support parenting we need to know what works
and how to deliver it. In order to do this we need to have some idea of what we
mean by 'parenting', what aspects of it we are trying to help with and whether
doing so makes a difference.

There are three ways to think about 'making a difference'. The first is that the
support makes parenting more enjoyable and manageable, even if parents can look
after their children perfectly well without it. Parenting with this kind of support
will be good, but even without it will be 'good enough'.

The second meaning of 'making a difference' involves some assessment of the
'outputs' from parenting as reflected in children's development; for example,
whether the children's education is going well or whether they are developing a
positive sense of themselves and who they are, and other outputs of that kind. We
might reasonably conclude that supporting parenting makes a difference if
children progress more satisfactorily in these ways, even if we are not able to be
specific about the ways in which the support changes parenting.

The third way of trying to 'make a difference' concerns making an impact on
issues and problems in parenting behaviour itself. These can range from problems
associated with emotional and behavioural difficulties or delays in intellectual
development, to more serious concerns about parenting that puts the children at
risk of 'significant harm'. Of course, this does not always mean that the problems
arise simply through the impact of parenting on the children's development. Parenting problems can arise because of the children's difficulties or there can be a
downwardly spiralling interaction in which problems in one feed off problems in
the other. Making a difference to parenting may need to be dealt with through
working with the children's issues.

Parenting

Behind all these notions around support for parenting is the other very large question: what do we mean by 'parenting'? If we are to support it and to know whether support makes a difference, we need to be clear about what we think parenting is – how and to what extent it is 'socially constructed' and how policy and the media help shape our views of it – and what we are trying to influence by our interventions. If we are not clear about this then deciding what to support and whether support made a difference is not possible.

Parenting tasks, relationships and parenting behaviour

In modern industrial societies the parenting task contains a formidable set of responsibilities. A well-used text on parenting (Pugh, De'Ath and Smith 1994)[1] includes the tasks outlined in Table 2.1.

Table 2.1 Parenting tasks	
Responsibility	*What parents have to do and provide*
Give physical care	Feeding, shelter, rest, health and protection
Give affection	Expressed overt physical and verbal warmth and comfort
Give positive regard	Give approval, sensitivity to signals, responsiveness
Provide emotional security	Consistent and predictable warmth, sensitivity and comfort
Set boundaries	Clear statements on what is acceptable, good supervision
Allow room to develop	Provide and allow challenges within the child's capability
Teach social behaviour	Model reliability, reasonableness and assertiveness
Help develop skills	Encourage learning and exploration, be responsive in play
Help cognitive development	Reading, constructive play, monitor schooling
Facilitate social activity	Facilitate peer contact and provide new experiences

In addition all these parenting inputs must be age appropriate, modified to the needs and temperaments of different children, adapted to resources and circumstances and, nowadays, usually in the context of outside work as well.

On top of all these tasks parenting is also a key social relationship. It has its own special relationship features but is also influenced by the quality and style of parents' relationships more generally. Although it is easy to agree that children need these inputs, it is important to recognize that putting these together as the

---

1   Pugh, G., De'Ath, E. and Smith, C. (1994) *Confident Parents, Confident Children: Policy and Practice in Parent Education and Support.* London: National Children's Bureau.

responsibility of parents is a fairly recent development within industrial societies. One consequence of this putting-together is that parents need resources and help in order to be able to pull it off.

Major lacks in resources or support make this list of responsibilities very formidable. Difficulty in meeting these aims does not mean that there is something missing in parents' capacity to do the job. Most of us as parents are usually good at some of these things and less good at others. Parenting is something that parents *do*, not something that parents *have*. Variation in what they do reflects what they have in the way of resources and support as well as their skills and characteristics. Indeed, it commonly reflects the interaction between the two. This is what is meant by the 'ecology' of parenting.

Key points about parenting

Parenting is something that parents *do*. It is not something they *have*. It involves:

- *Tasks* such as giving physical care, boundary setting and teaching social behaviour
- *Behaviours* such as responsiveness, affection and positive regard
- *Relationship qualities* such as giving emotional security and secure attachment

What parents do is influenced by many things, including:

Genetics, *childhood experiences* and *current circumstances* – especially *poverty*, their own *mental* and *physical resilience* and the *support* they get

Parents are the main organizers of their own support

The ecology of parenting

It is hard to imagine much dissent nowadays from the proposition that parenting has to be seen in an ecological context. Ever since Bronfenbrenner[2] set out the ecological notion with respect to child development and Belsky[3] and others developed it with specific reference to parenting, the ecological perspective has predominated.

---

2   Bronfenbrenner, U. (1979) *The Ecology of Human Development.* Harvard, MA: Harvard University Press.

3   Belsky, J. (1984) 'The determinants of parenting: a process model.' *Child Development 55*, 83–96.

The essence of the argument is that all sorts of ecological influences have an impact on parenting, especially material resources and the quality of relationships with partners, relatives and friends. These influences do not just go in one direction. Our own behaviour influences our relationships as well as the other way round. In addition there are those social and structural forces that we cannot influence, such as labour market changes or policies on benefits and taxation.

What this view emphasizes is that 'parenting' – what parents actually do with and for their children – arises from a very wide variety of influences. Some of these derive from parents' genetic characteristics, others from the consequences of their experiences of being parented, and others from their current mental and physical health. However, the translation of these differences into 'parenting problems' is substantially influenced by the circumstances in which they are trying to look after their children.

Some aspects of the ecology of parenting are beyond our control but others are not. The availability of support is not just a matter of happenstance. Support needs to be drawn on, organized, balanced and – in the case of informal support – reciprocated. As we shall see, being supported requires a lot of activity on the part of parents. Support does not just arrive, it has to be sought as well. In this the parents, and especially the children's mother, are the prime coordinators of support and services for the parenting task.

Later in this overview we will emphasize the value of 'key workers' in many formal services. At this point it is important to understand that *the great majority of*

Key points about support

We need to be precise about what we mean by 'support'

The whole pattern ('ecology') of support is a complex matter; it's not always easy to decide what influences what

The effect of support is influenced by the receiver as well as by the giver

Formal services are part of the ecology of parenting

Academics distinguish between:

- support from family and friends (*informal* support)
- support from community and self-help organizations (*semi-formal* support)
- support from services with special expertise (*formal* support)

These different kinds of support are used for different things but:

Relationships are at the heart of support

parents function as their own key worker: they analyse and diagnose problems, decide on actions, make contact with appropriate sources of support, try to articulate their needs to those sources and try to resist handing control to others or incurring obligations that cannot be reciprocated.

The ecological perspective forces us to recognize the complicated and often reciprocal relationships between all the influences on parenting. It follows from this that the best ways of supporting parenting may be far from obvious. For example, is it better to focus on the specifics of parenting or to deal with mental health problems that may be causing the parenting difficulties? Alternatively, is the best policy option to tackle the features of social structure and distribution of resources that are correlated with parenting difficulties?

Services as part of the ecology of parenting

There is one further point to make and that is to emphasize that formal services should be seen as *part* of the ecology of parenting, not just as something trying to influence it. Services have to take the ecological view as well. To use current jargon, they have to be 'holistic'. If this is not done then tackling one problem – say, adult mental health difficulties – may be ineffective, because tackling that problem should mean tackling related ones, such as poverty or the children's behaviour. The benefits of inter-agency working are now usually part of discussions on the delivery of services, but inter-agency working needs to be part of an effort to understand the whole of the parenting ecology, not just a desire to see agencies work together better.

Key questions

We have discussed above some key issues in the study of parenting and support. It is appropriate to conclude this chapter with some brief comments on which of these the studies address and to mention some methodological issues that readers need to bear in mind when drawing conclusions from the findings. The key questions on which the studies have something to say can be broadly grouped as follows:

1. What do parents and carers want in the way of support, how do they judge the support they get and what issues arise for them in getting it? That is, what are the users' views?

2. What is the nature of the relationship between informal and formal sources of support? Do these complement each other or deal with different aspects of parenting? Does one make up for lacks in the other? Does the informal network itself act as an advocate or key worker? Can the informal network be mobilized to enable better parenting?

3.   Does support make a difference to parenting? If it does, does this operate mostly through improving the 'permitting circumstances' (e.g. by improving housing, by giving grants or by providing short-term breaks) or does it also work through changing parenting behaviours and approaches?

4.   If support does appear to be related to better parenting, how well can we understand what leads to what? Does support genuinely lead to better parenting or does the association arise because those who have fewer parenting problems also get on better with their friends and families and are able to 'work' services better?

Research methods

The field of social research is full of passionate arguments about research methods. These arguments centre around the way data should be collected and the ways in which information should be extracted from them. This may be most familiar in the arguments about 'quantitative' and 'qualitative' methods. This debate extends to arguments about sampling and whether we can generalize from our data.

This brief section is not a review of methodological arguments. It has more humble intentions. The idea is to give a guide on what to look out for when judging the findings summarized in this overview.

Generalizability

All researchers have ambitions to 'generalize' in one way or another, although they may differ on what they mean by that. Whatever their stance, researchers do not really want their findings to apply only to the people from whom they get their data. They may primarily want to 'generalize to a theory'; that is, to add some new insight to a body of theory or to explore whether a theory seems right. Or they may want to generalize to the working of a particular service; that is, they might collect users' views on how the service is working so that it might be improved. They would be distressed if another sample of users came up with radically different views. Or they might want to generalize to some broader group, such as foster carers or disabled parents.

It is sometimes mistakenly assumed that researchers want to generalize to some very big aggregate, such as the population of the UK; but this grand aim is seldom the objective. Researchers in social care usually want to come up with findings that advance our thinking about a topic (generalizations to theory) and/or tell us something about how a service or intervention is working and what effect it is having. They often want to do both. The point is that they usually want to go beyond the data from their study to make points about or suggest changes in other services of the same sort.

Representativeness

If you are to judge whether research is able to make these more general comments it is important to know who is in the sample. There is much esoteric theory around sampling, but the question is easier for readers if they simply look at what data the researchers actually managed to get together and who they were actually able to talk to. It is reasonable to apply common-sense judgements when deciding whether the sample is such that the findings warrant the conclusions the researchers are drawing.

It is usually useful to check who is missing from the sample. These may be the parents with the most problems, a particular disabled group, some groups of imprisoned fathers or teenage parents – to mention just some of the subjects of studies in this initiative – or whatever. Missing data or groups seldom means that no conclusions are possible, but may limit the conclusions that can be made. For this reason, many researchers try to do some checks on the representativeness of their samples.

Who are the data from?

Most researchers would agree that data are stronger if they come from more than one source. Many of the studies in the initiative were able to use one source only, usually the parents themselves. This makes it impossible to know whether, for example, families and friends would agree with parents about the amount of help they had given them. Similarly, service users may give negative accounts of the help social workers have given. This account will reflect their subjective reality, but may be a harsh judgement on the amount of effort the social worker has put in. Interviews with children are usually very revealing, but they often come from a minority of the children the researchers would like to have talked to.

Is there a follow-up element?

It is very hard to get any purchase on the 'direction of effects' without some follow-up element in the study design. We can have much more confidence in whether some intervention or type of support has an effect on parenting if we are able to see how well it predicts parenting over time. Even so, simple follow-up designs are a relatively weak way of doing this compared with, say, randomized control trials.

All these methodological points are worth bearing in mind when reading this overview and especially when making sense of percentage differences between groups of people.

Satisfying all these requirements in research in social care is very difficult. Researchers deserve sympathy when they do not manage to recruit the samples or achieve the designs that would have answered their questions with more confidence. The designs used in these projects are able to answer key questions 1 and 2 with some certainty, although more fully for some groups of parents than others. Some progress can also be made on key questions 3 and 4, although these questions are naturally more difficult to answer.

Chapter 3

The Policy Context

Family policy

The major political parties in the UK all assert the central importance of the family to national life, the development of children, and social stability. The family is commonly characterized as one of the 'building bocks' or 'corner-stones' of society. All administrations bring forward policies intended to support or strengthen the family in the light of their political philosophies, and their views of what the family is and how it can best be helped in its central role. Of course, this involves difficulties in the definition of what a family is and who should count as a parent. This overview does not set out into this difficult territory.

The problem for policy formation is that nearly all people are part of a family and live for much or all of their lives with people who are related to them. Because of this almost all policies, whether directed towards the family or nor, have an impact on it. This is true for taxation, health care, transport, community regeneration, education and pensions, to mention but a few. This complexity inevitably leads to differences in emphasis in different policies and sometimes to contradictions, for example in balancing the needs for support *and* control, intervention *and* independence.[1] The current government has sought to emphasize both aspects of parenting: parents' entitlement to support and good services and their responsibility in caring for their children.

Since this research initiative began there has been a very active period of policy making intended to support families and to make a difference to parenting. Many of the studies in the initiative have fed into this process through interim reports and seminars. The purpose of this chapter is to set out – but not to evaluate – the policies intended to support parents and parenting that have come into play since the start of the research initiative and up to May 2003, effectively a period covered by a

---

1 These issues are well reviewed in Henricson, C. (2003) *Government and Parenting: Is There a Case for a Policy Review and Parents' Code?* York: Joseph Rowntree Foundation, for the National Family and Parenting Institute.

single administration: New Labour. The chapter is primarily concerned with policies intended to support parents or intervene in parenting directly. It is beyond the scope of this overview to take in all the policy areas that impact on the family, such as those focusing on education, health or juvenile justice, except where these have some direct provision for supporting or intervening in the parenting task.

This is still a rapidly changing field with frequent modifications to approaches to support, the consolidation or 'mainstreaming' of different programmes, and the introduction of new structures and policies. Most notable of these, at the time of writing, was the creation in June 2003 of a Minister for Children, Young People and Families within the Department for Education and Skills (DfES) and the bringing together within the Children and Families Directorate key initiatives such as Sure Start and Early Excellence, the Adoption and Permanency Task Force, the Children and Young People's Unit, the Teenage Pregnancy Unit, children's social care from the Department of Health (DH), family policy from the Lord Chancellor's Department (now the Department of Constitutional Affairs) and the Family Policy Unit, formerly at the Home Office.[2] These changes present some difficulties in presentation for this chapter. In general, policy formation will be attributed to the department in which it was located during the period in which the studies were being conducted.

The principles underlying policy on supporting families

Policy on families and parenting has been framed in the context of three broad agendas: the reduction in social exclusion, the abolition of child poverty and the delivery of support at a community level. Allied to these agendas is the conviction that 'work is the best form of welfare' and that policy should seek to make involvement in work easier and more rewarding.

A number of key principles are regularly repeated in many policy documents. These are:

- 'joined-up' thinking in services at a national and local level

- partnership with parents in providing services to meet family needs

- a serious attempt to listen to children's accounts of their views of services[3]

---

2   There are a number of websites that are useful in keeping track of changes. These include the sites for government departments and those maintained by the National Family and Parenting Institute, the National Council for Voluntary Child Care Organizations, the Social Care Institute of Excellence and Policy Watch and Community Care.

3   See, for example, (2002) *Listening, Hearing and Responding*. London: Department of Health, June, and (2001) *Learning to Listen: Core Principles for the Involvement of Children and Young People*. London: Children and Young People's Unit.

- an emphasis on parents' responsibilities as well as their entitlements to support

- enabling individuals and families to make the most of their potential but supporting those in difficulties

- the importance of good assessments of needs and a good evidence base for planning care and developing services.

The intention to be active in this field was signalled early on by the setting up of the Ministerial Group on the Family[4] and key policy units within government such as the Social Exclusion and Teenage Pregnancy units.

An early statement on policies on families and parenting was made in the consultation paper *Supporting Families*.[5] The guiding principles set out above have also been applied to policies for children whose families are unable to care for them either temporarily or permanently: the Quality Protects and Choice Protects programmes to improve services for looked-after children, and the changes in adoption law following the prime minister's review of adoption.[6]

The five broad policy areas set out in *Supporting Families* cover:

- financial support

- support services

- work/life balance

- strengthening marriage

- support for serious family problems.

The issues around work/life balance and strengthening marriage are important ones but not directly relevant to the research discussed in this overview. For this reason they will not be dealt with here. The other areas are much more germane. They provide a useful structure for, and outline of, the policy context for the research, especially if 'support for serious family problems' includes policy developments on substitute family care. Before summarizing the policies brought forward under these headings, it is appropriate to outline some of the mechanisms used in the formation and delivery of policy.

---

4   At the time of writing the Ministerial Sub-Committee on Active Communities and Family.

5   Home Office (1998) *Supporting Families: A Consultation Document.* London: The Stationery Office.

6   All the policy documents and information on units and task forces are easily found on the appropriate government websites. This overview of policy is entirely based on these sources.

Some key principles underlying policy on supporting parenting

'Joined-up' thinking in services at a national and local level

Partnership with parents in providing services to meet family needs

A serious attempt to *listen to children's views* of needs and services

An emphasis on *parents' responsibilities* as well as their entitlements to support

Enabling individuals and families to *make the most of their potential*, but *supporting those in difficulties*

The importance of *good assessments* of needs and a *good evidence base* for planning care and developing services

Addressing the *work/life balance*

Mechanisms of policy formation and delivery

There have been four key mechanisms for the formation of policy and the translation of policy into the improvement of services.

Units

The first is the setting up within government of a number of units whose purpose is to review particular areas, consult with stakeholders and advise government on the formulation of policy, long-term strategy and cross-cutting issues.

Amongst those most centrally concerned with policies related to children and parenting have been the Social Exclusion Unit, the Teenage Pregnancy Unit, the Early Years and Childcare Unit, the Sure Start Unit, the Connexions Service National Unit and the Young People's Unit.

FIVE KEY UNITS

The Family Policy Unit

The Family Policy Unit began life as a key Home Office unit with the purpose of encouraging greater awareness of the importance of family and parenting issues among voluntary, professional and statutory organizations and increasing the public profile of these issues. It also aimed to increase the support available to families by coordinating government policies and programmes to help families and by providing a grant for voluntary organizations working with families, the family support grant. The unit was responsible for the consultation document Supporting Families. The unit is now part of the Children and Families Directorate in the DfES.

The Social Exclusion Unit

The Social Exclusion Unit (SEU) was set up by the prime minister in 1997. It is staffed by civil servants from a number of government departments and external secondees from organizations with experience of tackling social exclusion. Since May 2002, the SEU has been located within the Office of the Deputy Prime Minister and reports to the prime minister through this route. This move brought together the SEU and others working on the overarching strategy on social justice and the quality of life for everyone, such as the Neighbourhood Renewal Unit, the Homelessness Directorate and central leads on local government and regional policy. The unit's remit covers England only.

The Sure Start Unit

Since 1998, when the first Sure Start programme was announced, Sure Start has sought to bring together early education, child care, health and family support to give a better start to young children living in disadvantaged areas. The new Sure Start Unit brings together a number of elements of support to young children and their parents. It works with local authorities, primary care trusts, Jobcentre Plus, local communities and voluntary and private sector organizations to ensure delivery of free early education for all three- and four-year-olds in disadvantaged areas, as well as affordable good quality child care and after-school activities, and health and family support in disadvantaged areas where they are most needed. The unit brings together free early education and more and better child care, with more support for parents through child tax credit, children's centres and ongoing support for Sure Start local programmes.

Children and Young People's Unit

The CYPU was set up in July 2000 to coordinate policies and services better for children. The unit supports ministers in more effective cross-departmental policy making. It is also concerned to promote active dialogue and partnership with children, young people and the voluntary sector. One of its main responsibilities is to administer the Children's Fund (see below), which aims to prevent poverty and social exclusion amongst children and young people.

Teenage Pregnancy Unit

The TPU was set up in 1999 as a cross-government unit following concerns highlighted by the Social Exclusion Unit on the high rates of teenage pregnancy and parenthood in the UK compared with other European countries, and the adverse consequences of early parenthood for education and employment. It was until recently located in the DH and is now within the Children and Families Directorate. Its targets are to halve the rate of conceptions to young women under 18 by 2010 and to increase teenage mothers' participation in education, training and work. The unit oversees the government's teenage pregnancy strategy at national level and supports local activities. It has commissioned projects on the sexual behaviour of teenagers and the effects of teenage births on education and life-chances.

Every top-tier local authority area has a ten-year teenage pregnancy strategy developed jointly with the local health trust and other partners and agreed by the unit. All local authorities receive a grant to support local pump-priming activities, add value to existing services and facilitate effective local coordination.

Task forces

Task forces are concerned with the translation of policy objectives into practice. Their membership is much wider than that of the units and commonly includes a 'diverse group of people from a wide variety of backgrounds',[7] usually people directly concerned with the organization and delivery of services. As with the units, a task force may start work on particular areas of policy and then be subsumed under larger groupings under the general impetus towards more 'joined-up' working. For example, the Children's Task Force, which is overseeing the development and implementation of the Children's National Service Framework, is now also taking forward work on Quality Protects and adoption.

Target setting

There has been an attempt to improve the quality of services through an emphasis on managerial efficiency and 'Best Value' using, as one of the key levers, the setting of targets and, in some instances, the use of 'league tables' to identify service providers who are doing well or not so well. Targets can be broad – such as to reduce the number of teenage pregnancies or to increase the number of publicly funded child care places – or more specific – such as to reduce the number of moves of children within the care system. The use of the mechanism of target setting has been accompanied by the development at the local level of formal plans and subse-

7   Department of Health (2002) *Children's Taskforce: An Introduction.* March.

quent reports to government departments on their success. In some instances the requirement for yearly plans and updates on progress are being replaced by longer-term strategic plans and shorter progress reports.

Information

Finally, there has been much emphasis on the quality of information used in the assessment of needs, planning and delivering services, the evaluation of progress in implementing policy and the dissemination of information. Two major developments were the setting up of two independent agencies: the Social Care Institute for Excellence (SCIE) and the National Family and Parenting Institute (NFPI). In addition, funding was provided to set up a National Parenting Helpline run by Parentline Plus, a new organization formed from a merger of the National Stepfamily Association, Parentline and Parent Network.

Key mechanisms for implementing policy

Units to review policy areas, consult with stakeholders and advise government on policy and long-term strategy

Task forces to help translate of policy into practice

Setting *targets* to improve managerial efficiency and deliver best value

Information:

- improving the quality of information used in the assessment of needs and for planning and delivering services
- improving the quality of information to parents

Specific policies to support parents and families

We can now outline, under the three headings from Supporting Parents discussed above, some of the specific policies that impact on parenting or are specifically designed to help parents: financial support, support services and support for serious family problems.

Financial support

Policies to support families through taxation and benefits involve both universal allowances and specific allowances or credits designed to help poorer parents. The commitment to end child poverty is a driving force behind these policies. But alongside this is a strongly held view that work is the best way out of poverty. The policies reflect the twin aims of providing support and encouraging responsibility.

BENEFITS

Direct financial support for parents has come through the universal child benefit and through the targeted tax credits, the children's tax credit and the working families tax credit.[8]

Child benefit, retained as a universal benefit in line with the 1997 New Labour manifesto, increased by 26 per cent in real terms between 1997 and 2000 and is intended to be up-rated 'at least in line with prices'.

The children's tax credit was introduced in April 2001 and is worth £520 a year for approximately five million poorer families. It was increased in April 2002 when it was doubled to £20 a week in the year after a child's birth.

The working families tax credit provides a guaranteed minimum income for a family with one child and one adult working earning a minimum wage of £225 a week (Home Office 2001).[9] Nearly 1.3 million families (2.5 million children) are on average receiving £35 a week more than under the benefit it replaced (Family Credit). There was a further increase of £2.50 a week from June 2002.

Three other financial supports can be mentioned here. The first is the one-off, non-refundable *Sure Start maternity grant* to help poorer families with the costs of caring for a new baby. From April 2002 it was set at £500, five times the grant when the programmes were first introduced in 1997. *Education maintenance allowances* are to be introduced from 2004. Models for their delivery are currently being piloted. They will provide up to £40 per week for young people during term-time. Finally, the *baby bond*, a new Child Trust Fund, provides for every child born from September 2002, with an initial endowment at birth of £250 rising to £500 for children in the poorest third of families.

Family support grants are administered by the Family Policy Unit and provide funds to many voluntary organizations working with families on parenting issues. The funding includes core support for the National Family and Parenting Institute as well as support for organizations undertaking parenting work, training facilitators and managers, providing parenting education and delivering support and services to parents.

8   These credits were replaced in April 2003 by the child tax credit and working tax credit.
9   Home Office (2001) *Supporting Families Progress Report.* Unpublished manuscript.

FINANCIAL RESPONSIBILITIES

Parental responsibilities have been emphasized in the New Deal for Lone Parents and the Child Support Agency.

The philosophy behind the *New Deal for Lone Parents* (NDLP) involves a view that 'work is the best form of welfare' (Gordon Brown 1999).[10] The philosophy unites the elements of support and responsibility, with tax credits used as way of 'ensuring that work pays'. The NDLP is primarily aimed at lone parents whose youngest child is of school age. Parents receive an interview at a job centre and support with training, access to child care and help in finding a job.[11]

The theme of responsibility has most notably been carried forward through the intention to make non-resident parents contribute to the support of their children through the *Child Support Agency*. Problems caused initially through the complexities of definitions and of administration, as well as issues of equity, resulted in a simplified scheme in the Child Support and Pensions and Social Security Act 2000, with a liability for the non-resident parent based on a percentage of income with some strictly prescribed exceptions and tougher sanctions for non-compliance.

Support services

NATIONAL INFORMATION AND ADVICE AGENCIES

The first element in the development of support involved plans for improving information and support for parents. The improvements in information involved the creation of the National Family and Parenting Institute and providing funding for a National Parenting Helpline to provide information and advice to parents. In addition, the Social Care Institute for Excellence was set up to put together high quality information on which to base the planning and delivery of services. In addition, a Parenting Fund was announced in the 2002 spending review, which will make available £25 million over three years in order to develop a network of parent support.

The *National Family and Parenting Institute* (NFPI) was set up in 1999 as an independent charity to develop and improve support for parents, provide advice and information on family policy, parenting, family relationships and the needs of children. Parentline Plus also undertakes research on the concerns of families and the support available to them, tries out new ways of providing support, brings together organizations and knowledge, works to influence policy makers, provides information directly to families and runs public campaigns.

10   Brown, G. (1999) 'A scar on the nation's soul.' *Poverty 104*, 8–10.

11   Home Office (1998) *Supporting Families: A Consultation Document.* London: The Stationery Office.

The National Parenting Helpline, run by Parentline Plus, was set up to give information to parents on parenting issues and problems. It is a free, confidential, 24-hour helpline for anyone concerned about their children and also gives information on parenting courses where parents can meet to get support. It also works with local and central government on initiatives to increase support for families, works to ensure that families have access to good quality information and works on projects to support children and adults when they are going through family changes such as divorce and separation.

The *Social Care Institute for Excellence* (SCIE) assembles 'knowledge about how to make social care services better'. SCIE has three main functions: to review knowledge about social care, to develop practice guides and other resources based on that knowledge and to promote the use of practice guides in policy and practice. As part of this, SCIE feeds into inspection and evaluation of social care services, works with education and training organizations and establishes partnerships with user-controlled organizations and with agencies in other sectors.

COORDINATED COMMUNITY-BASED SERVICES

The second element in providing support involved the setting up of a number of community-based programmes and initiatives. These developments were part of the agenda to reduce social exclusion, support for welfare-to-work policies and improve the life-chances of children. A feature of all of these initiatives was the attempt to develop partnerships between agencies to tackle problems at a local level. The most important of these are outlined below.

Early Years Development and Childcare Partnerships (EYDCP) were set up after the 1997 General Election as Early Years Development Partnerships and became Early Years Development and Childcare Partnerships in 1998, when their remit was extended to include child care for children aged 0–14. Their role is to find out what child care provision already exists in their area, to ask local parents and children about their child care needs and to produce a written plan describing how they will expand existing supply of child care provision to meet demand. Partnerships were required to submit yearly plans to the DfES, a requirement that has now changed to that of a three-year strategic plan and a shorter annual implementation plan.

The DfES *Neighbourhood Nurseries Initiative* gives financial incentives intended to stimulate the creation of 45,000 new full-time day care places for children from birth to school age in communities where there is currently little or no provision. It is the principal route through which the delivery of the *National Child Care Strategy* is planned. This strategy includes an ambitious plan to increase the availability of publicly funded child care from that available to 2 per cent of under threes in 1998, to 1.6 million places by 2004. Local authorities, voluntary sector groups and private nurseries are encouraged to submit plans for projects. Neighbourhood Nurseries are often able to take advantage of additional sources of capital funding from regeneration initiatives and other programmes, including the *New Opportunities Fund*, which is administered in parallel with *Neighbourhood Nurseries Initiative grants*.

Sure Start had its origins in an attempt to tackle social exclusion at the community level by developing comprehensive community-based programmes of intervention to tackle the consequences of social disadvantage early in children's lives. These programmes were intended to bring together the work of social services, health visitors and education. The development of the programme began with the identification of models of good practice at the local level fitted to local needs, rather than by setting out a top-down view of how such things should work. Sure Start projects are sometimes but not always building-based. The programme began by targeting on areas of social disadvantage but current plans are for the Sure Start style of integrated provision to become a 'mainstream' way of delivering services. As part of this development a number of related initiatives, such as the Early Excellence centres, have been 're-badged' under the Sure Start banner. The move now is towards children's centres offering integrated care and education and family support.

The *Early Excellence centres* (EECs) programme was set up in 1997, before Sure Start began, to develop models of good practice in integrating early education, child care and family support services, including parental involvement and outreach work, and to provide training and a focus for dissemination. A pilot phase between 1997 and 1999 involving 29 EECs chosen as models of excellence in integrated provision was followed by the commitment to have 100 new centres by 2004, one in each EYDCP area.[12] Ninety-one of these have been set up. EECs offer one-stop shops where families and children can have access to integrated care and education services delivered by multi-agency partners within one centre or a network of centres. They are also intended to raise the quality of local early years provision and disseminate good practice through training and exemplification of integrated practice.

The Children's Fund is targeted at 5–13-year-olds and is part of the strategy to tackle disadvantages and inequalities that derive from child poverty and social exclusion. It helps develop multi-agency working and brings together *preventative* services that work in partnership with the voluntary, community and statutory sectors and with service users. The CYPU encourages developments that identify children and young people with early signs of difficulty and provide them and their families with support to help them meet their potential. The intention is to build the capacity for support within local communities that involves children, young people and their parents in planning and developing services.

12 *Building on Success*. Green Paper, February (2001).

Funding is distributed through local partnerships that decide which projects to fund in their area, following local consultation that includes children and young people. This emphasis on local decision making makes the fund flexible in meeting the needs of diverse and changing communities, adding value to other services and working across boundaries of home and school. As a preventative programme, there is an emphasis on supporting children within the home and the school, and in the wider community as well. There is also a strong focus on supporting parents both in their parenting and with other issues, including domestic violence, counselling, family support and health awareness.

In the 2002 spending review the government announced the creation of a new *Parenting Fund*, which is intended to develop parenting support by building on existing voluntary and community sector approaches to support parenting and parenting organizations. The fund provides an opportunity for the government and the voluntary and community sector to continue to develop constructive approaches to working together. It is also a mechanism to increase the capacity of the sector through providing seed funding for an expansion in parenting support. At present the implementation of the fund is in a consultation phase.

Support for serious family problems

The third element from Supporting Parents central to this research initiative is that concerned with support for serious family problems. This covers a variety of rather different policies. Supporting Parents highlighted domestic violence, youth offending, teenage pregnancy and problems with children's learning (predominantly truancy, unnecessary exclusion, misbehaviour and under-performance).

DOMESTIC VIOLENCE

The inclusion of domestic violence in the list signalled recognition of the seriousness of this topic. The thrust of the policy approach has been to promote awareness of the problem at both a professional and a community level and to make perpetrators aware of how serious a crime it was considered to be. A further element in the programme includes better recording of incidence, developing support for victims and the development of preventative strategies. Proposals including improving the legal protection for victims have been brought forward in the recent Home Office consultation paper *Safety and Justice.*[13]

13   *Safety and Justice: The Government's Proposals on Domestic Violence.* Home Office Consultation Paper, June (2003).

PROBLEMS WITH CHILDREN'S LEARNING

The SEU's report on truancy and exclusion set out a framework for action involving a partnership between parents, communities, the police and social services. The aim was to reduce truancy and unnecessary exclusion by a third by 2002. The partnership with parents was to be taken forward through *home–school agreements*, intended to set out the responsibilities of each. With regard to behaviour problems, local education authorities (LEAs) were required to develop *behaviour support plans*, which give parents information on sources of help but also remind them of their responsibilities. LEAs in England were expected to have *parent partnership schemes* to work with parents of children with special educational needs. The most useful way to see how these plans and schemes are developing is to go to the websites of the various authorities and organizations that have information on what these approaches mean on the ground.

YOUTH OFFENDING

The policies on juvenile offending involve enabling parents to fulfil their parenting responsibilities and getting their offending offspring back on track. In addition, local *Youth Offending Teams* (YOTs) are intended to work with young offenders to reduce the likelihood of further offences. Three other initiatives involved setting up *Youth Action Groups* to involve young people in finding solutions to crime, developing a programme on *parenting education in prisons* and *action on drug misuse*.

The most direct action with regard to parenting behaviour came through *Parenting Orders* – through which magistrates can direct parents to take counselling or guidance to help them set consistent standards of behaviour. For children under ten at risk of an offending career, *Child Safety Orders* were introduced. These provide for a child to be supervised by a responsible 'officer', usually a social worker, and may include specific restrictions or prohibitions such as truancy from school. For these children also, *Local Child Curfews* may be applied to prevent them engaging in anti-social activity. Last, *final warnings* replaced repeat cautioning and ensured that action would be taken to address the offending behaviour.

YOTs are made up of representatives from the police, the probation service, social services, health, education, drugs and alcohol misuse, and housing. Each team has a manager responsible for coordinating the work of the youth justice services. The wide representation on the teams means that they can assess the needs of young offenders and respond to them in a more rounded way, with the intention of reducing the risk of further offending as well as protecting the public. YOTs are accountable to local authorities and the other local agencies and, through them, to the wider community.

Policy developments on children in need, looked-after children and adoption

Policy developments on children in need, looked-after children and adoption have been taken forward through three main programmes: Quality Protects, Choice Protects and the Adoption and Children Act 2002.

Quality Protects

The Quality Protects programme was launched in 1998 with the aim of transforming the management and delivery of children's services to children for whom local authorities have taken direct responsibilities – those looked after by them, and those in the child protection system – and also those who need active support from social services, including disabled children. Policies for disabled children are dealt with in a separate section below.

The main elements of the programme are:

- national objectives for children's social services, indexed by a range of performance indicators and targets

- a requirement to submit annual Quality Protects management action plans (MAPs) and progress reports

- guidance for local councillors in delivering the programme

- a five-year children's services special grant to help take this forward.

MAPs have been a key element in the development of Quality Protects. These give baseline data on the children in the community, analyse the local authority's strengths and weaknesses, and set out their strategic objectives for children's services and the actions proposed to meet them. Payment of the special grant is linked to plans of an acceptable standard, with funding targeted on improvements in the supply of adoptive, foster and residential placements; support for care leavers; services for disabled children; management information systems; assessment, planning and record-keeping; quality assurance systems; and listening to the views of children and young people.

From 2003–4 the requirement to submit annual MAPs has been replaced by a self-audit monitored through the normal Social Services Inspectorate Performance Assessment mechanisms.

Choice Protects

Choice Protects was set up in March 2002 as a review of fostering and placement services with the intention of improving choice and stability in foster care placements. An initial £113 million grant was established to help local authorities improve foster care services for looked-after children in 2003–4. In future the grant will be used to implement recommendations arising from the Choice Protects reviews.

There are two strands to the reviewing process: a review of the *commissioning of services* and a review of *different forms of fostering*. Including children's and young people's views is an integral part of these reviews. Weaknesses uncovered in the commissioning process have led to discussion with authorities on the role of consortia, joint arrangements with health and education, partnerships with independent providers and other agencies, training to support commissioning and contracting, and how to use financial and management information to support commissioning and develop placement choices.

A variety of forms of fostering and support schemes to help fosterers are included in the fostering review. These include *Friends and Family Care, Support Foster Care* – in which carers work with families on their parenting so that the children may remain at home – and *Treatment Foster Care* – an intervention tested in the USA for the most difficult-to-place children. Choice Protects is supporting six trial projects at a cost of £2 million.

In addition to these reviews, SCIE has been commissioned to undertake two reviews of the role of foster care in providing services for children and families. There is a *Practice Review*, which is looking at innovative fostering schemes and setting out principles of good fostering practice, and a *Research Review*, which examines arrangements that facilitate good outcomes in fostering, including 'user-defined' outcomes. The output from these two reviews will be web-based best-practice guides.

Adoption

Following the prime minister's review of adoption a commitment was made to increase the use of adoption as a route to permanent family life for those who could not remain at home and to shorten the time taken for adoption decisions to be made by social services and the courts. The Adoption and Children Act received the Royal Assent in November 2002, after a lengthy passage through parliament.

The Adoption and Permanency Task Force was set up in July 2000. Its purpose is to help councils in securing permanence for looked-after children and support for all parties to permanence decisions, especially adoptions. The task force does not carry out inspections or criticize councils. It works with councils that are performing well as well as with those with more problems, and has developed a range of practice materials.

Policies for disabled children and parents

Policies to help disabled parents and children are given separate treatment here because the research initiative contains three studies on parenting and disability.

Policy developments in this area have involved defining the rights of disabled people as well as taking forward the broad agenda on the integration and delivery of services.

Rights

THE DISABILITY RIGHTS TASK FORCE

The Disability Rights Task Force was established in 1997 to consider comprehensive, enforceable civil rights and the role and functions of a Disability Rights Commission. The task force published its report, *From Exclusion to Inclusion*, in 1999 and the government responded to this in 2001 with *Towards Inclusion*, a document that incorporated the views of disabled people, disability organizations, employers and service providers. These included opinions on legislative and non-legislative proposals on the definition of disability and views on employment; access to goods, services, facilities and premises; and barriers in the provision of services and equipment.

THE DISABILITY RIGHTS COMMISSION

The DRC was set up in April 2000 to work towards the elimination of discrimination against disabled people. The DRC is an executive non-departmental public body and is subject to formal management and reporting arrangements and accountabilities. These include the requirement to agree with the Secretary of State a strategic plan which sets out its medium-term objectives, and to produce a yearly business plan which sets out targets and measures of performance.

DRAFT REGULATIONS ON EMPLOYMENT

Draft regulations to implement the disability provisions of a European Union employment directive have been laid before parliament. The draft regulations go further than the task force recommendations in a number of respects. For example, they outlaw harassment of disabled people, bring practical work-experience placements within scope of the Disability Discrimination Act and ensure that discrimination motivated by prejudice can never be justified.

Supporting disabled people

Policies to support disabled people follow the principles for family support more generally and include a number of elements that directly parallel or are included in other developments. For example, support for disabled children is contained within the Quality Protects initiative and the New Deal for Disabled People follows the principles that lie behind the New Deal for Lone Parents.

NEW DEAL FOR DISABLED PEOPLE

The NDDP is a free voluntary scheme to help those with an incapacity, illness or disability return to work. It is part of the Welfare to Work strategy and aims to close the gap between the skills employers want and the skills people can offer. New Deal 'job brokers' give help with looking for a job and any support or training that is needed.

THE NATIONAL CARERS' STRATEGY

The National Carers' Strategy[14] highlighted the need for legislation to enable local councils with social service responsibilities to provide services direct to carers, including young carers under the age of 18. Following this the Carers and Disabled Children Act 2000 enabled local councils to offer any services that they judge will support carers and help maintain their health and well-being. Councils have the power to supply services direct to carers following assessment and carers have a right to an assessment of the needs of the person cared for, even if s/he has refused it. Those with parental responsibility for a disabled child also have a right to ask for an assessment. The local council must take that assessment into account when deciding what services, if any, to provide for the disabled child and the family.

DIRECT PAYMENTS

Local councils are given the power to make direct payments to 16- and 17-year-old carers and disabled young people as well as to those with parental responsibility for a disabled child. The purpose of these payments is to increase flexibility in meeting assessed needs and to give carers more control over their lives.

DISABILITY PROVISION IN QUALITY PROTECTS

The Quality Protects programme includes services for disabled children. Four QP objectives are especially relevant. These deal with the role of education and health care in improving life-chances, ensuring that the children's social needs are met and regularly assessed and reviewed, timely service responses and the active involvement of users and carers in planning services and packages of care. Each objective has an attached set of areas or actions through which the objective is to be achieved.

VALUING PEOPLE

The White Paper *Valuing People* (Department of Health 2001) outlined a strategy for improving services for people with learning disabilities across the whole age

14   Department of Health (1999) *Caring about Carers: A National Strategy for Carers.*

range. *Valuing People* is set in the context of four principles: enforceable civil rights, promoting independence, choice – such as a say in where to live, what work to do and who will look after them – and inclusion. In this context 'inclusion' means being enabled to do everyday things, make use of mainstream services and be fully part of the local community.

As with Quality Protects the programme has a set of formal objectives and a set of mechanisms for achieving these, including a National Citizen Advocacy network, the extension of direct payments, improving information through a National Learning Disability Information Centre and Helpline, the development of Health Action Plans, introducing the Learning Disability Awards Framework (April 2001) to provide a new route to qualification for care workers, giving local councils responsibility for establishing new Learning Disability Partnership Boards within Local Strategic Partnerships and with joint investment plans, establishing a Learning Disability Task Force, and setting up a national Implementation Support Team and an Implementation Support Fund.

SPECIAL EDUCATIONAL NEEDS ACTION PROGRAMME

A programme for supporting children with special educational needs (SEN) and their parents was set out following a Green Paper and a consultation exercise.[15] The main elements of this programme are to provide high quality early years education and child care, including support for parents; to encourage earlier identification of difficulties and early intervention; that every LEA should have a parent partnership scheme, and that every parent should have access through these schemes to advice from an independent parental supporter; that LEAs should develop conciliation arrangements for dealing with disputes; and that arrangements for involving children in the SEN process should be strengthened.

Policy developments bringing together work to support parents and children

At the beginning of this chapter we pointed out the current emphasis on bringing together a range of programmes and initiatives in a more efficient and coherent way and the translation of special initiatives into mainstream provision. The creation of a Minister for Children, Young People and Families, and the gathering together of many units and programmes previously located in a variety of departments, is part of this process – notably the collecting together of community-based programmes designed to promote integrated services under the Sure Start banner. Two other

15   DfES (1998) *Excellence for All: Meeting Special Educational Needs: A Programme of Action.*

major integrating initiatives should be outlined here: the National Service Framework for Children and the Integrated Children's System.

National Service Framework for Children

A Children's Task Force was created in November 2000 to take forward the NHS Plan as it applies to children. The purpose of the task force is to help improve the lives and health of children through the delivery of needs-led, integrated, effective and evidence-based services to 'secure the health and well-being of all children throughout childhood and into adult life'. Its most important task is the production of the Children's National Service Framework, which covers children, young people and maternity services.

The purpose of the framework is to tackle variations in care and to improve services by setting national standards. A key element in improving services is seen to be the breaking down of professional boundaries and the development of partnership between agencies. A second element is the setting of national, evidence-based standards linked to good service models. The standards are intended to ensure better access and smoother progression in the provision of health and social care services that meet children's needs and involve them and their carers in choices about their care. The standards are developed through External Working Groups (EWGs) made up of experts and service providers on particular areas such as acute services, maternity, mental health and disability. The documents produced by the EWGs emphasize the recurring themes of partnership, assessment, early intervention, families' and children's views, and information for management and users.[16]

CAMHS GRANTS

An important element in the development of mental health services has been the introduction of child and adolescent mental health services (CAMHS) grants, which are intended to ensure that all local CAMHS mental health professionals are available to support services for children and young people within primary care, education, youth justice and social services settings. Grants also support mental health care and consultative advice to social services, schools (especially through multi-disciplinary behaviour and education support teams or BESTs), children with special educational needs, Youth Offending Teams and Connexions workers. It is expected that all local CAMHS should, by the end of 2003–4, have a minimum of four child and adolescent mental health workers or similar CAMH professionals.

---

16 This is well described in Aynsley-Green, A. (2003) *Practical Implications of the Emerging NSF for Children.* www.doh.gov.uk/nsf/children/agreenspeech.pdf

The integrated children's system

The integrated children's system (ICS) takes forward the overall strategic emphasis on information, assessment and individually tailored and coordinated care. The ICS is now integral to the development of the Children's National Service Framework. The system was developed by the Department of Health and the Welsh Assembly Government as a conceptual framework to help managers and practitioners in social services improve the outcomes for the children and families with whom they work. It builds on the Assessment Framework and the Looking After Children materials to offer a single approach to assessment, planning, intervention and review, based on an understanding of children's developmental needs in the context of the parenting capacity of their families and their environmental stresses and supports.

The ICS was originally developed for work with children in need but its scope has been widened in recognition of the fact that all providers of services for children and families will benefit from a common approach to assessment, planning, intervention and review and from being able to share relevant information with each other. The system provides common terms for understanding and describing the developmental needs of children, which can be used by all those who work with children and families. Its purpose is to enable a more effective use of information gathered during assessments in making plans and deciding on the best supports. It also provides the basis for reviewing a child's progress in seven important areas of development, including health, education, family relationships, emotional and behavioural development, social presentation and self-care skills. Use of this conceptual framework across local agencies should help them to work together better and share information more easily. It also helps families understand what information agencies want and why they want it, and judge whether they are getting the help they need.

For social services, the ICS will provide core information about children in need and their families. These data are part of the Children's Social Services Core Information Requirements. The ICS also provides a set of exemplars that illustrate how the information can be collected and used to generate reports for, for example, child protection conferences or reviews. The exemplars are intended to help social workers collect, organize, analyse and retrieve information. The data they collect will constitute the e-social care record required by government by 2005.

Discussion

The extent of policy developments and activities during the time of our research initiative that are related to supporting families is apparent from this brief account of the main features of policy that relate to our studies. The intention of this summary has been to set out the thinking behind the policy developments and the ways in which these ideas have been translated into a range of proposals and initiatives. A central theme across a whole range of policy developments to support parents and children has been the need to move towards much more integrated services that are able to respond to a range of needs and organize their responses on the basis of what the family requires rather than on the basis of what the service traditionally supplies.

This push towards 'joined-up thinking', 'partnership', 'inter-agency working' and other ways of characterizing this process sets a formidable challenge to service providers and managers and a formidable challenge to policy makers in taking this agenda forward. It is easier to set out the principles, targets and mechanisms than it is to bring about the changes, not only because services are hard pressed and often face longer-term training and workforce issues, but also because everyone, from policy makers to 'front line' workers, needs to learn how to bring this off. It is not surprising, therefore, that there is fluidity and reorganization in the composition and attachment of policy-making groups or that the evidence on the ground can point to slow or patchy progress in more integrated working. For example, the national mapping of family services in 2001 by the NFPI showed both encouraging signs and slow progress. Thus, 40 per cent of family support services in their survey had been established within the previous five years. On the other hand, the intention to provide six-week post-natal visits by health visitors has little hope of being realized in the foreseeable future.[17]

Developing and implementing complex policies such as these will benefit most from applying the principles underlying the policies to the process of developing them. The ideas of working together, partnership and the like are powerful ones. Seen from this point of view, policy development should also be part of a process of partnership between policy makers, service users, service providers and managers. It seems clear from the policy documents that the will to do this is there.

---

17   Henricson, C., Katz, I., Mesie, J., Sandison M. and Tunstill J. (2001) *National Mapping of Family Services in England and Wales – A Consultation Document.* London: NFPI.

Part 2
Parenting and its Supports

Chapter 4

Studies in the General Population

Introduction

The studies in this group have one thing in common: all the samples were drawn from the population as a whole, rather than from those who had come to services for one reason or another. Even so, most of the samples were chosen because the families were in situations where parenting might be stretched and where additional supports might be helpful. But this was not a return to a focus on problems. The researchers were just as interested in how parents *coped* and how they thought about the support they needed and got.

Because of this, the studies have much to say on what support parents want, how independent of it they want to be, and the extent to which they see informal and formal sources of support as something they can draw on to help them solve problems on their own. The research also has something to say on how community-based services might reach parents who do not see themselves or their children as having difficulties.

The studies are discussed in two groups:[1]

- First we summarize the three studies that drew representative samples from the general population. The first two of these looked at parenting under stress and change – that is, parenting in poor environments and step-parenting. The third looked at one aspect of normal parenting, the study of everyday injuries.

- The second group of studies are those dealing with parents' responses to their children's behaviour problems. These are the study of parenting styles and children's behaviour over several years and the community-based intervention to help parents with their children's behaviour and literacy.

---

1   For brevity and ease of reading, short ways of referring to the projects are used in the text. This shorthand is given on the first page on which the findings of a project are discussed.

The findings of each study on the kinds of support parents used and what was related to are discussed first. At the end of the chapter the findings are brought together to look at what these studies can tell us about the balance between different kinds of support and whether it makes a difference to parenting.

1. Studies of family circumstances and events
Parenting in poor environments[2]

The study *Parenting in Poor Environments* is an ideal starting point for looking at parenting and its supports. It opens up many of the issues and themes that recur in other studies. It also tells us a lot about the links between formal and informal supports and the relationship between support and parenting. This study has the most wide-ranging coverage of these topics in this group and, for this reason, is heavily drawn on in this chapter. The areas in which the parents lived were chosen because census data showed them to be high in family and environmental factors associated with the maltreatment of children.

Family life and stresses
NEIGHBOURHOODS AND FAMILY DISADVANTAGE

From the parents' point of view the areas were, indeed, depressing. They saw them as dirty, run down, crime-ridden and dangerous, and they were concerned about drugs, burglary, theft and graffiti. But what got them down on a day-to-day basis were the daily reminders of the poverty of their neighbourhoods, such as litter and dog fouling. It was these physical manifestations of their disadvantage that they found most depressing. They did not feel isolated or that their neighbourhoods lacked a sense of community, a finding that runs counter to some academic theories on the effects of poor environments on family life. Indeed, none of these depressing features of where they lived were related to feelings of stress in their lives once family poverty was taken into account.

So the second feature of the study that should be emphasized was the extent of material and social disadvantage amongst the families. Half were living in social housing, 39 per cent were single parents, 55 per cent had been at their current address for less than four years and 43 per cent had no or low academic qualifications. The average[3] household income was low (£7013 p.a.) and 43 per cent of families relied more on benefits than on work. Sixty per cent could not afford

---

2   Ghate, D. and Hazel, N. *Parenting in Poor Environments.* Referred to as 'the *Poor Environments* study' or 'Ghate and Hazel'.

3   As measured by the median.

holidays and less than two-fifths (38%) could afford all of a list of basic requirements including warm winter clothing, a cooked main meal every day, family outings or basic toys and sports gear.

FAMILY HEALTH

Research has consistently documented the strong associations between poverty and problems with health, family life and children's development. Not surprisingly, these associations were repeated here. The parents had high levels of ill health – 40 per cent had long-term problems such as arthritis, rheumatism or respiratory difficulties. One in twelve had mental health difficulties and two-fifths scored high on an index of anxiety and depression (the 'malaise' score).

The children, also, had physical health problems such as asthma and skin disorders, which affected 15 per cent of them. In addition, 15 per cent of the children were rated by the researchers as 'difficult' based on standardized scales filled in by the parents. Strikingly, however, ill health and emotional and behavioural problems were not much higher in these children than in the population as a whole, according to standard measures. This suggests that the parents were managing to care for their children well despite the fact that their lives were substantially more stressed than those of parents in more advantaged circumstances.

CHILDREN'S BEHAVIOUR DIFFICULTIES

The view that their children were difficult relied on the parents' own accounts. These reflected the pressure that parents felt under, especially the combination of low income, having younger and less healthy children and feeling anxious and depressed. Seeing a child as difficult was *not* related to lone parenting, once income was taken into account. Of course, these associations do not mean that children's problems were just a reflection of how the parents felt rather than of the children's behaviour. Children's problems *are* more common when families are disadvantaged and stressed to the point that anxiety and depression affects their parenting.

How the parents saw support and how they used it

Although a priority must be to alleviate poverty and disadvantage, improving informal and formal supports to parents should also have a major part to play. But what should be done? The best place to start is by looking at the supports parents have, what they like and dislike about them and what they find helps best.

SOCIAL CIRCLES OR 'NETWORKS'

The families said that they did not feel isolated and very few of them were. Only 3 per cent did not have a 'social network'[4] of some kind. The average[5] size of networks, including partners, was six. Most of these people lived within ten minutes of the family and were seen or spoken to on the phone on most days. The key people for mothers – apart from their partners – were their own mothers and their female friends. Social circles were somewhat smaller in the poorest areas and for those with the lowest incomes, but for most families they were of a reasonable size.

KINDS OF SUPPORT FROM FAMILY AND FRIENDS

These circles generally got on well with each other and wanted similar things for their children. Parents thought that their kin and friends could be counted on when needed. Most support was around child-minding (42%), help with chores (23%), having a shoulder to cry on (39%) and general advice (25%). Help was lowest with respect to loans of money or care when a parent was ill. There were no differences in the support received by larger families, single parents, poorer parents or parents from ethnic minorities.

Was there a connection between having more problems and having less support? This might be expected to be so if there were a simple link between the two but the opposite was the case. Those who said they had more problems also reported *higher* levels of support. These problems included poor relationships with partners, financial difficulties and stresses at work or with the children. Support was also higher for those with higher levels of anxiety and depression.[6]

Formal services

Most of the input from services around children and parenting came from the family doctor, the health visitor and the school. These, of course, dealt with health and education. Input on parenting and child-rearing were the concern of health visitors, antenatal classes and social services. The researchers also checked the use of more specialist services such as clinical psychology, psychiatry and speech therapy.

---

4 'Social network' is a jargon term referring to people's circle of family and friends. In the past academics were interested in whether the people in the network knew and influenced each other. In the studies in the initiative the 'social' or 'informal' network simply refers to family and friends. The latter is used wherever possible.

5 As measured by the mean.

6 On the Malaise Inventory.

In fact, 46 per cent of families said they had never used *any* services related directly to parenting. Indeed, one-third (32%) said that they had never had contact with a health visitor and two-thirds had not used antenatal classes. These figures may have been affected by people forgetting, but the lack of use still seemed to be substantial. Thirteen per cent had had contact with social services around parenting and a similar proportion with speech therapy. Parents made contact with these services mostly through referral from other services or through contact by the service itself. Self-referral was rare except for advice over child behaviour, or personal circumstances. Once parents were in contact with these services they used them a lot and nearly always saw them as helpful (83%).

WHAT DID PARENTS LIKE AND DISLIKE ABOUT SERVICES?

Parents liked services to be practical, professional and well organized. They disliked services that did not give practical help, whose staff were not understanding, that were badly organized, inconvenient and expensive to use and, most important, that did not pay attention to their needs as they saw them. Services needed to steer a fine course between being seen as supportive to parenting and being seen as interfering. Bad feelings about a service were not because people felt that it was 'not for people like us' but because they felt that they had not been listened to or had been made to feel like bad parents.

Semi-formal support[7]

Semi-formal supports such as play groups, special needs groups and groups for lone parents were used by parents on a 'take it or leave it' basis, depending on how well they fitted with current needs. Use was less common amongst those most in need. Indeed, it was associated with relatively higher family incomes.

Use was also low on a day-to-day basis, but 40 per cent of families had used such supports in the previous three years, overwhelmingly for child care or for children's activities. Use of semi-formal supports was not related to any measures of need except for children's special health problems.

It would be wrong to conclude that these supports were unimportant, simply because regular use of them was generally low. Rather, the pattern of occasional use points up their value in increasing the flexibility of provision available to parents. This is what a high proportion of parents wanted: support that was there for them and could be activated when they needed it. On the other hand, it seemed that

7   It was pointed out earlier that 'semi-formal' sources of support include community groups and schemes and also users' groups, such as foster carers' groups or those for people with physical or mental health problems.

Messages from the study of parenting in poor environments

CIRCUMSTANCES

- The parents had poorer physical and mental health than parents in other areas
- Major stresses arose through low incomes, unemployment and anxiety over finance
- Two-fifths of families had serious problems with housing

but

- Families did not feel isolated and were not
- Parents were remarkably resourceful and had a strong sense of pride in their neighbourhoods

SUPPORT

- Poverty was seen by parents as at the root of most problems
- Lone parents, those with unsupportive partners and those with poorer health struggled more with parenting

but

- Those with more problems had more formal *and* informal support
- Those with more support needs feared a loss of independence

SERVICES

- 46 per cent of families had never used any services related to parenting
- Semi-formal services were mostly used for social contact but were important
- Parents were mostly positive about services

Parents wanted services

- To be accessible
- To be professional and well organized
- To be responsive and to treat them as equals
- To be 'there for them' and available when needed, especially in crises
- To pay attention to their needs *as the parents saw them*

Parents wanted to feel that they remained in control

Services need to

- Be able to deal with overlapping family and parenting needs (be 'holistic')
- Help parents fell in control of solving their problems
- Steer a fine line between support and interference, or 'taking over'

parents needed sufficient energy and resources before they were able to add this to the supports they used. This study is discussed further at the end of this chapter when we consider general issues on the nature and mobilization of support.

Parenting in new step-families[8]

Background

The second study in this group was about family and parenting issues in new step-families, another context in which parenting may be challenged and in need of support. The researchers wanted to see what life was like in families that had come together in the previous four years and had children between the ages of seven and eleven. To do this they found 434 step-families fitting this definition through questionnaires to roughly 10,000 parents. Most of these (82%) were families with step-fathers. They then interviewed the parents, step-parents and children in 184 of these families. They were strikingly successful with interviews with the children, talking to 78 of them.

There are many myths about step-families but relatively little research – especially about life in them – although this is increasing. For example, this study found that at the time of their survey, only 7 per cent of children in the schools surveyed were living in step-families (although, of course, more children will spend time in a step-family at some time during their lives).

The information on how the families came about also challenges many preconceptions. Most (85%) of the couples got together after the mother's previous partnership broke up. The new relationship was not involved in that break. Moreover, this was the first cohabiting relationship for one-third of the step-fathers.

Parents' problems and relationships

Compared with the parents in the *Poor Environments* study these were not disadvantaged families. On the other hand they did have more problems than families in a previous study by this team.[9] For example, anxiety and depression was twice as high (31%) and moderate to severe depression four times higher, although this was not reflected in their self-ratings of anxiety and depression.[10] This may be because the episodes of unhappiness could have occurred over the time of the break up of

---

8   Smith, M., Robertson, J., Dixon, J., Quigley, M. and Whitehead, E. *A Study of Stepchildren and Step-parenting.* Referred to as 'the *Step-family* study'.

9   This comparison was with families in Marjorie Smith's other normative studies conducted with other colleagues at the unit.

10   The Malaise Inventory.

previous relationships, whereas the self-ratings were about how they felt now. There were no differences in the rates of alcohol problems.

Some level of violence occurred in 14 per cent of the new relationships compared with 8 per cent in the previous study, and this was related to violence in previous partnerships. But looked at overall their relationships were better. Twice as many were rated good and half as many poor as in the previous study.

Children's problems and relationships

Emotional and behavioural ratings made on the children were compared with those of the children in the studies used as a comparison. The step-children did not show increased rates of difficulties. Higher scores on these ratings were not related to the history, structure or complexity of the step-families. Rather, they went along with the quality of relationships within the family, the most important being the relationship between the new parents, followed by the child's relationship with its own mother or father. These findings repeat those in many other studies.

The effects of how the children got on with the new step-parent were more variable, depending on what was being considered and who was reporting on it, but better relationships with the step-father went along with fewer emotional problems in the adults' but not the children's accounts. The high rates of adult anxiety and depression caused problems for the children only if they affected relationships in the family, but not otherwise.

Establishing the new family and the problems in relationships that went along with it were not negatively reflected in parenting styles. Compared with the previous study, mothers were significantly less likely to smack their children. This difference was even more marked for step-fathers. On the other hand, they were also seen as having less control.

How did the families think about themselves?

The accounts of the parents and the children reflected common dilemmas for step-families. The parents worried whether they should let the children get away with more while they were adjusting to the new family, and whether the step-father should punish his step-children and what his role in child care should be. There was clearly much uncertainty on what being a step-family might mean. There were hints that families may have shied away from this issue. Seventy-nine per cent said that they did not think of themselves as a step-family. Comments in the interviews suggested that they were worried that to do so might get in the way of them becoming a 'normal' family.

The children's comments were also revealing. Most (86%) included the step-parent in their definition of who was in the family, most referring to him as 'mum's partner or boyfriend' and commonly addressing him by his first name

(75%). On the other hand, 29 per cent did not know what a 'step-family' was. Some said 'he's step-family, we're not'. They generally defined who was in the family with respect to themselves, especially the younger children.

Support

INFORMAL SUPPORT

The study did not collect information on reactions to the new family from the couple's own relatives, nor on whether they got support from them. Many parents had difficult relationships with their former partners and problems over the children's contact with them and with the grandparents. Forty per cent of children were worried, sad, angry or withdrawn following contact with the absent parent and 45 per cent of parents had tense or hostile relationships with him.

Children in nearly two-thirds (64%) of families continued to have contact with the absent parent's family, usually organized by that parent, but also by the parent they were living with (22%) or by the extended families themselves (18%). Over the previous year 88 per cent had had contact with these grandparents and 78 per cent with uncles or aunts.

FORMAL SUPPORT

One of the most striking findings, given the complexities of forming a new family and the emotional adjustments asked of adults and children, was the lack of use of semi-formal or formal support services. Fifty per cent said they had at least one problem associated with getting their new family together that they would like help with. Moreover, these problems were not trivial ones. They included relationships in the family (20% of families), the children's behaviour (18%), relationships between the couple (14%), problems with the absent parent (11%) and legal issues (10%).

Nevertheless, their overall level of contact with formal services, private agencies or self-help and voluntary groups was *lower* than that in two-parent birth families in the comparison study. Only 12 had spoken with lawyers, four with the Citizens' Advice Bureau, one with 'Step-Family', two with formal support services, two with other private agencies, two with other voluntary agencies and one family with friends who were also step-families. Moreover, only three families had sought any advice in the previous year.

Messages from the study of step-families

- These new step-families were not generally disadvantaged

but

- They had more anxiety, depression and other problems than families headed by both birth parents
- 79 per cent did not think of themselves as a 'step-family'
- Children referred to their step-father as 'mum's partner or boyfriend'

THE CHILDREN

- The children did *not* have higher rates of emotional or behavioural problems
- What problems the children did have were associated with poorer family relationships, not with the history or complexity of the step-family
- 45 per cent of children were worried, sad or angry following contact with absent parent

THE STEP-FATHERS

- Were not strongly involved in discipline and worried about what their role as a father should be

THE FAMILIES

- Were keen to establish themselves as families and, maybe for this reason, used formal and semi-formal services for family problems much less than comparison families

---

A normative study of children's injuries[11]

Background

The study of normal injuries was one of the three projects funded by the Department of Health (DH) outside of the initiative funding. It was added to the programme because of its importance in understanding a particular parenting issue. Because it was not initially intended as part of the programme, it only has a small amount of data on support.

---

11   Smith, M., Boddy, J., Hall, S., Morse, C., Pitt, C. and Reid, M. *A Normative Study of Children's Injuries.* Referred to as 'the *Injuries* study' or 'the *Normal Injuries* study'.

We know surprisingly little about the pattern of children's day-to-day injuries and whether particular patterns predict more serious ones. Most of what we know comes from attendance at accident and emergency (A&E) clinics. These data have shown that injuries are associated with family disadvantages and difficulties of the kind that also show up with a wide range of psychosocial difficulties in children. It has been suggested that these associations arise because of differences in parental supervision, but no studies of injuries had looked at this.

The study

The researchers sent letters to a representative sample of 1350 families and contacted about three-quarters of these in person. In the end 766 took part in the study, including 671 who were interviewed about the family and the child's history of injuries that needed treatment. Mothers completed a diary recording injuries – even very minor ones like small bruises or scratches – over a nine-day period.

Incidents and injuries

INCIDENTS

Mothers recorded the number of incidents they knew about – such as tripping or falling or running into things, whether or not these resulted in visible injuries. The 685 children on whom there was this information had 2127 incidents over the nine-day period; an average of three per child, with a peak – not surprisingly – at about the age of two. These incidents were the same for boys and girls and occurred mostly in the kitchen or the living room. Mothers saw about 60 per cent of these.

INJURIES

There were 1345 injuries whose cause was known by the parents and 3042 injuries where the causes were unknown, sometimes because they were only discovered later and sometimes because they happened when the child was not in their parents' care (for example, when they were at school). These were mostly bruises and cuts and most usually on the legs (51%), head (20%), arms (18%) and torso (11%). Injuries to the buttocks, groin or genitals were very rare. About 6 per cent of injuries involved more serious harms such as deep cuts, puncture wounds to the head or burns with blistering.

For seven-year-olds 61 per cent of injuries were on the legs, while for the under ones they were nearly all self-inflicted injuries to the head. Bruises to the torso and arms were very rare for babies. The average number of injuries over the nine days was 8.9, again with a peak at around age two and again with no differences between boys and girls. The data made it possible for the researchers to provide a profile of the pattern of normal injuries for different age groups.

MORE SERIOUS INJURIES

Nearly half (46%) of children had had injuries that needed treatment and about half had been to hospital for these at least once, mostly for cuts and head injuries. Thirty-five per cent of those who went to A&E were examined and discharged without further treatment. Again the peak for these was between the ages of one and two.

Children with more frequent minor injuries had more frequent serious injuries as well and were also more likely to have hospital visits. There were few other predictors of more serious injuries. Predictors of day-to-day injuries went against what might be expected. Single parents reported fewest and better-off married women in intact families the most. White families reported more injuries than ethnic minority ones. The most likely explanation for these findings was that they were a consequence of the complexity of diary recording, which took time to complete.

What influenced the frequency of injuries?

THINGS THAT DID NOT RELATE

Strikingly few of the commonly canvassed reasons for frequent injuries held up. There was no association with the child's health, impairments, independence or emotional or behavioural problems. There was some association with children's clumsiness and with naughtiness, but none with how warm or critical the mothers were nor with their anxiety or depression or life events. However, daily 'hassles' were weakly but fairly consistently related to minor injuries.

THINGS THAT DID RELATE

The most consistent predictors involved the parents' own relationships and aggression. The frequency of smacking was associated with the number of injuries, with non-trivial injuries and with bruising. A poor relationship between the parents went along with a higher frequency of minor injuries, and domestic violence with more hospital visits. Mothers' verbal aggression outside the family was also associated with minor injuries, and mothers' physical aggression to others with non-trivial injuries to the head and torso. This may indicate, along with the findings on daily hassles, that a lower threshold of tolerance and a tendency to fly off the handle is in some way implicated in raising the risk of minor injuries. Fathers' aggression outside the family went along with hospital visits and hospitalizing injuries to the children.

Did parental safety consciousness and the use of safety equipment help?

The use of safety equipment went along with more advantaged social circumstances, but there were more minor injuries and more hospital visits in families that

Key points from the normative study of children's injuries

MINOR INJURIES

- Minor injuries are the stuff of life
- The average number in a nine-day period was 8.9, with peaks at age two and age five
- Parents' attitudes to safety, supervision and use of safety equipment did not relate to the frequency of minor injuries, although supervision and safety consciousness are clearly important
- Parents know about the cause of less than one-third of minor cuts and bruises
- Nearly half of the children had been to hospital for injuries at least once in their lives, mostly for cuts and head injuries

PREDICTORS

- Few child or parent factors predicted the frequency of injuries

but

- Parents' relationship problems and aggression in and out of the home did so

and

- Those with more frequent minor injuries had more frequent serious ones as well

ABNORMAL PATTERNS OF INJURY AT DIFFERENT AGES CAN BE IDENTIFIED

For example:

- Injuries to the torso are unusual at any age
- Injuries on the legs for children under one

had more equipment. The impact of the possible reporting bias discussed earlier may explain this odd association.

Another measure of safety consciousness was a count of the number of safety hazards in the home. Only just over a quarter of households (28%) had no hazards. However, there was no association between the number of hazards, nor of the interviewers' ratings of safety consciousness, nor of the parents' accounts of how they supervised the children and any measure of minor injuries or a history of more serious ones. Nor did it make a difference whether the child was sometimes cared for outside the home (including school), except for the frequency of leg injuries.

Mothers' attitudes to safety were not related to injuries. Indeed, mothers whose children had been to hospital were less anxious than those who had not. Mothers were most anxious about extremely rare dangers and least anxious about common ones. It is, therefore, not surprising that there was no association between the level of anxiety and the use of safety equipment.

Ethnicity

One final set of findings needs comment. These were the ethnic differences in the recording of injuries. Parents from minority ethnic communities recorded fewer bruises and cuts on their children. These differences remained even after other social factors were taken into account. One reason for this might be that it is true: their children do sustain fewer day-to-day injuries. Certainly, the children were also taken to hospital less often because they were hurt. On the other hand, the families might have been less willing to use services and more reluctant to discuss injuries with the researchers, all of whom were white. There may also have been cultural differences in deciding what counted or what showed up as significant because of the children's skin colour. Certainly, there were no differences between ethnic minority and majority families in attitudes, safety consciousness or the use of safety equipment.

2. Studies of parents who find their children's behaviour problematic

The second group of 'general population' studies was about helping parents who found their children's behaviour difficult to deal with. In both studies the families were found through questionnaires filled in by parents or teachers and designed to pick up possible difficulties in children's behaviour. However, although parents' answers on these questionnaires suggested that there might be problems, this did not mean that the parents themselves thought of the behaviour as something out of the ordinary, even though they may have welcomed help and advice.

Effective strategies for parents with young children with behaviour problems[12]

This investigation was a follow-up to an earlier study of children's behaviour in the New Forest area, first begun when the children were three. The researchers wanted to see whether there were styles of parenting that predicted whether problems would not occur or would begin, cease or persist during the follow-up period, according to the parents' questionnaire scores. The questionnaires were repeated and interviews and further measures completed with the parents when the children were ten.

Styles of parenting

The first task was to devise a classification of parenting styles. This was done statistically[13] and came up with two slightly different classifications. Examination of the questionnaire data alone found four parenting styles:

- *Sensitive* – characterized by an adaptive, non-critical, reflective, non-restrictive and warm approach.
- *Consensual* – this involved high agreement between parents and consistency in behaviour.
- *Potent* – a style that was efficacious, nurturing and 'not-dissatisfied'.
- *Firm* – parenting that was strict and not indulgent.

When additional data from the interviews and other questionnaires were included, four other styles were discovered:

- *Engaged* – relaxed but not boundaried parenting, i.e. somewhat indulgent.
- *Disengaged* – somewhat negligent and lacking in warmth.
- *Engaged but strict* – engaged parenting associated with firm boundary setting.
- *Hostile/disengaged* – hostile and aggressive parenting.

A third approach to classifying parenting used the qualitative interview data to identify parenting styles through a thematic analysis of their answers to how they dealt with their children's behaviour. The main themes were about physical punish-

12 Stevenson, J., Sonuga-Barke, E., Thompson, M., Cornah, D., Rayner, A., Sizer, C. and Taylor, G. *Effective Strategies for Parents with Young Children with Behaviour Problems.* Referred to as 'the *New Forest* study'.

13 Parenting style types were derived by factor analyses from the questionnaire data and by cluster analysis from the combined questionnaire and interview data.

ment, the use of reasoning and failure to follow through on threats. Thirty-seven per cent of parents used physical punishment (smacking) and 31 per cent shouting. Reasoning was reported by 42 per cent. The parents admitted to permissive behaviour only infrequently and only 19 per cent said that they failed to follow through on a threat. Parents either gave accounts of physical methods of control or said that they used reasoning; only one person mentioned both methods, although similar proportions of punishers or reasoners used praise as well.

Parenting style and children's problems

The only parenting style associated with *persistent* psychological disorders in the children was the hostile/disengaged type. It was apparent by the time the children were three and was associated with persistent maternal depression and a view that the child had been difficult from infancy. Changes in children's behaviour were only predicted by parts of the first (questionnaire) classification of styles. The disappearance of problems between the ages of three and eight was associated with highly consensual and efficacious behaviours, and the appearance of new problems with less nurturant and less effective ones.

Neither 'sensitive' nor 'firm' parenting styles related to change. It should be pointed out that these classifications of parenting were done from the data collected when the children were ten but the change ratings for the children were based on data collected when they were three, eight and ten. For this reason the links between parenting and change or persistence in children's problems are not strictly predictions. Some of the parenting styles might have been consequences of the children's behaviour and changes in it, as well as being things that changed behaviour.

There was *no* association between any of the styles uncovered in the thematic analysis and behaviour problems.

The conclusion from these different ways of looking at parenting was that a wide range of techniques are used within ordinary parenting without increasing the risk of behaviour problems. The researchers concluded that services to improve parenting should be targeted on those with markedly hostile and disengaged parenting.

Support for parenting

A final part of this study dealt with the supports that parents used and valued. A number of features stood out:

- Although emotional support was more common from family and friends, 30 per cent of families said they received this kind of support from formal sources as well.

- Mothers with mental health problems were dissatisfied with the practical help they got from friends but not with that they were given by the family or from formal services.

- Parents with children with behaviour problems received similar amounts of support as did those with children without such difficulties.

- Health visitors were seen to have an important and valued role, especially by mothers with children with behaviour problems. This support contained both an emotional component and the giving of helpful information.

- Lone mothers felt less well supported by GPs and health visitors than parents in two-parent families and also relied on friends more.

There were no data on how support related to parenting styles or whether it had any impact on the onset of disappearance of problems.

Messages from the study of parental strategies with children with behaviour problems

- A wide variety of parenting styles was identified, but none of these increased the risk of persistent behaviour problems except for a *hostile and disengaged* style

- This was identifiable when children were three and was associated with maternal depression

- Disappearance of problems between three and eight was associated with highly *consensual and effective* parenting

- Parents were generally satisfied with the support they got from services

- GPs and health visitors were valued for their emotional support

- Lone parents felt less well supported by services

Parenting services should be targeted on those with markedly disengaged and hostile parenting

---

A community intervention to address behaviour difficulties[14]

The last study summarized in this chapter is different in kind from the other four. Two were 'snapshot' studies of parenting situations that might make parenting harder to manage. The third was a snapshot of everyday injuries and the fourth a 'catch-up' study of children who had behaviour problems earlier in their lives. All these studies relied on the parents' accounts of their experiences, what made parenting harder and what kinds of help they had or wanted. What they generally lacked was an analysis of the relationship between support and parenting. Did support make a difference to the ways parents parented, as the ecological model would suggest?

The study

The *SPOKES* project took a different approach; it tried directly to intervene in parenting in families where children were showing some behaviour problems. It deliberately set out to see if one kind of 'support' could have an effect on children's 'outcomes' through changing parents' behaviour. To do this, the researchers identified children whose scores on parent and teacher behaviour questionnaires were outside the usual range. They then encouraged parents to join a programme to help them deal with this, whether or not the parents themselves saw their children's behaviour as a problem. Thus the definition of a 'problem' was based on previous research data, not on parents' perceptions. Likewise, the parenting strategies the parents learned came from research findings, not from techniques chosen by parents themselves. This programme uniquely worked both on parenting skills *and* on helping parents enhance their children's literacy. Thus it addressed the two most common routes into disaffected and challenging behaviour.

The study used the optimum method for evaluating the effects of the programme by randomly assigning parents with 'high scoring' children to the programme or to a basic telephone support through a helpline; that is, it was a randomized control trial (RCT). The randomization was done independent of the research team and the assessments of behaviour and of reading before and one year after the intervention were blind to the group in which the children were placed.

The programme

The programme involved weekly sessions conducted at the children's primary schools over three terms. The first term began with six sessions to help parents

14   Scott, S. and Sylva, K. *Enabling Parents: A Community Intervention to Address Behaviour Difficulties (The SPOKES Project)*. Referred to as 'the *SPOKES* project' or 'the *SPOKES* study'. SPOKES stands for 'Supporting Parents on Kids' Education'.

STUDIES IN THE GENERAL POPULATION / 75

work with their children on constructive activities. The second six weeks worked on misbehaviour and on getting the child to take responsibility for his or her actions. This order was deliberate and parents who came to learn what to do about misbehaviour often found the earlier sessions on constructive activities most useful. All parents were visited at home at least once to discuss how the programme fitted into their lives and about any difficulties they had in taking part.

The second term concentrated on development of the child's literacy through activities for the parent and the child around reading. The final term worked on both parenting and literacy to address communication and problem-solving issues.

The outcomes

It was clear that the intervention was very effective. There were highly statistically significant changes for the intervention group on conduct problems and overactive and restless behaviour ('hyperactivity'). The improvement on conduct moved the children from a level of behaviour problems that placed them within the 15 per cent most problematic children in the community to the group outside the 35 per cent most problematic. The intervention produced significant improvements in the way parents saw the children's behaviour as well. Reading outcomes similarly greatly favoured the intervention group with a gain of seven months in reading skills. Over 90 per cent of parents were highly satisfied with the programme. None of the changes in children's behaviour were explained by demographic factors such as family composition, ethnicity or income.

Multi-agency and community working

Gaining the confidence of parents made it possible to develop multi-agency working. For example, links were developed with child and adolescent mental health services (CAMHS) and the local authority's literacy coordinators, and referrals were made to them.

The formal test of the transfer of this intervention from an expert specialist centre to a service delivered by the community has yet to be tested. Despite the effort put into gaining cooperation through positive approaches and parental involvement, about one-third of the parents selected for the intervention did not take part and those who did attended, on average, only 60 per cent of the sessions. The robustness of the findings, given the incompleteness of attendance, is very encouraging. Support directed at helping change parenting practices can clearly have an effect despite the fact that it was delivered to parents in a deprived area with many family and social stresses.

Messages from the SPOKES community intervention with behaviour problems and reading

This was a *community-based* and highly *focused programme* that was:

- tailored to parents' perceptions and needs
- took account of the barriers to participation
- was delivered in a non-threatening community setting

The programme made highly *significant improvements* in:

- conduct problems
- hyperactivity
- reading skills

Changes in children's behaviour were the same regardless of family composition, ethnicity or income

Gaining parents' confidence helped multi-agency working with CAMHS and LA literacy coordinators

Despite efforts, about one-third of those invited to take part in the programme did not do so

BUT

The effects were striking, despite the fact that parents attended, on average, only 60 per cent of the sessions

THAT IS

The programme is robust and had a positive effect in a deprived area with many social stresses

What the general population studies tell us about support

These 'general population' studies have much to say about four important questions asked in this initiative:

- What is 'support' and what do families feel about it?
- Can informal and semi-formal support be 'mobilized' to support parenting?
- Does support make a difference to parenting problems?
- How should formal support services help parents?

All these themes will recur in subsequent chapters when we discuss the findings on foster parents, parents with disabilities or with disabled children, teenage parents, imprisoned fathers and parents who reject their children. Although these different groups of parents have specific support needs, many issues are prefigured in the general population studies and go across all the other groups.

What is 'support' and what do families feel about it?

The good relationships we have with our families and close friends help define the behaviours we value and think of as 'supportive'. Since the *Poor Environments* study had the most complete discussion of informal support we begin with what those parents had to say about that.

Support from family and friends

It is easy to think of relationships with family and friends as the model for what support should be. They have the responsiveness, flexibility and understanding that more formal systems often lack, but the *Poor Environments* study brought out the difficulties and balances in these relationships as well as their positive aspects.

GIVE AND TAKE

The first issue concerned the question of balance in giving and taking.[15] If we accept support we feel that we should pay it back sometime, perhaps in kind or at least in a way that feels equal. If this balance is hard to maintain then we may feel a loss of independence or, indeed, open the way to interference and intrusion.

It is probably for these reasons that the most common forms of support were those that could be 'traded'; that is, those that were easy to give and were inter-changeable, such as child care, sharing chores, and comforting and giving advice, rather than those things that we might be expected to give back in return, such as money or care during times of sickness. Even with the close family, where a kind of trade in support might be less calculated, the receiving of support can still involve a trade with independence.

INDEPENDENCE

The families in the *Poor Environments* study were very committed to maintaining their independence, so, not surprisingly, those most vulnerable to losing it were the most apprehensive about accepting support from family and friends. Moreover,

---

15   Often called 'reciprocity' in the academic literature.

these were parents who saw themselves most in need of help. Thus, those who felt they needed help most had the most negative attitudes towards it; they feared that asking for help was a sign that they could not cope and this weakened the independence of the family.

Support as a relationship

So far in this discussion we have used findings about informal support to highlight some issues for parents. Support from family and friends is important because these people understand the family's needs and can respond to them quickly. But the families also needed to be able to give as well as receive and in this way to retain their independence.

A distinction is often drawn between this kind of support, which is based on personal relationships, and support from services, which is based on expertise. There is an element of the obvious in this, but it is quite clear in all these studies that parents want semi-formal and formal services to aspire to these characteristics as well. The parents in the *Poor Environments* study liked the services they used to be practical, professional and well organized. But they also wanted them to pay attention to their own view of what they wanted, to be responsive to them and to treat them as equals. In the case of formal services the sense of balance and equality cannot come through the parents giving something back to the service. Rather it comes from service being respectful to parents and treating them as experts on their own needs so that they feel they are partners in problem solving.

The need to feel competent and in control is just as important in people's relationship with formal as it is with informal sources of support. Ghate and Hazel's aphorism that 'relationships between individuals lie at the heart of support' is one to be taken seriously. Although the degree of intimacy in relationships within the social circle and with service providers is obviously different, support from either source needs to be given in a way that does not make people feel vulnerable, small or obligated. If 'support' does not have these features it is, simply, not 'supportive'.

None of the other studies in this chapter had enough data on informal support for the detailed analysis that the *Poor Environments* study provided, but what data they had were consistent with these findings on independence and give and take. For example, the families in the *Step-family* study felt a need for formal support but seldom used services. This reluctance may have arisen because of the newness of their families. In these circumstances the need to feel competent and maintain control may have turned the families inward onto their own resources. Amongst the parents in the *New Forest* study, those with mental health problems were less satisfied with the practical support they got from friends, and also showed increased reliance on GPs and health visitors for emotional support.

Can informal and semi-formal support be 'mobilized' to support parenting?

The second issue for the initiative was whether help from family, friends or the community could in some way be 'mobilized' to help parents. This idea contains two sub-questions. First is the narrower one of whether there are untapped sources of support within families or in the community that might be drawn on to help parents. Second, there is the more general question of the extent to which one source of support can be organized to replace or complement another.

Mobilizing family and friends

Policy makers have been interested in informal forms of support, especially the potential for the use of family and friends in child care or fostering. The general population studies do not have direct evidence on this matter. It is clear that these sources *are* heavily used to help in day-to-day parenting but there appears to be little scope for mobilizing them – except, perhaps, through financial incentives. This is the case because parents and their social circles are themselves the natural and most effective means of drawing on this source of support. If this is not being done already, it is unlikely that it can be promoted, because the use of these sources depends so strongly on the quality of relationships.

A further powerful piece of evidence from the *Poor Environments* study also goes against the idea of mobilizing informal support. That is that parents who 'consumed' support from one source already tended to get it from another. There were relatively high and relative low consumers overall. Parents who felt unsupported even when they were actually getting quite a lot of help tended to have problems about which the informal system could not be expected to do much; for example, long-term health problems, high levels of current family difficulties, financial problems and children with health and behaviour difficulties. Finally, of course, informal networks in poor neighbourhoods are themselves likely to be stressed and to have fewer material or emotional resources to spare.

Mobilizing community supports

What about beefing up semi-formal sources of support? These sources are important, are inexpensive since they rely on a substantial amount of goodwill from their staff, and can be facilitated with relatively low financial inputs. They try to deal with all sorts of family and community issues and deserve all the support they can get. But, although they meet specific parenting needs – mostly around child care and socializing – as the data from the *Poor Environments* study made clear, they are not used by the most needy families. Rather, they are drawn on by parents with more resources as part of the range of sources they use.

Does support make a difference to parenting problems?

There is a common-sense notion that many problems in parenting arise because of a lack of support and therefore that they would be ameliorated by provision of supportive services. There is plenty of evidence in the research literature to confirm that parenting difficulties are *associated* with a lack of support. This 'ecological' evidence mostly concerns support from family, friends and partners.

The direction of effects

The main problem in looking at the association between support and parenting is a methodological one. The problem is that it is very difficult from 'snapshot' studies to decide on the *direction of effects*. That is, if a family has a particular parenting problem *and* lacks support, how can we tell that the latter is a contributor to the former, rather than the other way round? Conversely, if well-supported families have fewer problems how can we tell whether this association simply reflects the families' ability to manage their lives, part of which is their ability to attract and manage support themselves? An understanding of the direction of effects is essential if we are to devise appropriate forms of help.

Only one of the studies in this chapter followed the principle: 'If you want to understand something, try to change it.' That was the study of the SPOKES community intervention in parenting and literacy. The other studies looked more generally at support, with an assumption that support would translate into parenting behaviour. The *SPOKES* study was successful in demonstrating that a well-delivered community-based programme can modify what parents do and also be popular with parents. The *Poor Environments* study provided an extended analysis on the relationship between support and the parents' sense that they were coping, but without looking at whether support actually modified the way they parented. None of the other studies looked at the relationship between support and parenting either directly or in terms of coping. Conversely, the *SPOKES* study did not look at the impact of other informal or formal supports on, for example, the capacity of the parents to take part in the intervention.

Support and coping

Did the *Poor Environments* study tell us anything about whether support made a difference to parents' sense that they were coping, even if it did not look directly at parenting behaviour? The associations between coping and support were complex. Those who were not coping clearly wanted more support but so did a third of those who were. However, those who felt they were coping were actually getting less support than those who were not. This was true both for support from family and friends and from services.

More use of services went along with a feeling of not coping, but service use did not go along with the negative feelings these parents had towards help from their families and friends. Perhaps in this case the input from services helped to protect parents from the dangers of obligation to their social circle. As the researchers point out, this is encouraging in that needy families accept that organized support services are there to help them. On the other hand, their very 'neediness' may lead formal agencies to treat them as less competent and to take over their parenting rather than support it.

How should formal support services help parents?

Finally we draw some conclusions on what these studies tell us about the place and style of formal services in helping parents.

Parents are generally positive about services

The first message is a positive one. Despite their frequent bad press, parents using services were usually positive about the help they received and felt less ambivalent about drawing on their help than they did with their families and friends. Then they liked services best that helped them in a way that ought not to be a surprise to any service user – which we all are. They wanted service providers to be practical and professional, to take their needs seriously, to listen to them and to be emotionally supportive as well as practically helpful.

What parents wanted services to be like

In short, parents wanted services to treat them like adults and to see them as partners in solving their problems. These key elements in service delivery are matters of style. They have few implications for resources. But parents also wanted things from services that are harder to achieve. They wanted them to be fast and responsive, and to meet the family's needs as the family saw them and when the family wanted. Some of these demands are unreasonable things to ask of services, as they are to ask of family and friends as well. But a lack of response also arises because families know that needs in one area of their lives – say health – impact on other parts, while service responses usually come from services that address one issue but not another. This problem will recur in many of the studies we are going on to discuss. Things are usually better when someone organizes the support. In the discussions to come the role of key or link workers in this will be prominent.

Parents as their own link workers

Key and link workers figure in these studies in a formal way only in specialist services, but these general population studies show just how much parents act as their own 'key workers', but without the official status that helps the professionals argue for services.

Engaging parents

The *SPOKES* project provided a number of lessons on how to deliver one kind of parenting support. The project made great efforts to follow the principles of 'partnership' that parents clearly wanted. The researchers point out that it is not just what interventions do that matters but also how they are delivered. 'Professional' approaches that give the message that parents need to be taught something have a high dropout rate. Much better are approaches that invite parents to participate and to choose the elements that they would like to try for themselves. That is, they fitted the programme to the parents' needs rather than fit the parents' 'problems' to the prescriptions of the service. This proved very effective even though the basic content of the intervention was based on research findings, not just on parents' self-defined needs.

Dealing with family stresses

Of course, this does not mean that dealing with family stresses more generally can be downgraded in favour of direct interventions in parenting. The *Poor Environments* study showed that a feeling of not coping went along with a whole range of stresses including lone parenting, the number of children, anxiety and depression, and having a difficult child.

These stresses were all strongly related to poverty as an underlying factor that acted on parenting through these stresses. Poverty should be addressed regardless of its effects but relieving poverty will not be sufficient. For example, having a difficult child was the strongest predictor of not coping even when poverty was taken into account. The evidence that positive parenting programmes work gives us one route into these difficulties, providing that these parents can be encouraged to take part. But the links with other services need to be made as well if 'support' is to make a difference.

Parents in control

Perhaps the point to re-emphasize at the end is that in most cases parents have a strong desire to solve problems for themselves and for advice and services to give them help in this, not to take the solving of the problems away from them. When faced with a parenting problem the parents in the *Poor Environments* study first wanted leaflets, videos and advice. As one mother said:

> Support means that you are still in charge; the parent is still in charge and that you are asking for help, advice or whatever – but you are the one in charge. You are not handing over...your kids to someone else to take over. You are still in charge of them.

Messages from the general population studies

PARENTING

- There are *many styles of parenting* that do *not* cause problems for children

SUPPORT

- Relationships are at the heart of support. This is true for formal as well as informal support
- Accepting support depends on feeling that there is *a balance in give and take* and *respect* in the relationship
- Different sources of support provide *different* things; one cannot make up for another

so

- *Diversity* and *flexibility* in services are important
- *Parents* are the *best organizers* of their own informal support.

PARENTS

- Parents are very committed to retaining their *independence*. They want to feel in *control*
- Parents with long-standing problems such as *mental health difficulties* can be especially concerned about *a loss of control* if they accept support

Parents wanted services

- To treat them like adults
- As partners in problem solving
- To be practical and professional
- To take their needs seriously
- To be fast and responsive

but

- It's not just *what* is offered but *how* it is offered that engages parents

Tackling poverty and lack of resources is a key part of tackling parenting problems

Chapter 5

Studies of Foster Care

There were two studies on foster care: a large questionnaire-based study of foster carers and foster children[1] and an intensive interview-based study of fostered adolescents for whom the expectation was for long-term placements.[2] Both studies had followed up their samples and were thus able to look at what predicted the outcomes of placements. Both, also, had information from some children and young people.

In this chapter we deal with the relationship between foster carers' parenting approaches and the success of placements. We also consider what difference informal and formal support makes to caring and placement success.

Foster care and parenting

Nowadays foster caring is considered to be different from parenting – a view reflected in the change in terminology from 'foster parents' to 'foster carers'. Carers may be advised to resist the temptation to become too attached to the children in their care because this makes moves within the system more difficult for the children. It also complicates attempts at reunification with birth parents and the management of contact. As Sinclair, Gibbs and Wilson put it, foster carers are 'ordinary parents recruited to a special task'. Foster carers are a key part of a formal service offered to children and young people in need of support and protection. But they are also recipients of formal support from agencies, including payment.

Despite these differences, foster caring *is* a kind of parenting. Children are taken into the household, become part of the family, are looked after and controlled and, one hopes, develop positive feelings towards their carers that are

---

1   Sinclair, I., Gibbs, I. and Wilson, K. *Supporting Foster Placements*. Referred to as 'the *Supporting Fostering* study'.

2   Farmer, E., Moyers, S. and Lipscombe, J. *The Fostering Task with Adolescents*. Referred to as 'the *Adolescent Fostering* study' or 'the *Adolescents* study'.

reciprocated. But because foster caring is a special kind of parenting, what makes it effective and the supports that help it may not be the same as those that make the parenting of birth children successful. For example, the kin network may take a different view of their obligations to foster carers than they do with parents who are bringing up the kin group's 'own' children.

For these reasons there are likely to be ambiguities in the carers' perceptions of their role. They need to be *like* parents but to be something else as well. Social services need to see carers both as part of their service and also as recipients of support. For agencies, there may be ambiguities as to the purpose of support: is it mostly to maintain a stable pool of carers and to support and monitor their performance? Or is it to help them care for the children in a way that will enhance their development? If both objectives are taken on board, how are they to be balanced? Of course, these aims are not necessarily in conflict. Carers want the children to do well and anything that helps the children should also support the carers. Nevertheless, we need to know what kind of caring 'works' and does support make any difference to it?

The studies

The *Supporting Fostering* study surveyed a large representative sample of 596 foster placements through questionnaires sent to social workers, carers and fostered children. Some qualitative data were also obtained from the questionnaires. There were, in addition, a small number of case studies of successful and unsuccessful placements.

The *Adolescent Fostering* study used interviews with foster carers, young people and social workers to look at the task of caring for 68 teenagers who had a history of emotional and behavioural difficulties and whose placements were intended to be long term. Both studies took the dimensions of parenting they looked at from existing research literature, but both also collected qualitative data on the carers' own views and priorities.

Carers', social workers' and young people's views

What the carers said and did

WHAT THEY THOUGHT WAS IMPORTANT IN FOSTERING

The carers in the *Supporting Fostering* study stressed the need to provide stability for the children. They also stressed the importance of liking the children and responding to them as individuals. They emphasized the need to provide social training – that is, to set limits and to give direction and encouragement – and they stressed professionalism, having realistic expectations of the placement and getting something back from the child.

Even more, they stressed the need to provide responsive parenting that would help the children attach to them. It was also important, in their view, to provide a secure base to help the children come to terms with their experiences and begin to act positively in the world. Providing this involved sensitivity, availability and consistency, understanding and empathy. Successful caring also involved setting predictable limits and helping the child understand these. Finally, there is a need to help the child make sense of who he or she is, through linking their current and past experiences – that is, to help with the development of 'identity'.

LOVING, 'FIT' AND PROFESSIONALISM

The profiles of successful cases illustrated the pull of contrary elements in foster caring. The carers emphasized their positive feelings – 'loving him to bits', 'thinking he's wonderful' – but also the professionalism needed to allow them to stand back and think through problems without becoming enmeshed in them. The case studies also illustrated an element related to both of these – the intangible element of 'fit' or 'click'. This describes those instances in which the carers and children just took to each other, often despite the ambivalences and challenges in the children's behaviour. Placements were more likely to succeed if the children wanted to be there. The less successful placements also started with positive intentions but, in the absence of this kind of connection, caring could become overwhelmed by its negative features and the children's behaviour difficulties.

ENGAGEMENT AND SENSITIVITY

Many of these themes are echoed in the *Adolescent Fostering* study. The great majority of foster carers were good at recognizing and responding to anxieties and developmental needs. A particularly noteworthy feature of this was the ability of the more successful carers to respond to and work with a young person's *emotional* age rather than his or her chronological one. Two-thirds of carers gave examples of parenting that illustrated this kind of responsiveness.

The *Adolescent Fostering* study team also looked at the carers' 'engagement' with the young people: a measure of acceptance and commitment and of active attempts to understand the young people's emotional and material needs. Just over half of carers were engaged with the children in this way. A lack of engagement reflected a lack of 'fit'. Fifteen per cent of carers actively disliked the young people in their care. Dislike was more common when the young people seemed unprepared to have a relationship with the carers or to accept support from adults more generally.

BOUNDARY SETTING

Most carers in the *Adolescent Fostering* study were able to set boundaries and control the young people's behaviour, although they found this easier with the younger teenagers. A special aspect of boundary setting for them was highlighted. This was the need initially to set limits that might be *more* liberal than would be the case with birth children and then gradually to make them more firm, in order to get the young people used to boundaries. This process is contrary to the more usual parenting of teenagers, which involves a steady relaxation of control and an acceptance of independence. Boundary setting with teenagers is particularly problematic for foster carers because of restrictions on what they are allowed to do.

This problem was reflected in supervising activities outside of the home. Although this was generally satisfactory, it was unacceptably low in 16 per cent of placements. In one case a young man was involved in auto crime (TDA and no licence) but the carers were unaware of this. In another case carers seldom knew the whereabouts of a young person seen to be at risk of prostitution.

Inappropriate or dangerous sexual activity was one of the most worrying things for these carers. This was the case with six of the young people, two of whom were very poorly managed. Supervisory issues also showed up in more ordinary things like the young people's dating behaviour. Twenty per cent of carers knew little about the young people's relationships. Only 8 per cent had good knowledge and were able to establish appropriate rules and be sympathetic about upsets.

What social workers liked

Social workers in the *Supporting Fostering* study joined the carers in stressing the importance of the carers' ability to commit to the child alongside the need for a willingness to part from a child without being swayed by their feelings. The social workers in the *Adolescent Fostering* study liked placements that provided stability, nurture and clear boundaries.

What the children and young people said

The children in the *Supporting Fostering* study stressed their need to be cared for and given encouragement; to feel that they were treated equally and to be made to feel that they belonged – indeed, the word 'love' was often used by them. On the other hand they also wanted their distinctness recognized. Despite these tensions, more than two-thirds of the children and young people who answered the questionnaire wanted to stay where they were until age 18 or beyond.

Nevertheless, they wanted their wishes and feelings to be taken seriously. For example, they wanted their *own* views about contact with their birth families to be recognized by both carers and social workers. They were more likely to want to see more of their families rather than less but they were often specific about the type of contact they wanted. Some wanted to see their mother but never their step-father; see an older brother but with supervision; or have telephone contact with a sister but no-one else. If children had been abused previously, unrestricted contact with any family member was associated with placement breakdown.

The adolescents also said they felt close to their main carer (81%) and that they received praise or rewards for things they had done well. Most thought that the rules and regulations were reasonable (71%) but a few had some complaints; for example that they were not allowed to eat in their bedrooms, had to have lights out at a particular time and had to ask to use the phone. Given the fact that these placements frequently broke down, these accounts have a self-protective flavour about them, with the young people telling the interviewer what seemed safe. Despite this, 22 per cent said that they would rather be at home and 6 per cent that they would rather be somewhere else.

The emphasis by the carers in the *Supporting Fostering* study on stability matched the children's wishes. Nevertheless, long-term placements were rare in practice. Thus, the researchers estimated that out of 100 children who were in placement for under one year, only 34 would be there just over a year later and after a further 14 months the figure would be about 17. This in the context of the fact that only 18 per cent of children overall were expected to return home or to relatives at the end of the current placement.

Foster caring or foster parenting?

Parenting qualities

It is clear from these two studies that, broadly speaking, the caring styles that fosterers follow and that are approved by social workers, children and young people are the characteristics of good parenting more generally: warmth, commitment, sensitivity to anxieties and worries, tolerance, boundary setting and providing a sense of security. These are the well-established features of positive parenting for foster as well as birth children and are highly desirable.

Differences from birth parenting

Nevertheless, there are clear differences between birth parenting and foster caring. Thus, although 'commitment' is stressed in these studies, the commitment of foster carers to the children and of the children to them is of a different order from that between birth parents and their children. Birth parents and children seldom think seriously of ending their relationship or denying their obligations and attachments to each other. In foster care commitment seldom has the same lifelong or 'come what may' characteristic. It can much more easily be ended by the carers, the children or by social services.

A further difference is the acceptance of responsibility for a child's emotional or behavioural problems. Birth parents will usually respond to such difficulties by asking themselves 'Where did we go wrong?'. Although foster carers may also question their handling of problems, foster children come to them with baggage for which the carers are not responsible. In the absence of 'fit' or commitment, the children's behaviour can become a major driver of placement instability. As the *Supporting Fostering* study shows, 'fit' can help the carer commit to the children and deal with emotional and behavioural problems that would otherwise become intolerable.

'Fit' or 'click'

'Fit' is a two-way affair. The children must want to be in the placement and the carers to have them. 'Fit' is for the most part unpredictable, intangible and often immediate. However, it does not always occur this way. Relationships can also develop; people can get to like one another. For carers, a key element in this is the experience of getting something back from the child, signs that the child has positive feelings for them, no matter how difficult their behaviour may otherwise be. Both studies show that there are fewer disruptions in the face of emotional and behavioural problems if the carers get some reward from the child's positive feelings for them.

Professionalism

Both studies emphasize the professionalism needed in foster care. That is, the ability to commit to the child in the longer term but also, if necessary, to see caring as a temporary involvement in a child's life that is intended to help him or her, not to provide the carer with another member of the family. In some respects the ability to stand back and to try to understand problems dispassionately – which is an aspect of professionalism – is a feature of good parenting for all children. But foster carers need to be able to go beyond that. They cannot make themselves like, feel close to or feel warmly about the children. But professionalism can enable them to be committed to the child's well-being, to respond sensitively, to be tolerant, to set boundaries and to foster a sense of security, even if they do not feel committed to the child him- or herself.

This professionalism requires training, a recognition of the carers' own practical expertise, support from other professionals and services and being treated as part of the team caring for the child. In short, being professional involves being treated like a professional.

Predictors of placement success

Do the positive parenting styles outlined above make a difference to the success of placements? And does support make a difference to parenting?

The *Supporting Fostering* study looked at predictors of disruption and at carers' and social workers' views on whether the placements met the children's needs. If anyone thought that the placement had not gone well it was rated as less successful. If everyone was positive about it the outcome was considered good. The remainder of the placements were put into a middle category. At the time of the first survey 54 per cent of placements were in the 'good' group, 38 per cent were in the middle group and 8 per cent were not going well.

The *Adolescent Fostering* study also looked at predictors of disruption. In addition, a follow-up measure of outcome combined placements that had already disrupted with ones that were at risk of doing so. Forty per cent had disrupted by the time of the follow-up and a further 13 per cent were considered at risk. Thus, 47 per cent of the placements were rated as 'successful' at the time the study ended.

Age and earlier history

In the *Supporting Fostering* study the child's age at placement and a history of previous disruptions – but not the number of placement moves *per se* – predicted disruptions, as did emotional abuse, which had probably been experienced by nearly half of the children (49%). When emotional abuse was taken into account neither sexual abuse nor neglect predicted poorer outcomes.

Attachment

A further predictor of poorer outcomes was attachment behaviour. The children showed one of two kinds, either *aloofness* – showing little affection and hiding emotions – or *childish attachment* – that is, seeking attention through misbehaviour or indiscriminate friendliness. These two styles are similar to the two main forms of attachment disorder, although the ratings cannot be assumed to be a measure of these. Childish attachment predicted breakdown as did aloofness, albeit to a much lesser degree and then predominantly for the younger children.

These findings were not repeated in the *Adolescents* study, even when the comparison was restricted to children in the same age group. This may have arisen because the high level of relationship problems in the adolescents swamped more subtle manifestations of attachment style, or because the measures are less reliable as children get older. Nonetheless, young people whom the foster carers felt had little or no attachment to an adult at the first interview were significantly more likely to have disrupted placements.

Special needs

More hopefully, poorer outcomes for the children in the *Supporting Fostering* study were not more common in children with special needs – apart, of course, for emotional and behavioural problems. Predominant amongst other special needs noted but not defined by social workers were learning difficulties, which were recorded for about 29 per cent of children. Indeed, allowing for their age, special needs children did *better* on all the measures of outcome. Placements of children with physical disabilities were very unlikely to disrupt.

Birth children

Finally, and contrary to most previous research, poor outcomes were *not* more likely among the families in the *Supporting Fostering* study if there were birth children in the family. This may have been a chance finding but it might also have been due to social workers' greater awareness of this issue and more care in making placements. Carers said that their own children were generally positive about fostering unless the behaviour of the fostered child was especially difficult. This was true in the *Adolescents* study as well. Bad effects of the fostered child on the birth children made carers less warm and committed and made their parenting more aggressive and control more difficult.

Emotions and behaviour

Behavioural problems were one of the strongest predictors of a lack of success in the placements in both studies. Challenging, overactive and restless behaviour were particularly implicated. These difficulties only led to placement breakdown in the *Supporting Fostering* study if they prompted the carer to reject the child. Conversely, success was much more likely if the young person wanted to be in the placement and was happy with it. Success was also more likely if carers had realistic expectations of the young people's behaviour, even if this included emotional and behavioural problems.

Not all aspects of emotional and behavioural problems pointed towards failure. Indeed, in the *Adolescents* study some problems appeared to be 'protective' of the placement, even if they were worrying in terms of the young person's development. For example, the placements of depressed, lonely and socially isolated adolescents were more likely to remain intact. These problems went along with lower levels of engagement with other children in the household.

Foster carers' characteristics and experiences

In neither study were foster carers' social characteristics or past fostering histories related to success. For example, there was no association between the outcomes of the *Supporting Fostering* study and the age of carers, the length of their experience or whether they were lone carers. There was one exception to this. In the *Adolescents* study, carers who had previously had experience in relevant occupations – such as nursing, teaching or social work – achieved better outcomes. On the other hand, current and previous stresses were associated with poorer outcomes. In the *Adoles-*

cents study, placements were more at risk if carers' lives were more generally stressed. In the *Supporting Fostering* study carers' experiences of two recent life events – previous disruptions or allegations of abuse – were predictive of poorer outcomes.

What are we to make of these predictors? They may just reflect a 'last straw' phenomenon. Pile on enough stresses and something is bound to give. But this does not seem to be the whole story. Some carers had fewer breakdowns and better current outcomes. In neither study were these characteristics simply a consequence of having easier children to look after. The inference must be that this has something to do with parenting styles. Was this the case?

Parenting styles

The *Supporting Fostering* study approached this question by creating summary measures of parenting:

- a *parenting score*, covering things such as caring, accepting, having clear expectations, not being easily upset and seeing things from the child's viewpoint

- a *rejection score*, involving a lack of fondness for the child, a view of him or her as incorrigible and uncertainty about whether the carer wanted him or her to stay

- a *child orientation* score that assessed the level of practical involvement and facilitation of the child's activities. (In practice, this score was very strongly related to the other two and did not explain much once they were taken into account.)

The broad question of whether carers' parenting style made a difference is easily answered. The parenting and rejection scores were strongly related to the outcome measures *even after the child's level of disturbance was taken into account.*

POSITIVE PARENTING

The associations between the parenting style, rejection scores and the number of previous disruptions the carers had experienced help to disentangle the meaning of all three measures. The experience of past disruptions went along with lower parenting scores but not with higher rejection scores. This suggests that the two scores measure different things. The parenting score would seem to be a reflection of more enduring parenting styles while the rejection score is mostly a consequence of a lack of 'fit' in the current placement. A higher parenting score indicates the features of positive parenting mentioned earlier: sensitivity, boundary setting, supervision and child-centredness. The evidence from the *Supporting Fostering* study shows that differences on these features do influence the success of placements.

Many of these findings are repeated in the *Adolescents* study even though a high level of difficulties for the young people was deliberately part of the sample selection. In this case the measures of parenting style were taken from interviews with the carers. They were used to predict disruption or, as in the *Supporting Fostering* study, placements that were at risk of disruption, as well.

In the case of the *Adolescents* study, it was not so much a question of how sensitive the carers were in a general way but how well they were able to fit their responses to the child's 'emotional age'; that is, it was a good indicator of responsiveness. As in the *Supporting Fostering* study, sensitivity, warmth and responsiveness were relatively stable parenting characteristics. There were few changes between the first interview and the follow-up in these features of parenting.

ORGANIZING ACTIVITIES AND DOING THINGS WITH THE CHILDREN

In neither study was the amount the carers did with the children or how much they organized activities for them related to outcome, although in the *Supporting Fostering* study the child orientation score – which asked about 'doing things' – did predict better outcomes. The direction of this association in unclear but in both studies it was relationships that mattered. Once a child became rejected or the carers lost commitment the placement was very likely to end. In the *Adolescents* study one element in declining commitment was the impact of the fostered young person on other children in the household. Commitment declined markedly in 25 per cent of cases, and, if this turned into rejection, 73 per cent of placements broke down within a year compared with 37 per cent where rejection was not part of the picture.

DOWNWARD SPIRALS

A familiar scenario occurred under these circumstances. Loss of control over the young people's behaviours went along with the tendency of carers to let young people get away with things and to increased irritability and aggression on the carers' part. Loss of control within the home went along with ineffective supervision outside it. As relationships deteriorated, new problems appeared.

Summary of parenting style and outcome

In sum, the two studies show that well-tuned and responsive parenting – associated with commitment, the development of rewarding relationships and effective boundary setting – contributes to placement success; but the high disruption rates with the teenagers suggest that these characteristics on their own are not enough. Responsiveness, commitment and a good working relationship can contain challenging behaviour but the task remains formidable. Any additional stresses within or outside the household can destabilize the situation, and once negative spirals develop the likelihood of success is low. In the end, the lack of 'fit' or the level of difficulties can push through the best attempts to provide a stable and secure placement. We turn next to the extent to which 'support' can act as a modifier of these dangers.

Foster Caring, Support and Outcomes

In this section we look at whether support makes this task easier, whether it has an effect directly on caring behaviour, whether it has an effect through reducing other stresses and whether it has an effect through changing the child's behaviour. Inevitably the burden of this discussion will involve support from the formal system – that is, social and other services. However, informal sources of support may also be very influential and semi-formal organizations, especially foster carers' groups, may also play an important role. It is appropriate to begin with these two sources of support first.

Informal supports

SUPPORT AND STRESS AT HOME

Earlier in this overview we made the point that support begins at home but, frequently, so do stresses. First among these stresses are the effects of the placements themselves on family organization and relationships. Both of the studies highlight these. For example, outside work can make meeting the fostered children's needs more problematic; meeting the needs of birth children often needs careful balancing against the needs of the fostered children; even rooms and clothes may need to be shared. In addition, there may be major wear and tear on the house that is not adequately compensated by social services. In short, carers and their families may find that it is hard to stretch their emotional and physical resources to cover the task.

Partners

Stresses in relationships with partners were quite common. At some time in their fostering careers 31 per cent of the carers in the *Supporting Fostering* study had experienced severe family tensions (including marital) because of a difficult foster placement.

Fifteen per cent of carers in the *Adolescents* study mentioned stresses with their partners – a figure similar to the number who stressed the positive impacts of the placement. Overall, 30 per cent of the carers reported 'tensions within the family'.

Only fragmentary data were available from either study about the kind of support that partners gave but carers in the *Adolescents* study ranked their partners top as supporters. Their overall ranking of day-to-day helpfulness was: partners,

Messages from the foster care studies 1: Views and outcomes

Foster carers stressed the need:

- To provide *stability*
- To set *limits* and give *direction*
- To be *responsive* to the children
- To be *professional* and have *realistic* expectations

Social workers added:

- The need to *commit to the child* and to be willing to part from him or her

Children and young people wanted:

- To be *cared* for
- To be treated as *equals,* to feel that they *belonged*
- To have their *distinctness* recognized
- To have their own views on *contact* taken seriously
- Often to *stay* until they were 18, although stability was rare

PREDICTORS OF SUCCESS

- The 'click' or 'fit' between carer and child
- The child or young person wanting to be there
- Willingness of the child to have a relationship with the carers
- A developing relationship ('attachment')
- Sensitive child-oriented parenting
- Meeting the child's emotional needs
- Good boundary setting
- Absence of severe behaviour problems
- Lower age at placement

Foster caring is a kind of parenting but also requires the ability to stand back and let go

Effective foster caring has the same characteristics as all effective parenting

Differences in carers' parenting seemed to reflect relatively stable styles. Good caring contains behaviour problems rather than changing them dramatically link workers, own children, other foster carers, the child's social worker, their own parents, and then friends. For day-to-day help 34 per cent turned to partners if they had them and 24 per cent to other fosterers. Nine per cent turned to their own children.

Stresses for birth children

Sharing the foster mother's time can affect relationships with birth children. The foster children can monopolize the mother's time because of their attachment needs and this can lead to the birth children feeling cut out. Fostered children sometimes stole from birth children or were aggressive towards them. Rejection of approaches of friendship by one or the other caused difficulties. Birth children also worried about the effects of the fostered children on their parents.

Both studies record these stresses. Twenty-four per cent of birth children in the *Adolescents* study had things they disliked about the placements, including sharing their bedrooms and having their possessions damaged. Two-fifths of carers in the *Supporting Fostering* study rated the effects of the placements on their children as neutral or positive (41%), a figure very similar to that in the *Adolescents* study (40%). The most common view of carers in the *Supporting Fostering* study was that the impact depended on the individual child and how they fitted into the family.

Even birth children who were no longer at home were not immune to stresses and jealousies. This occurred in seven families in the *Adolescents* study and in a further 11 there were things that adult children disliked about the placements, including the carers' neglect of their grandparenting role and worry about the effects of the fostered children on them. This particular stress occurred for over a quarter of carers (26%).

Positive aspects for birth children

It is common for social workers to record and worry about these risks to placements. Much less attention has been paid to birth children as a positive source of influence and support. Thus, the carers in the *Adolescents* study ranked their children second only to their partners as sources of useful and available help overall – above even link workers and other carers. The impression is that birth children generally want to be helpful to their parents and continue to try to support them. They want to help the fostered children as well, but features of the latter's behaviour could impact on them directly, especially attachment-related behaviours and conduct problems, and also make them worry about their parents. Qualitative data from the *Supporting Fostering* study strongly supported this view.

KIN, FRIENDS AND NEIGHBOURS

A similar picture was evident with regard to support from kin, friends and neighbours. On the positive side, relatives could be emotionally and practically helpful and could support the family in their belief in what they were doing. However, being a foster carer was an activity that fitted with the life of the informal network to a greater or lesser extent.

Risks and stresses

Support and understanding from relatives and friends was especially needed when life in the home had to change to fit in with fostering. But this did not always work out. Changes in the regular pattern of seeing each other or shifts in the balance of give and take could have a bad effect on support. For example, grandparents' help and support could be limited if they disapproved of the impact of the fostered children on the family or if they simply did not like them. Kin could be critical if they thought that the carers were ignoring the 'real family'.

Neighbours, also, could be a source of stress: 20 per cent of the carers in the *Supporting Fostering* study had neighbours who did not think fostering was a good idea and one-third of the neighbours were sometimes upset by the foster children. Twenty-five per cent of carers had experienced criticism or hostility. Similarly, 38 per cent of the carers in the *Adolescents* study had suffered criticism or hostility. Neighbours were the main source of this but friends could also be critical or relationships could end because of disagreements. Amongst the sources of criticism or jealousy were beliefs about the supposed earnings of the fosterers.

Positive features

Despite these risks, the picture of informal support was predominantly positive. In the *Supporting Fostering* study 63 per cent of carers had a lot of informal support from the immediate family, 24 per cent from other relatives, 35 per cent from friends and 15 per cent from neighbours.

Semi-formal support

FOSTER CARERS' GROUPS

Support through foster carers' groups was especially valued. These groups are often organized by the agencies and in some cases foster carers are expected to attend them. Both studies showed that meeting other carers was a very important source of emotional support and advice.

In the *Adolescents* study 84 per cent of carers knew about local groups and about half went to them. Attendance was compulsory for nine carers, all of whom worked for a specialist scheme. Timing and child care arrangements were the main barriers to attendance for 26 per cent of carers. Probably for these reasons, attendance was much higher for couple carers, where at least one of them could attend, than it was for lone parents. A quarter of carers were dissatisfied with these organized groups, although only 17 per cent thought them not worth going to. In addition, groups organized by the carers were available to 21 carers and about half of them went.

Finally, 89 per cent of carers, mostly couples, had personal contact with other carers. Those who were more satisfied with their social workers also had more contact with other carers. Thus, as in the case of the parents in the *Poor Environments* study, carers who got one kind of support were more likely to get another.

The findings from the *Supporting Fostering* study are comparable. Eighty-five per cent of carers said that their authority organized groups. About one-third who had groups to go to did not do so, but one-third did regularly. Nearly 70 per cent said they could turn to another foster carer for practical help and advice. A quarter did this a lot. This kind of contact was related to whether there were local organized groups, suggesting that these individual contacts were often forged at these meetings. Thus, nine out of ten of those who went to groups regularly also had other carers to call on.

Formal support

SOCIAL WORK

The carers in both studies had link or family placement social workers and children's social workers. In the *Supporting Fostering* study, 95 per cent of carers had a link worker who worked like the carers' own social worker. All the carers in the *Adolescents* study had link workers. In both studies the carers were distinctly more favourable to the link worker. Fifty-five per cent of the carers in the *Supporting Fostering* study said they gave a lot of support. They said this about 36 per cent of the children's social workers. Similarly, 74 per cent of the carers in the *Adolescents* study said that their link worker gave good support and advice, compared with only 46 per cent of children's social workers. Indeed, the latter were often felt not to take their views seriously.

What carers wanted from social workers

The carers in the *Supporting Fostering* study were quite clear what they wanted from social workers. They wanted them to be there for them, respectful of their views, considerate, supportive (that is, warm, approving and ready to listen) and practical. This meant sorting out finance and transport, arranging professional services, working with the birth family, working with the child, enabling carer to work with the child and supporting the carer. In nearly all these things the link/family placement workers were seen much more favourably.

The carers in the *Adolescents* study echoed these sentiments and added some things of their own. They wanted workers who listen in a supportive way, help them unravel an issue and give practical support, such as arranging child care. They liked workers who could see both sides of an issue and were impartial. For them, the key element was availability and responsiveness, especially as evidenced by answering phone calls. Forty-four per cent saw responsiveness as a characteristic of their link workers, whose advice was particularly valued (61% said so). Children's social workers, on the other hand, got poorer marks for accessibility or ringing back. Of course, it was not an entirely positive story. Carers gave examples of an apparent lack of interest in them by their link workers and 13 per cent were dissatisfied with them.

What they meant by responsiveness

Responsiveness was also evidenced by the way in which the link workers were used as a source of advice and support over day-to-day matters. Three-quarters of the carers in the *Adolescents* study said that they used the link worker in this way, compared with the use of only 33 per cent of children's social workers. Indeed, when it came to a ranking of sources of support that were both useful and available, link workers came top (85%), followed by the carers' own children (82%), other foster carers (71%), partners (69%) and children's social workers (64%).

These carers ideally wanted a formal support system that had the responsiveness and flexibility of the informal system and the knowledge and authority of the formal one. But, much more important, they wanted to be regarded as full members of the team caring for the child. Only 46 per cent felt that they were. Overall, about half of the carers were unhappy with the way that the professionals treated them.

Being treated as a member of the team

A number of factors added to the feeling of being a team member: the availability of specialist out-of-hours services, useful help from the children's social worker and feeling included and involved by the outside professionals who were helping the child. Again, being professional means being treated like a professional.

Does support make a difference to outcomes?

We have drawn the distinction earlier between responsive behaviour that makes people feel supported and support that makes a clear difference to caring and to the stability of placements. Supporting carers in the first sense is the right and proper way to treat people. We do not need research to tell us that, nor do we need to demonstrate 'effects' before we try to make 'support' behave in that way. Research can mostly tell us when this is not the case.

This initiative is interested in both these meanings of 'support'. It is especially interested in effects but these are not easy to explicate. It is not hard to find connection correlations, but it is much harder to understand how those connections come about or what the 'direction of effects' is.

The follow-up design in these two studies does give some purchase on this issue. Support might have an effect on outcome either because it changes parenting itself – for example, by encouraging responsiveness or helping the carers understand attachment – or it might have an effect through making carers' lives less stressful, thereby giving them more scope to use the parenting skills they have.

Effects of informal stresses and supports

In both studies stresses in the carers' family and social lives went along with poorer outcomes. In the *Adolescents* study bereavements, poor relationships with kin and friends, illness and similar stresses were related to disruption. Feeling the pressure of these events was associated with not feeling supported more generally. In the *Supporting Fostering* study also, family tensions, criticisms and lack of support were related to how carers felt about fostering, and whether they felt stressed and intended to give up. Conversely, carers' accounts of feeling supported were associated with a more positive commitment to continue fostering. There was a strong correlation between support for fostering from relatives and the carers' positive attitude to it. The *Adolescents* study found that a feeling of strain around the young person's behaviour was less when their own children or their friends provided useful help.

The need for formal support

Encouragement from family and friends is clearly important, but foster caring usually needs emotional and practical supports that are beyond their skills and resources. Other carers can act as knowledgeable advisers on parenting, a part that family and friends would usually play in birth parenting. But again this is not enough. The social workers are essential providers and coordinators of specialized support and information.

Carers were clear that they wanted these inputs to include sympathy and responsiveness and also effective coordination and delivery of specialist inputs. Sympathy and responsiveness are essential to morale. Professional input ought also to improve parenting in a practical way, either by training carers to handle the special needs of these children or by modifying the children's problems by working with them. Did this happen?

The *Supporting Fostering* study found that a number of features of the social workers' behaviour that carers liked came together as a bundle of 'good' behaviours. The core of these was listening carefully, visiting, responding, showing appreciation and being practical. All these skills were seen as much more common for link workers than children's social workers. These attributes went along with the carers' views that they were given enough information, were consulted over placement planning and seldom had disagreements. That is, effective social workers combined the characteristics of sympathy and action. It should be stressed that most of the carers in this study *liked* their social workers and made excuses for their shortcomings.

Did good support from services make a difference?

Yes and no. In neither study did the quality of social work support make any difference to disruptions, but in the *Supporting Fostering* study, good ratings by the child's social worker was associated with success – that is, whether the general opinion of carers and social workers was that things were going well. Carers in the *Supporting Fostering* study who had frequent contact with their link workers were more likely to continue fostering – a kind of success in itself.

In the *Adolescents* study too, good support from the young person's social worker was significantly associated with more successful placements. Since most link workers were well regarded, their input did not vary enough to know what would happen if their input were poor. Views on the children's social workers varied a lot. For this reason these findings probably mean that good support from the children's social workers on top of good link working did seem to make a difference.

But is that so? The authors of *Supporting Fostering* took a different view. They did so because support did not make any difference to disruption, which is a much harder test than their other outcome measures because it is independent of carers' and social workers' judgements. Because support did not make a difference to disruption their more conservative conclusion was that good foster carers had better outcomes and got on well with their social workers because of this. That is, the effect was from parenting to support, not support to parenting.

This somewhat pessimistic conclusion is in line with other research: *everyday* social work support does not have much effect on outcomes, which are driven by much more powerful forces, especially the extent of difficulties the children are themselves facing.

On the other hand, this issue is far from settled because, as we have strongly argued in Chapter 2, it is necessary to look at the whole ecology of parenting, not just at specific elements in it. The *Adolescents* study team have argued that, for the foster carers, support is like a net: it is only as strong as its weakest link. In that study there were many associations between a variety of supports and whether placements broke down or not. These included support from link workers as well as the immediate family and specialist services.

To be sure, disruptions were most strongly driven by the young people's behaviour and a lack of 'fit'. On the other hand, it would be premature to conclude that formal supports had only weak effects. As yet, however, it is not clear how positive effects come about. It may be through direct help in reducing stresses caused by behaviour and relationship difficulties, or it may be indirectly through reducing life stresses more generally. It does seem clear, because of the positive findings on link workers, that there is an important difference between general support and support better fitted to carers' needs and concerns on a day-to-day basis. We next check whether any specific specialist service inputs made a difference.

What about specific inputs?

These studies considered a number of specific inputs.

SHORT BREAKS FOR CARERS

The *Supporting Fostering* study was able to look at these. Short breaks did not improve outcomes. If anything, the associations were in the opposite direction – that is, breaks were associated with poorer outcomes. This, of course, was almost certainly because breaks were a marker for more problems, especially anti-social behaviour in adolescence.

INPUT FROM SCHOOL

Social workers in the same study certainly thought that support from the school was a major factor in the placements that went well. Certainly, children who liked school had better outcomes, but this link is hard to interpret because children who did well at school had fewer problems to start with. The findings in the *Adolescents* study were the same. The type and amount of education and the frequency of school attendance were not related to disruption or to 'success'. Low confidence in relationships and in school work predicted disruption. In both studies the links are real but it is hard to be sure of the 'direction of effects'.

SPECIAL PSYCHOLOGICAL INPUTS

Contrary to many expectations, specialist psychological input was quite common. Thirty-seven per cent of children in the *Supporting Fostering* study had seen specialists, including psychiatrists, psychotherapists, counsellors, clinical psychologists or educational psychologists. A further 10 per cent were awaiting an appointment. The outcomes from these individual services could not be assessed because only a few children went to each of them, but disruption rates were somewhat higher for these children. Success ratings were not significantly different. The *Adolescents* study followed these findings in most respects. Sixty-four per cent of children had some special psychological input, including life-story work, play therapy, group therapy, behaviour therapy and family therapy. None of these had any discernible effect on disruption or success. The carers of the adolescents felt better supported if counselling was arranged for the young people and if the adolescents, in turn, say that they are getting it.

A common finding and what to make of it

These findings illustrate a common problem in analysis. That is, that outcomes tend to be *poorer* amongst those with more input and support, almost certainly because these are the most troubled children. This is illustrated in the *Supporting Fostering* study, where outcomes were not significantly different once allowance was made for the difficulties of those involved. This does tell us that, in the short run, these inputs make little difference to outcomes overall on the kinds of measures used. It does not mean that they are not helpful to some children. Nor does it tell us whether they may make a difference in the longer term. We are at the point where only more systematic trials of different approaches will answer the question.

The *Supporting Fostering* study had one interesting anomalous finding. That was that children seeing educational psychologists did significantly better even on disruption rates, even when the level of behaviour problems was taken into account. What are we to make of this? The cautious analyst would worry that the finding was sample specific – that is, a rogue finding. This concern would be strengthened by the fact that these children were different in many other ways from those not getting this help. They were more likely to be forbidden contact with some adults and to have carers with high parenting scores. They were also more likely to be receiving other specialist help; but the number of services they were getting made no difference to outcomes, only the use of educational psychologists did. The interpretation of this tantalizing finding must remain open at present.

Messages from the foster care studies 2: Support and its effects

SUPPORT

- Support within the family was very important and the main source of emotional support
- One-fifth to one-third of carers had criticism from neighbours and friends
- Support from other foster carers was especially valued; most carers had informal links with other carers
- Link workers gave good support and advice and were more highly regarded than children's social workers

Carers wanted social workers who:

- Were 'there for them'
- Were respectful of their views
- Were considerate
- Were supportive and practical, i.e. sorting out finance, transport, professional services
- Worked with the birth family or child
- Helped the carer to work with the child
- Supported the carer emotionally by:
  - listening carefully
  - visiting
  - responding to calls
  - showing appreciation and being practical

Foster carers should be treated as *part of the team* around the child

If we want carers to be professional we should treat them like professionals

THE EFFECTS OF SUPPORT

- Good support did not lead to fewer disruptions

but

- The whole pattern of stresses and lack of supports did

Support tailored to carers' and children's needs is more effective than general support

Fostering is an extremely complex task, given the children's needs, so all supports need to be working well. Support is like a net; it is only as effective as its weakest link

Discussion

Two final comments need to be made.

Does support change parenting styles?

We asked at the beginning of this chapter whether support might work by directly changing parenting styles or whether it might have a more general effect through making the context of parenting less stressful. It is clear that the kind of 'support' offered at present is not capable of changing parenting styles. More direct approaches, such as that used in the *SPOKES* project, will be needed to see if this is possible. These two studies illustrate the formidable complexity of deciding on what influences what – that is, what the 'direction of effects' is. The ecological model acknowledges this complexity.

What is much clearer is that in many of the cases nowadays, perhaps the majority of them, fostering is extremely taxing, and 'support systems' need to be working well and in harmony if fostering is to be successful. In these two studies all kinds of personal stresses and strains were associated with poorer outcomes. In the *Adolescents* study, poor support from social workers contributed to these stresses. These stresses seemed to affect parenting in individual placements and become associated with negative spirals in relationships. Although parenting behaviours could be changed in this way, as well as by the behaviours of the children and young people, differences in parenting seemed to reflect relatively stable caring styles. Some carers were better at this kind of caring than others.

Treating carers as professionals

Service providers can do little about relationships in the family and informal networks, but they can note them and take them seriously in their planning. More important, if they expect carers to be 'professional' they should treat them like professionals. The fact that so many carers did *not* feel that they were treated as part of the team caring for a child or young person is worrying. Thinking about inter-agency working should include the carers. As the *Adolescents* study team noted, foster carers experienced support services like nets – they were only as strong as their weakest link.

Chapter 6

Parenting and Support
in the Context of Disability

Three studies in the initiative looked at issues around parenting and disability. Two were concerned with parenting disabled children, the other with disabled adults as parents. The studies of children dealt with two special but very important circumstances. The first was concerned with caring for technology-dependent children, where the usual boundaries between the private life of the family and the public input from services become blurred. The second dealt with learning-disabled children in South Asian families. The study of disabled adults took a broader approach, to look at issues of support for parents with physical, sensory and mental health impairments.

Models of disability

Researchers into disability generally make a key distinction between an impairment and a disability. An *impairment* is some difference in physical or mental functioning outside the usual range that makes a person's life potentially more problematic. A *disability* usually refers to the way in which an impairment becomes a social disadvantage because of the failure of society to adapt to the needs of the person with the impairment. This view is usually referred to as the 'social model of disability'. The older term 'handicap' is seldom used nowadays, probably because it confuses the two meanings and leads to the assumption that problems lie predominantly in the individual.

In practice the terms 'impairment' and 'disability' are not always used consistently, but it is important to keep both of them in mind. If it is not, the arguments from the social model can read as if it were believed that there would be no disability if it were not for society's failure to adapt to impairments. Minimizing disability may sometimes require exceptional input from support networks and services. The strength of the social model is to do away with any idea of the disabled as passive recipients of service inputs. The three studies in the initiative fully support this.

They all highlight the active role of the parents of disabled children and of disabled parents themselves. Their service needs may be very specialized and specific but, as far as the parents are concerned, one purpose of these inputs should be to allow them to care for their children themselves. They want to stay in control of their lives and solve problems in their own way.

We deal first with the experiences and needs of parents caring for technology-dependent children and then move to the issues for parents with learning-disabled children and parents who are themselves disabled.

Caring for technology-dependent children[1]

Background

Because of advances in medical technology, more children with chronic conditions are surviving. Technology-dependent children are a sub-set of this group. What distinguishes them is the need for a medical device and ongoing substantial nursing care to compensate for loss of vital bodily function. Otherwise they are a very diverse group of children in terms of the nature of their problems, the associated disabilities, whether the dependence is continuous or intermittent and whether it is permanent or temporary. This study extends the idea of what parenting is because, as we shall see, the private sphere of parenting can become the public when medical personnel come into the home to help parents care for their children.

As the number of these children has increased, so policies for the children to be cared for at home have begun to develop, but in an *ad hoc* way and not at a local level. Because of the level of the children's impairment, the parents' task has progressed far beyond ordinary caring activities to performing complex clinical nursing procedures. Partly in response to this, Community Children's Nursing teams have been developed to help parents. At the time this study was done this specialist provision was patchy. Only 50 per cent of health authorities purchased this service. Support for parents came most usually from health visitors and district nurses as well as from specialist outreach nurses attached to hospitals. Some medical specialist units had specialist nurses who worked in the family home as well as the hospital.

---

1 Kirk, S. and Glendinning, C. *Supporting Parents Caring for a Technology-Dependent Child*. Referred to as 'the *Technology-Dependent* study'.

The study

A small purposive[2] sample and exploratory qualitative interviews were used to study a wide range of technologies. The researchers interviewed the parents of 21 children who were under 18, four of the children themselves and 38 professionals from 26 different professional groups associated with their care. In addition to these 21 families, three further families were followed from before discharge from hospital and as they returned home, to look at the hospital discharge planning process, the purchase of services and the transfer of nursing skills from staff to parents. Six professionals involved in commissioning services or discharge planning were also interviewed. The children were continually or repeatedly dependent on a medical device or technology, including mechanical ventilation, oxygen therapy, tracheostomy, parenteral nutrition, intravenous drug administration or renal dialysis.

The small sample meant that the data could not sensibly be presented numerically. Because of this we do not know what proportions of the families received different kinds of support or had particular kinds of problem, but the overall messages are clear.

Parents' experiences

THE PROFESSIONALIZATION OF PARENTING

For most families, looking after their children at home meant that they had to organize family life around the children's care. The special requirements for this often left little room for 'ordinary' family life. Parts of the home might have had to be turned into extensions of the hospital, even containing professional carers, and the parents themselves became the providers and managers of a wide range of technical procedures. They sometimes even felt that professionals taught them these as if they were clinic staff, to the extent that the professionals concentrated on teaching the technical aspects of care and neglected the emotional impact of the tasks on the parents.

Although the parents were keen to bring their children home they had little to go on as far as deciding what 'parenting' these children meant. There are no cultural 'models' for this kind of parenting. This may also have led the professionals to concentrate on the technicalities and to deal less adequately with the emotional side of things.

---

2   A 'purposive' sample is a sample specially chosen to cover the range of characteristics or experiences in which the researchers are interested. It is often used with small or rare samples. It is not intended to be statistically representative but is designed to illuminate important issues.

The tasks parents had to undertake were often not comforting to their child. Indeed, performing some procedures was distressing because they involved inflicting pain or physically restraining their children. They had to make clinical decisions, adjust therapies to changing conditions and assess when to seek help, often when the course of the disability or illness was uncertain. Sometimes they asked themselves whether they were parents or nurses – albeit nurses with no time off.

This professionalizing of parenting also involved them in coordinating and organizing services and getting supplies and equipment. In this way, a family-centred policy that encouraged the care of children at home could make the parents themselves responsible for coordinating help from multiple inputs, which should have been coordinated by the agencies. Parents stressed the obligation and duty they felt to care for their children at home. Nevertheless, some felt that the decision to do this was not negotiated with them and some professionals feared that the parents were being exploited in order to cut costs.

THE IMPACT OF CARING AT HOME

In order to maintain some normal family life in the midst of all this, coordination between parents was essential. They set themselves high standards and usually worked as a team, often adopting specific roles; but the tension between being a parent and being a nurse remained a major element in the stress they felt. Over and above this their lives were made more difficult because their sleep was often severely disrupted and family activities restricted by cumbersome equipment. Outings could be stressful because of the need to get home to administer therapies. Public reactions could be hurtful, especially if parents had to administer procedures when they were out. Thus even times of pleasure had to be organized with military precision.

The parents' own life as a couple was also affected: many could not use babysitters because of their child's special needs, their own relationship could become strained because of an inability to spend time together and their other children might miss out on parental attention. Some mothers and fathers had had to give up work, thus reducing family income when there were often marked additional costs for electricity, laundry or other necessities.

Many parents felt that they would have been unable to care for their child at home without the support of professional home carers but, equally, the presence of home carers medicalized their home. It is hardly surprising that the overall intensive nature of caring led to feelings of anxiety and exhaustion, which sometimes led to a need for counselling.

The organization and impact of support

INFORMAL AND SEMI-FORMAL SUPPORT

Because the study was concerned with the needs of the families for specialist input, there were fewer data on other kinds of support. Nevertheless, it was clear that the special skills and knowledge needed to care for the children limited the practical support that family and friends could give. They were often not able to babysit, take the children out or pick them up from school. They helped with other things such as doing housework or caring for the other children when they could, but support was necessarily limited. Specialist voluntary agencies were sources of information, advice and emotional support, and sometimes loaned equipment.

FORMAL SUPPORT

It might be thought that the provision of well-thought-out services with good inter-agency working would be *de rigueur*, given that the task of caring for these children at home was so complex and the policy for parents to do so firmly established. For most parents this was far from the truth. Their faith in the system could be shaken early on when the children were still in hospital, through errors in medication or other slip-ups. Even at this early stage in the process the lack of clarity about the parents' role was often apparent and the professionalizing of their parenting began. Both they and the professionals mentioned these issues. Parents felt that professionals assumed that they could and would care at home and that the professionals' task was to teach them how, often with a disregard of their feelings and anxieties. There was little planning of services once the children returned home. This led to problems through the lack of clarity over professional roles and responsibilities.

Once home, power began to shift towards the parents, who became clearer and more assertive about what they should do and what should be 'given back' to the professionals. Over time, the parents themselves became the experts in the management of their children's disabilities and the most sensitive interpreters of many clinical signs. This expertise was seldom a problem to specialists but became so for some primary care professionals who seemed reluctant to admit the parents' expertise.

SPECIFIC PROBLEMS IN SUPPORT

There were three specific problems in formal support.

Information

Good information helps parents practically and gives them a sense of control but, in practice, getting information on caring for the children and managing the illness was hard. It was even hard to get information on services, benefits and equipment. Parents often wanted to think beyond the immediate problems and to understand the trajectory of the illness. Honesty and openness on the limitations to professional knowledge were important to them, but information was often inadequate or conflicting, leaving parents confused and anxious. There were concerns about the lack of expertise in local district hospitals, which led parents to prefer specialist children's facilities. They reported many instances where professionals, especially hospital staff and GPs, did not listen to them.

Equipment and medication

The supply of equipment and medication was a major worry. Community health services lacked experience in supplying the range of specialist supplies and equipment the children needed. Parents were often left to organize supplies themselves or to battle with local health agencies for them. Community professionals noted that there had been no increase in funding to deal with the increased numbers of these children and that funds had not 'followed the child' out of hospital. Ordering was also a problem for community nurses, especially if trusts did not employ a Community Children's Nursing team. For many families the supply of consumables could be split between two or more providers. It was much better when some or all supplies were received directly from a commercial company.

Short-term care and home support

Parents were reliant on formal services for short-term care and home support because of the care needs of the children. Short-term care ranged from a few hours once a week to 24 hours 365 days a year, but the home support available was not always tailored to the children's needs. The availability of short-term care was very much a 'postcode lottery'. Even where it was available, local short-term care services did not always have the specialist knowledge to enable them to help these families. For this reason home-based care services were most usually employed, sometimes with teams specially trained to care for that child. Families overwhelmingly preferred home-based care, even though this could lead to a lack of privacy.

THE ORGANIZATION OF FORMAL SUPPORT

Inter-agency working

The three problems discussed above and poor inter-agency working went together. Arranging short-term caring could be difficult because of the lack of specialist caring teams, but problems arose much more often through funding disputes between local and health authorities over who should pay for these services. Similarly, there were wrangles between GPs, hospitals, community trusts and health authorities over the funding of supplies and equipment.

These problems were resolved in areas where care packages were jointly and equally funded by health and local authorities, but in general short-term care suffered from a lack of strategic planning and post-discharge multi-disciplinary meetings to plan care were rare. GPs and nurses could even be unsure about who was responsible for the children when they returned home and communication between hospital and community services was often poor. Parents' concerns for needs beyond the medical services were even more patchily addressed, especially worries over education.

Sometimes professionals did work well together, jointly visiting families and negotiating their visiting patterns to avoid too much intrusion and to enhance support. Clinical nurse specialists appeared to have a clear sense of their role with this group of families, sometimes devolving care to community children's nurses, health visitors and others. Thus, models of good practice did exist, but were the exception rather than the rule.

Key workers

Help was always better when there were specialist or 'key' workers – sometimes now called 'service or care coordinators' – for the family. These helped with organization of supplies, argued for services and coordinated support. Clinical nurse specialists and community children's nurses were especially effective in this. Families stressed the importance of being able to talk to professionals they knew and trusted. The use of mobile phones made these professionals especially accessible. This gave the important message to the parents that they were 'there for' them. Regrettably, most families did not have a key worker. Rather, they were left to be their own key workers, providing care, organizing supplies and services, not to mention writing to the media and to their MPs.

Messages from the study of technology-dependent children

PARENTS' LIVES

- Parents were determined to care for their children at home

but

- Family life, leisure, work and even sleep were markedly disrupted
- Children's special needs made organizing babysitters or outings difficult, and limited the help that family and friends could give

PARENTING

- Parents lacked *good information* on caring for the children
- Predicting and coping with the *trajectory of problems* was hard
- *Parenting became professionalized* and the home often an extension of the clinic
- Professionals concentrated on practicalities and ignored the emotional side of things
- Parents often become more expert than the professionals

SERVICES

- There was little planning of services prior to the child's return home
- Well-thought-out services were the exception rather than the rule
- There was often a lack of clarity about the parent's role
- Parents were often left to battle for services and equipment and medication
- The availability of short-term care was often a matter of postcode lottery

WHAT IS NEEDED

- Honesty on the limits to professional knowledge
- Professionals the families know and trust
- Readily accessible help, e.g. via mobile phones
- Integrated purchase of equipment and services
- Flexible, skilled short-term home care
- Collaborative working between health trusts, local authorities and voluntary associations

Services are best when coordinated by a key worker

Parents' expertise should be recognized and valued

Supporting South Asian families with a child with severe disabilities[3]

Background

Severe learning difficulties are three times greater amongst South Asians than among other ethnic groups in the UK. It is estimated that by 2021, 7 per cent of all British people with these difficulties will be of South Asian origin. The nature of the children's disabilities and their families' cultural circumstances suggest a special set of support needs, but equally striking is the commonality of issues these parents share with others caring for their children in many different circumstances.

Cultural issues did add an important dimension to the problems facing these families. Ease of service access went with English language use. Services seldom met religious and cultural needs. This was not only because these things were not well understood but also because of mistaken assumptions about the nature of support from the families' relatives and friends. Contrary to belief, the research literature shows that these families have quite small extended families and receive *less* support from them than white families do, a fact confirmed by this study.

The study

The study took a representative sample of 136 families with learning-disabled children, which they recruited through special needs services. They were mostly originally from Pakistan (70%) but also from India and Bangladesh. Eighty-eight per cent were two-parent families and 20 per cent had two or three disabled children. Ninety-three per cent of the families were Muslim. English was generally not the preferred language spoken at home.

The lives of the families

FAMILY HARDSHIP

Family hardship was common even though over half (57%) were home owners. Indeed, the general picture was of pervasive disadvantage: the majority of families had less than £200 p.w. (only 13% had £300), most families had no-one in the household in full-time employment (55%), only 63 per cent had a family car in which to take the child out and less than half of the main carers could drive. Fifty-three per cent thought that their housing was unsuitable for looking after a learning-disabled child. Despite this level of disadvantage, a substantial proportion

3 Hatton, C., Akram, Y., Shah, R., Robertson, J. and Emerson, E. *Supporting South Asian Families with a Child with Severe Disabilities.* Referred to as 'the *South Asian Families* study' or 'the *South Asian* study'.

of the families were not receiving any benefits – for example, 42 per cent did not have mobility needs allowances.

THE CHILDREN

Nearly all the children were described by their parents as happy and affectionate, but there were many day-to-day difficulties. Eighty per cent had problems with eating, toileting and bedtime routines, 81 per cent had no involvement in organized activities, 73 per cent had no social activities with friends and 27 per cent had no social activity of any kind, including with siblings. The children's disabilities, combined with the parents' lack of resources, meant that the parents' lives were very restricted. Forty-three per cent of children could not be left unsupervised and a further 41 per cent could not be left for more than one hour. Less than one-third of the parents ever went out in the evenings or for a weekend.

IMPACTS ON PARENTS

The effects of all this on the parents' health were stark. Compared with other Asian parents, they were twice as likely to have longstanding illness and disabilities, diabetes, respiratory problems, hypertension or angina or be overweight. Over 74 per cent were high on self-ratings on anxiety and worrying[4] and their levels of depression (40%) and anxiety (27%) was much higher than in the fourth national survey for all Asians.

The process of support

This brief summary of the families' lives shows a group of parents manifestly in need of all the help they can get. But this is not simply a question of assessing what is needed and providing it. The *South Asian* study, like the *Technology-Dependent* study, shows the importance of seeing the provision of support as a *process*, with each step in the process important to a family's confidence in their ability to cope.

For the South Asian parents the process began when they were told about their child's disability and the advice they were given about what to do and about what help could be organized. Important elements in this were the availability of useful and culturally appropriate information and help in coordinating services. The process does not stop there. It also has to anticipate and adjust to the parents' changing experiences and circumstances. Not all needs can be known or anticipated at the beginning, nor should any assumptions be made about the family's

---

4   The Malaise Inventory. The comparable figure for the parents in the *Poor Environments* study was 21 per cent. See Chapter 4.

knowledge or capacity to deal with what they are facing. We can follow through these stages in this process as they affected these families.

'TELLING'

Parents were often aware that 'something was wrong' before this was confirmed by specialists and a diagnosis given. Sometimes tests before the child was born told them that there were problems, but only about one-sixth of parents were aware of a problem at this time. The great majority (83%) were told some time after the child's birth; nearly all by the time their child was four. By the time a diagnosis was given – usually by a specialist medical consultant (71%) – about half the parents had suspicions that something was amiss and had consulted their GP about it. In a small number of cases the child was already in a special educational provision before the parents were told what the problem was (9%).

These bald figures disguise the fact that the process of telling was often unsatisfactory. Although English was generally not the preferred language for these families, 67 per cent were told in English. Written information was given to only 33 per cent of parents. Even when it was, it was nearly always in English (88%) and 20 per cent of families found it too technical or hard to understand. Only 5 per cent were given advice on how to explain the child's disability to the rest of the family, although one-third would have liked it. 'Telling' met established criteria for good practice[5] in only 15 per cent of cases. Given this, it is not surprising that only 48 per cent of parents were satisfied with the way in which they were told and a full 31 per cent were clearly dissatisfied.

INFORMATION

Clear information at the time of telling is very important, but the need for good information is part of the ongoing process. Parents were more likely to say they had enough information if they could speak English. They would have liked more written information and videos, but this was not enough. Indeed, the great majority wanted ongoing information from a key worker or other professional. Information providers needed not only to answer parents' questions but also to be proactive in providing information on sources of help that the parents did not know about. The majority of parents desperately needed more information on available services, and then help to access them. The lack of information and advice was apparent even with respect to statementing. Only about half (53%) of parents understood the

---

5   Sloper's criteria for 'disclosure' is a 47-item index measuring good practice. See Sloper, P. and Turner, S. (1993) 'Determinants of parental satisfaction with disclosure of disability.' *Developmental Medicine and Child Neurology 35*, 816–825.

statementing process, only 54 per cent said that their child had a statement and 28 per cent didn't know if their child had one or not.

Formal support

Parents were well aware of general health and welfare services and used these reasonably frequently, especially if they spoke English; but their awareness of and use of specialist services was generally low. Language problems figured large in this but parents also mentioned the cultural insensitivity of many services (72%) as well as discriminatory practices (40%). Their views of services for the child's disability were no more sanguine. It took too long to get them organized (87%), they did not know what services were available (82%) or where to get information (81%), they had to fight to get services (75%) and often had services reduced or withdrawn (74%). Although these problems are also common for all parents with learning-disabled children, lack of use of English made things even more difficult for these families.

RELATIONSHIPS WITH PROFESSIONALS

The overall quality of relationships between the parents and the professionals showed 43 per cent to be ones in which parents were shown respect and treated as equals; in 33 per cent parents and professionals simply did not get in each other's way; but for 18 per cent the relationship was confused, with no clear understanding of roles. The remaining 6 per cent of cases either showed professionals as completely taking over or parents and professionals having competing agendas. Thus relationships were poor for nearly a quarter of the families.

SHORT-TERM CARE

Issues of information and culture were especially apparent in short-term care. Very few parents were even aware of 'respite' services and only 10 per cent had had any formal short-term care, usually in specialist social services centres. When care was available it was most likely to be by unpaid members of the family. It was not just lack of awareness that limited the use of short-term care services. Many parents did not use them because of worries about their quality or because of fears of cultural inappropriateness, especially issues around the gender of the child and concerns about religious observances. At the extreme there were worries about abuse.

THE LINKING OF SERVICES

A recurrent theme across this initiative is the importance of supports that link families to services, provide information, argue for services and give emotional support and comfort. These needs are especially apparent for these families because of the language and cultural barriers that exist between the parents and service providers. An obvious need was for interpreters. Sixty-five per cent of parents wanted an interpreter but only 40 per cent had them. Even for those with interpreters there were problems with flexibility and availability as well as the fact that interpreters often knew little about disability. In the absence of interpreters people relied mostly on their spouses or another of their children.

Many of the studies have argued for the advantages of 'link' or 'key' workers in the coordinating role. Only 28 per cent of these families had key workers but those who did valued them (89%). A majority of those without one wanted one (59%). In the absence of specified key workers some social workers and health visitors took on this role, but it was a matter of chance whether families were lucky enough to have this support.

EDUCATION SERVICES

In the absence of link workers it was often schools that were the primary source of ongoing support. Nearly all the children (84%) were in special schools. These often enabled access to other services as well as being an important source of emotional support themselves. On the other hand there were limitations to the support they could give, most obviously during school holidays when parents received very little help.

The findings on education were not all good. There were shortages in speech therapy, physiotherapy and educational provision in their family language, and a lack of awareness of the children's cultural and religious needs, including diet.

Semi-formal and informal support

SEMI-FORMAL SUPPORT

Cultural and language barriers affected the parents' use of support groups. These were generally not available – or not known to be available – to these families. Only 19 per cent belonged to a support group. They generally did not find them helpful. They used groups as sources of information, for contact with people with similar problems (a reason for 91 per cent of those who used a support group) or for contact with parents with similar cultural and religious affiliations.

INFORMAL SUPPORT

The amount of support from family and friends went against the stereotype of large and supportive social circles – a finding repeated in other studies of black parents with disabled children. Black and South Asian families report *less* support from extended family networks than do white families. This difference largely arises because relatives do not live near the family. In this study, 37 per cent of families had no kin living nearby. It is thus not surprising that 68 per cent of families had no help from relatives or friends. Only 11 per cent had a lot. The support they got involved emotional support, looking after children, making loans, help around the house and similar activities.

Although geography was important, it was not the only reason for a lack of help from family and friends. It sometimes arose because kin were too busy, but 21 per cent said that relatives were 'not interested' in the child or could not cope with him or her. Eighteen per cent did not understand the disability, how it arose and what might be done about it. Support was given by friends in only a minority of cases again because, in the parents' view, 'they didn't understand'. Some parents also reported negative attitudes from local communities.

Support at home

Most mothers received most of their support from within their own homes. Families tried to be 'like a normal family'. Support from partners was high and decision making was shared between the parents. About 53 per cent of partners gave practical help and 70 per cent emotional help. In about 35 per cent of households another child helped a lot with the care of the disabled child, a percentage that would have been higher if the calculation were restricted to older children.

The balance between formal and informal support

The situation for parents was best when all sources of support were available and complemented one another. As in the *Poor Environments* study, those who were well supplied from one source of support also did better from another. Parents knew more about services if they had better informal and semi-formal support. If they were aware of more services they had fewer problems in fighting for services.

Better support tended to go with other advantages. For example, parents had a wider range of services if someone in the household was employed. The mechanism for this link was unclear but may have been through a greater feeling of confidence and competence as well as having the personal resources to pursue help. The link did not arise through more help from the informal network. More help from family and friends did not seem to help families organize formal supports.

It was certainly the case that services were not targeted on those without support from their social circle. Parents without help from family and friends tended to use formal services to compensate for the lack of informal ones, crucially to meet their need for emotional support and reassurance, a role frequently filled by schools.

Discussion

We have emphasized the importance of seeing support as a process starting with 'telling' and continuing through the coordination of services that are adaptable to changing circumstances. The researchers put this together neatly. The ideal process is summarized in Figure 6.1.

> Telling the parents and giving clear information in a supportive way helps parents accept the disability and helps mobilize services

> Acceptance by the parents makes kin and friends more accepting and supportive, even if the level of disability itself limits what they can do

> Support from kin and friends and from disability groups helps make parents more aware of services, but

> Mobilizing these services needs good language support, a trusted professional or key worker and a collaborative relationship between parents and professionals

> Good service supports reinforce the collaborative relationships, reduce unmet needs and improve parental health

Figure 6.1 The pathway to good support

Messages from the study of South Asian families with learning-disabled children

FAMILY LIFE

- Family hardship was very common
- Parents were twice as likely as other South Asian parents to have longstanding illnesses
- Levels of anxiety and depression were very high
- The parents had small extended families because of geography
- They had less informal support than white families who have learning-disabled children

'TELLING'

- Being told about the child's disability was often badly done
- Most were told in English, which was not the first language for most parents
- 'Telling' met criteria for good practice in only 15 per cent of cases

INFORMATION

- Written information was not given in two-thirds of cases
- Parents wanted more *ongoing* information
- They wanted it from a *key worker* or other professional
- The needed it to be responsive to their questions and proactive
- Only about half of the parents understood the 'statementing' process

SERVICES

- Services were often culturally insensitive
- Relationships with professionals were confused or the professionals took over in nearly a quarter of cases
- Cultural insensitivity was especially evident in the provision of short-term care
- Interpreting services need improving
- Interpreters need to know more about disability
- Only 28 per cent of families had a key worker
- Education services were often a primary source of ongoing support

Things were best when all sources of support complemented each other

Of course, this neat summary should not be taken as the royal road to success. Each step is hard to achieve and each link only increases the chance that the next step will be achieved – it does not ensure that it does. Nevertheless the process is neatly summarized in this analysis.

Parenting and disability: The role of formal and informal supports[6]

Background

The third study was concerned not with supporting parents caring for disabled children but with support for parents who are themselves disabled, through physical, sensory or mental health impairments. Discussions of this topic have often focused on the question of 'young carers'; that is, the extent to which the children's lives are taken up with caring for their parents and the impact this has on them. This study took a different perspective. It set out to examine 'the ways in which disabled parents can be enabled to maintain control over providing care for their children'. This is important in challenging the assumption that impairments affect the capacity of disabled people to parent successfully.

The study

The intention was to look at a range of disabilities and family circumstances to find out how these affected parenting, to see what help they might need. An additional idea was to see how families changed and what supports were needed following the onset of a new disability. Families were recruited to the study in a 'purposive' way. Sixty-seven parents were recruited through disability organizations, community facilities and GPs, but not from young carers' groups. All these were interviewed, as were 60 children and 37 partners. Most of the disabled sample were women (85%), two-thirds of whom were in two-parent families.

In practice the sample was very heterogeneous with respect to the kind of impairments experienced. The mental health group was the most diverse and included many people with neurological problems such as Multiple Sclerosis (MS). There was some overlap between the broad categories of disability: 20 of index parents had mental health impairments, 32 had physical impairments, 12 both kinds of impairment and three physical and sensory impairments.

---

6   Olsen, R. and Clarke, H. *Parenting and Disability: The Role of Formal and Informal Networks.* Referred to as 'the *Disabled Parents* study'.

Family circumstances

HOUSING, TRANSPORT AND EDUCATION

The sample that was painstakingly collected is unlikely to be representative of disabled people in its social circumstances. Sixty per cent were home owners and over two-thirds had been in the same home for more than five years. The great majority (84%) of households had a car available for private use and 36 disabled parents were able to drive. Nearly half (48%) had A-level or degree-level qualifications. This educational bias in the sample may have enabled the articulation of support issues, but the atypicality of the sample should be borne in mind when interpreting percentage figures from the findings.

WORK AND FAMILY INCOME

Despite this bias, the level of disadvantage in the sample was high. Only 18 per cent were in regular paid employment and 60 per cent were permanently sick or disabled. Nearly one-quarter of families had a household income of less than £8000 p.a., although a small minority (15%) had an income over £29,000, usually through a partner's occupation. Hindrances to normal family life were also apparent, especially for those without a car. Many parents commented on the usual problems for wheelchair users and difficulty in using buses. Using public transport was also hard for those with mental health impairments, especially those with agoraphobia or panic disorders.

BENEFITS

Thirty-two households were on Income Support and 47 had some kind of disability living allowance – 42 with a mobility component and 44 with a care component (39 got both) – and 18 had Incapacity Benefit and 16 severe disability allowances. Receipt of disability living allowances was much less frequent for the mental health group but there were no differences in receipt of incapacity benefit according to the type of impairment. Only one family received direct payments. This family also got Independent Living Fund payments, as did three others. All those that had these really liked them.

Young caring

One-third of parents (33%) described their children as 'young carers'. A further third said the children were involved in caring. In practice, however, involvement of the children in caring was low. Indeed, parents actively tried to protect their children from this happening. Children in single-parent families were more likely to be involved in housework and caring (59% v. 38%) but seldom in caring for the impaired person. All the instances of direct caring (12%) were for physically impaired parents.

Certain external factors influenced the need for children to help. In one case the withdrawal of home help when the child reached 12 necessarily put some extra responsibilities onto her. Even good support from services could not always eliminate the need for the children to help, especially in single-parent families, and outside normal service hours. However, it is clear that 'young caring' was infrequent in this sample.

THE CHILDREN'S VIEWS

The children themselves were somewhat more likely than the parents to report that they helped in personal care or stayed in to keep their parents company. Their reactions to caring varied greatly depending on their own sense of what was right and wrong for them. This ranged from resentment at any 'interference' in their freedom to be kids to a real sense of contributing to the family. We have no comparison with the normal level of involvement in household tasks in non-disabled families.

Formal support

Most formal support services were used infrequently by these families apart, of course, from hospital services (consultants, occupational therapists and physiotherapists). On the other hand, the range of services having some input to the families was wide – 22 or more services in all. The most important other services giving ongoing help were social workers (25%) or home care workers (18%). Two-thirds of physically impaired parents had some help from formal services at that time, compared with 43 per cent of parents with mental impairments.

THE SUPPORT PROCESS

These parents, although predominantly white and generally more advantaged than the South Asian parents, nevertheless echoed many of the points the South Asian parents made about being told about their impairment and the process of support. Most talked about the paucity of good information on benefits and services at the time of onset/diagnosis, even, for example, entitlement to a free wheelchair. Language problems were also apparent in this study for ethnic minority families.

The part of the study on the onset of impairments highlighted problems around 'telling' and the giving of a diagnosis. This was often not well handled. The problems raised by these parents are remarkably similar to those raised by the South Asian parents, even though in this case the diagnosis involved the patient him- or herself rather than a child. The parents emphasized the importance of clarity and sympathy at the start and the importance of putting supports in quickly.

SERVICE ASSUMPTIONS ABOUT FAMILY SUPPORT

An additional complication for these families was that assumptions were made about the capacity of partners or families to care, without any additional financial or other help or any consideration of the impact of caring on the partner's work.

KEY WORKERS

These families generally did not have a 'key worker', although support was much more satisfactory when some took this on, as was the case with a particularly effective consultant. Many families stressed their need for someone to argue their case for services and to battle for them.

RELATIONSHIPS WITH SCHOOLS

Most parents were satisfied with their relationships with their children's schools but issues of disclosure did crop up. These mostly concerned the mental health group, who worried about the judgements the school would make about their disability and its consequences for the children's absences and behaviour. Other parents had difficulties in communicating with schools, which could be frustrating if the children were themselves having a difficult time at school.

Schools were generally well regarded for their understanding of parents' problems around education. They worked hard at the best ways of communication with them – for example, through home-school books – even if this still needed working on. A perennial issue concerned access for the physically impaired, especially when the children moved from primary to secondary school. Problems arose for a variety of reasons, including physical access, geographical distance and less close relationships with teachers.

Barriers to the use of services

PRACTICAL BARRIERS

The study has many useful examples of the barriers to the use of services, which point up the realities behind the 'social model' of disability, especially with regard to parenting. The location and timing of services sometimes failed to fit the parents' lives and the limits to their getting around. For example, some parents were offered play-school places on the other side of town, when there was little chance of their being able to take the children there.

Mobility and access issues meant that building-based services were often not helpful. In addition, the use of community provisions for children, such as clubs and groups, was limited by transport problems faced by parents as well as by cost. In addition, community provision could fail to see impaired parents as parents. In one case, a mother was told that she could not take her children with her when using low-cost transport provided by a voluntary agency, because of insurance issues.

INFLEXIBILITIES IN BENEFITS

Some problems in support were related to the rigidity of support systems in the face of fluctuating impairments, such that benefits could be withdrawn and parents find it hard to get them reinstated. Application for benefits was particularly problematic, as were reductions in allowances following reviews, an event with a particular impact on MS sufferers. In addition, some conditions – bipolar disorder, for example – were not recognized as impairments eligible for disabled living allowances. This issue of flexibility relates not only to the response of formal support systems to change but also to their ability to maintain continuity and stability in the parents' lives in the face of fluctuations in illness; for example, in keeping work or returning to it following an episode of illness.

PATIENT-CREATED BARRIERS

Parents themselves were often willing to discuss their own contribution to their under-use of support services. Indeed, some – especially the mental health group – said that this sometimes arose through their own difficulty in taking responsibility for arrangements or a reluctance to have others take over housework during periods of illness. They also mentioned their own forgetfulness; for example, in not telling a partner that arrangements had been changed or cancelled.

SERVICES' RELUCTANCE TO SUPPORT PARENTING

The researchers' view that services often concentrated support on the parents' impairment and neglected their parenting was illustrated in a number of ways. There was sometimes simply a reluctance to see parenting as a legitimate support need; some parents said that help with parenting was not allowable as part of community care or direct payment packages. In addition, relationships with social services could turn into conflicts; for example, around 'at risk' registrations – with the implication that social services tended to see parents' disabilities as cause for concern, not as a parenting need to be helped through support.

Informal support

FAMILY AND FRIENDS

Disability could compromise parents' ability to make and sustain relationships with their social circle; for example, when the houses of others became inaccessible to them. Restrictions on mobility naturally affected the ability of the disabled parents to keep in touch with family and friends. But there was more to it than that. Family and friends did help and the parents gave help themselves, an often over-looked fact. On the other hand, help from family and friends was often not taken up because they felt that they could not return favours. Parents were often wary of leaning on friends too much because they worried that this might jeopardize friendships.

As in the other studies, family and friends could be a source of stress as well as of help. Sometimes this was because the family was seen as a source of the parents' difficulties, through their perceived role in the origins of the parents' mental distress, in their negative attitudes to the parents having children at all or because of relatives' difficulty in understanding the impairments.

Discussion

The case for supporting these parents so that they can go on parenting, rather than looking for 'parenting deficits' caused by their impairments, seems clear. Of course, this is rather more easily said than done since 'disabled parents' are a very varied group in the nature and severity of their impairments and in the extent to which these fluctuate. Heterogeneity makes service planning difficult. Heterogeneity is even more of an issue when the diverse kinds of mental impairments are considered alongside physical and sensory ones.

However, the authors are right to point out that disabled parents' needs *as parents* can be invisible to services that consider the impact of the impairment too narrowly. Assessments should include what is needed to help them continue to parent. This is obvious for practical things such as offering nursery school places that cannot be taken up because of lack of mobility. The study highlights two major issues: the variability of impairment and the needs of children as they get older. The first is a problem when fluctuations in illness lead to fluctuations in support, which in turn affects parenting. The second causes problems if benefit entitlements are related to children's ages or if children's developmental needs at particular ages are not taken into account.

Messages from the study of parenting and disability

PARENTING

Parents felt they needed

- To have housing that made parenting easier
- To be able to get out with their children
- To have access to schools and teachers
- To have practical and emotional support in their parenting

but

- There were barriers because houses were not adapted

or

- Schools and child care provision was inaccessible

CHILDREN

- Children's involvement in caring was low and irregular
- Parents and children were concerned to keep it that way

SERVICES

- Services often concentrated on the parents' disability and ignored their needs as parents
- Parenting was sometimes not seen as legitimate support need
- Services made assumptions or demands about the partners' ability to care
- Services were more effective when someone took a key worker role, but most did not have them
- Rules on benefits did not deal well with fluctuating illnesses
- Changes in children's needs as they get older were not taken into account in benefit entitlement

What these studies tell us about support, parenting and disability

The balance between formal and informal support

The messages from these parents are the same as those from those in the general population and foster care studies. Informal and formal sources of support do not balance or replace one another. Rather, those people who receive more of one kind of support get more of the other. The parents in the *South Asian Families* study were more aware of services if they had better informal and semi-formal support. They also had a wider range of services if someone in the household was employed. Those who spoke English got more services. Better 'telling' was also associated with getting more services. In short, there seemed to be a general process of inverse targeting, although there was no suggestion that this was deliberate.

For *disabled* parents as well as *parents of disabled children*, relationships with family and friends were complicated by problems of balance of help and its availability, as well as understanding and tolerance of the impairment. Parents were wary of making too many claims for help and kin and friends were wary of helping because they did not understand the disability, had negative feelings about it or did not have the skills to provide what was often most needed – babysitting, day care or giving the parents a break. *South Asian* families got less support from their social circle than white families, mostly because of geography but also because of attitudes to disabilities.

Because of these limitations to help from the informal system, formal support was used to make up for the lack of informal ones, especially in the provision of information, comfort and support. Services clearly need to provide emotional as well as practical support. There were examples of this happening in all three studies, both in the actions of individual professionals and schools and in the input from 'key' or 'link' workers. All three studies emphasized the positive response of parents to these services.

Was support related to better parenting?

None of these studies had direct measures of parenting and therefore could not look at the effects of support on the details of parenting. But they all dealt with major impairments in children or parents and we can reasonably assume that making parenting less burdensome will have a positive effect on parent–child relationships. For all these parents formal inputs were essential, so we can focus the discussion on these.

Despite the differences in sampling strategy and type of disability, the extent to which parents and partners were thrown back on their own resources and relationships was striking. Because of this it was essential that services were delivered in an emotionally supportive way. The *South Asian* parents relied heavily on the schools for emotional support. Everyone liked key workers not only because of their practical helpfulness, but because they were emotionally supportive as well. Relationships lie at the heart of support.

It is easy, when a service is technically very specialized, for service providers to concentrate on their technical skills. This was apparent in the *Technology-Dependent* study even when this expertise was used in the parents' own homes. Thus distinction between emotional and specialist practical support, which is sometimes seen to distinguish informal and formal support systems, is questioned as service providers learn to be more emotionally supportive.

Messages from the studies on disability

FAMILY LIFE

- Parents worked hard to maintain a normal family life for their children

but

- The extent to which parents were thrown back on their own emotional and physical resources was striking

INFORMAL SUPPORTS

Informal supports were limited by:

- Geography
- Mobility
- The children's special needs
- The attitudes of kin and friends in some cases
- The parents' concerns about being able to return the help

SERVICES

For these reasons services need to think beyond their expertise and their responsibility for the disability alone. Unfortunately:

- Support was too easily determined by service agendas
- Sensitive telling and information was not sufficiently in evidence
- Ongoing information and partnership tended to be lacking
- Services were often culturally insensitive

NEEDS

- Parents with disabled children need their own physical and mental health needs addressed
- Disabled parents should have their needs as parents recognized
- Services need to be especially careful about providing emotional support
- Provision for short breaks needs to be flexible and appropriate
- Support should include paying attention to material disadvantage and employment opportunities

Key workers should be a central element in service coordination

As yet services are not based on reliable, valid and holistic assessments

Parenting and disability reconsidered

The studies discussed in this chapter are placed together for an obvious reason: they are all concerned in one way or another with 'disability'. However, apart from the fact that they involve impairments in children or parents that make parenting more challenging, we need first to consider whether this grouping is any more than a matter of convenience – or indeed prejudice. We should ask whether having a group of 'disability' studies at all is counter to the ideas behind the 'social model'.

In practice, it seems impossible to frame policy or devise services that do not make a special case for support in relation to impairments of one kind or another. On the other hand, the heterogeneity in the type, severity and variability in the impairments and their associated disabilities is striking. Heterogeneity makes service planning difficult. All the studies make a strong case for more flexibility in service provisions but do not specify the limits to flexibility or to set out specific models for flexible services.

In all the studies parental satisfaction with services was most positive when they were responsive to needs, culturally sensitive and respected the parents' expertise on their own problems. This was all much more likely if services were coordinated, usually by a key worker. Involving children and families in planning is crucial to designing responsive services. Greater satisfaction was associated with more helpful services, more collaboration and fewer communication problems with professionals.

None of the studies was able to show that services paid particular attention to support around parenting itself, apart from care in the context of the child's disability or concern over the parenting of disabled parents. There was no evidence of help with parenting approaches or with relationships.

Services have a long way to go to meet these objectives. Service responses were clearly not based on reliable, valid and holistic assessments. Instead, parents often had to fight for services, some of which proved unsuitable.

Chapter 7

Supporting Parents who may be Hard to Help

Introduction

This chapter summarizes the findings from the final four studies in the initiative. These studies are a diverse group. They include research on:

- support for teenagers in public care who are pregnant or already have children
- inputs to strengthen the parenting roles of imprisoned fathers
- identifying and understanding the rejection of children
- the role of family centres in coordinating support.

This apparent diversity nevertheless has an underlying common theme. Parents in the first three of these are ones of whom society sometimes has a negative view, for one reason or another. At the extreme they may be seen as responsible for their own misfortune and 'get what they deserve'. These attitudes may have an impact in subtle ways on our ideas on their right to services or support, or their place in the queue for services, or the way that services treat them. The response may be to supply the minimum input required to mitigate some of the worst effects of their actions.

The studies cover groups whose culpability may be ordered in the public mind in a direction of increasing severity. Teenage parents may have been careless but deserve our help. Imprisoned fathers may be seen as responsible for their actions but their children and families generally are not. Rejecting parents show parenting behaviours that most of us find hardest to be sympathetic to or to understand.

Family centres do not necessarily work with parents with these kinds of difficulties. Indeed, they began as centres that have a philosophy of community-based and holistic services that are best provided in a preventative way to meet a wide range of parenting needs. Increasingly, however, they have been pushed towards providing assessments of and services to families with complex and intractable problems. For this reason it is appropriate to include them in this chapter.

Preparation and support for parenting[1]

Background

This study was about young people whose early sexual behaviour causes particular concern: looked-after teenagers. Adults have ambivalent feelings about teenage sexuality but concern for these young people goes beyond that, especially for girls. The worries include their vulnerability to sexual exploitation and the very high rates of pregnancy and teenage parenthood, amounting to one-quarter of girls discharged from care in one sample.[2] Early parenthood can have very serious consequences for the life-chances of young women.

Earlier policy changes to address early pregnancy tended to focus on changing individual behaviour. An acknowledgement of a link between early pregnancy, social disadvantage and poor educational attainment was made with the transfer of the responsibilities of the National Task Group on unwanted and unintended teenage pregnancies to the Social Exclusion Unit in 1998. Nevertheless, the focus has remained more on prevention than support, perhaps because the rates of teenage pregnancy are higher in the UK than in any other modern industrial economy besides the USA.

One favoured route to prevention has been through better sex education. Rates of teenage pregnancy are lower in countries with good sex education and contraceptive services. However, the links between culture, policy and teenage pregnancy are likely to be more complex than a simple correlation between education and pregnancy rates.

Of course, good sex education has a far wider purpose than lowering rates of unwanted pregnancies. It is essential for young people's health as well. This may be particularly the case for looked-after children who may miss parental guidance or be led into early and dangerous sexual activity. Unfortunately, sex education in the UK is very patchy, especially so for looked-after young people. This arises partly because they are more likely to miss schooling through school changes, truancy or exclusion. But it also arises because of the lack of clear policy within social services on this topic. At the time this study was done there was a striking lack of policies

---

1   Corlyon, J. and McGuire, C. (1999). Published as *Pregnancy and Parenthood: The Views and Experiences of Young People in Public Care.* London: National Children's Bureau. Referred to as 'the *Teenage Pregnancy* study'.

2   Biehal, N., Clayden, J., Stein, M. and Wade, J. (1995) *Moving On: Young People and Leaving Care Schemes.* London: HMSO.

within the social services departments studied. Few of them even had figures on pregnancies in the children they were looking after.

Sex is a personal and emotive topic, and educational or other programmes are unlikely to be effective in getting information across to young people unless we find out from them what is wrong with the way it is currently delivered and unless we see sex as a normal activity for them, even quite early in their teens. Of course, the gap between knowledge and passion will always be hard to bridge, but we shall not do so unless we know whether early pregnancy is the result of choice, ignorance or the pressures of the moment. For looked-after children we also need to understand the need for something to love amid the uncontrollability of their lives.

The study

This study looked at how looked-after teenagers differed from their peers in the general population in their ideas about pregnancy and parenthood, what they thought lay behind pregnancy in adolescence and whether to continue with or terminate it and, finally, at the support pregnant looked-after teenagers got from services. The focus was very much on the young people's perspectives.

The study was done in two parts between 1995 and 1998. First, there were interviews with 30, mostly white, young people in 11 local authorities who were expecting babies. There were also interviews with 20 social workers and with social work managers. In this chapter these are called the pregnancy sample.

Second, there was a questionnaire study of equal numbers of looked-after children and children in the general population (the school group), 106 in each group between the ages of 13 and 17. They were mostly age 14 or 15. There were interviews with 67 volunteers from amongst these young people – 38 looked after (mostly in residential care) and 29 in the school group.

Attitudes, motivations and behaviours

What light does the study throw on the personal thoughts and motivations around pregnancy and its prevention?

IDEALS OF FAMILY LIFE

Young people often give surprisingly conventional answers on their ideals for love and family life, especially before they have much experience. This was true here. There were no differences between the looked-after and school groups on the ideal family, which was a couple with babies. They aspired to be trustworthy parents who gave responsibility to their children and told them that they loved them and showed it. Few saw single parenthood as a good deal, although the pregnancy group girls, who were nearly all single parents, did not want the children's fathers around. Even they hoped for stable partners, despite their experiences and negative views of men.

EDUCATIONAL ASPIRATIONS

The aspirations of the looked-after children on work or education were as high as those of the school group and exposed the gap between hopes and reality. A surprisingly large proportion hoped that in four years' time they would have stable jobs or be in college or university (62% of males, 83% of females). The pregnancy sample wanted work with animals, children or the elderly, or in social work, although only three were attending college or taking higher qualifications at the time of the interview. One interpretation of these commonly chosen jobs is that the girls looked to follow the few positive caring models they had experienced, but with no understanding of what was needed to get there.

EXPECTATIONS OF PARENTHOOD

Their expectations regarding parenthood were more likely to be realized. Early partnership and parenthood were more attractive to the looked-after group than the school children. Forty-seven per cent of them thought they would have children in four years' time compared with 17 per cent of the school group.

Factors in early pregnancies

FATALISM

Was early pregnancy related to lack of a sense of any other future? Certainly the looked-after sample had little sense that they could do anything about the future. Only a third of the girls and half of the boys felt that they were involved in plans and decisions about their lives. There was a generally fatalistic attitude about what would happen to them, which applied to pregnancy as well.

This fatalistic attitude did not show up in differences from the school sample on when it was okay to start having sex. Seventy to eighty per cent of boys and girls in both samples thought it was all right at 14 or 15, providing that the boy and girl wanted it and used contraception. We do not know which of the children had had intercourse or whether they had followed their own rules if they had. Their answers probably just tell you that for most young people of this age sex is very much on their minds.

PEER PRESSURE

Interestingly, both samples said that social pressure to have sex came more from their *own* gender. It was a badge of maturity and a way of being part of the scene (and probably of normalizing everyone's activity). However, looked-after young people *of both sexes* were much more likely than the school group to say that partners had pressured them.

INVULNERABILITY

By far the most commonly agreed reason for pregnancy across all the samples was that teenagers didn't think it would happen. Invulnerability and carelessness were the big drivers as the young people saw them. Three-quarters of every sample held this view. However, the looked-after children differed markedly from the school sample in their belief that teenagers also want someone to love and that the girls want a baby.

GETTING PREGNANT TO GET A HOUSE OR KEEP A BOYFRIEND

Ideas that pregnancy is used to keep a boyfriend or to get housing benefits received no support. The young women in the pregnancy sample had a very low opinion of the fathers. Care leavers are a housing priority anyway. On the other hand, these girls did suggest that having a baby confers a kind of transition to adulthood and gives girls the status and attention that they might not otherwise have achieved.

USING CONTRACEPTION

The injunction to sex only in loving relationships and protected by contraception was contradicted by other views and attitudes. One-third of girls in the looked-after and school samples agreed that they would be too embarrassed to talk about contraception with a new partner. Looked-after boys ignored the possible consequences of their actions. The looked-after girls were somewhat more concerned but less so than the school girls.

Other studies have highlighted the lack of contraceptive use in younger teenagers. The experience of the pregnancy sample suggested why. Some were simply overtaken by the moment. A larger proportion thought they were unassailable. This involved much magical thinking. If they had 'got away with it' once, it strengthened their beliefs that it would not happen to them. Some simply did not mind if they got pregnant. The lack of contraceptive use was nothing to do with distaste for it. No young people in either study thought that using contraception implied promiscuity.

Abortion and adoption

The school samples were twice as likely to think of abortion if unwanted pregnancy occurred. The pregnancy sample showed how much more complicated it was for them. There were pressures from adults who favoured abortion and peers who favoured keeping the baby. Adoption hardly came into consideration, but there seemed to be some pressure from parents against it.

From their accounts, the situation of the pregnancy sample was dire. They were very distressed when they found that they were pregnant but two-thirds had no counselling, only two felt supported by services and there was seldom any support from their birth mothers, although it was hoped for. Sometimes the girls felt over-whelmed by the weight and variety of other people's opinions. Making decisions is generally hard for this group. Keeping the child often seemed the least worst option for girls unused to planning and generally not in a position to take a long-term view. They said that parenting should be fun and that praise was impor-tant but few had been given advice or support on child care and parenthood.

Informal support

There were naturally big differences in the questionnaires on the frequency with which young people saw their parents. Only two-fifths of looked-after children said that they got on well with their mothers, compared with 88 per cent of the school group. The gap in their relationship with fathers was even greater. The parents of the looked-after children were not seen as helpful. Indeed, girls said that they had a better deal from their carers than from their parents. Trust and respect were the main things they felt they lacked in their relationships with significant adults.

Relationships with parents were especially bad for the pregnancy sample girls. Many had been rejected by their mothers in favour of a new partner. Although their mothers sometimes visited them, this was often to get support from the young people, not the other way round. Their friends were also likely to be seen as untrustworthy and exploitative.

Formal supports

Two aspects of formal support can be considered: the young people's views on sex education and their relationships with specific services.

SEX EDUCATION

Better sex education is seen as key to reducing unwanted pregnancies, but the views of the young people in all samples was not positive about what they got.

Sex education is compulsory in maintained secondary schools. If schools do not provide this for looked-after children then the local authority should. At the time of the study this was an intention, not actuality. No local authority staff in the 11 authorities in the pregnancy study were aware of *any* policy. Some developments were under way, focused primarily on residential care, perhaps because of the clear risks in this sector. Carers and social workers were uneasy about giving contraceptive advice without parental agreement. Sexual activity was seen as a problem with no local authority policy framework.

For these reasons sex education relied almost entirely on what the young people got at school. Many of the pregnancy sample had effectively finished education by 14 and missed out on some input. Anything they got in care was from individual staff, not part of a policy. Those that had had sex education at school were negative about it but had no real ideas on how it might be different. All the samples complained about content and timing (that it was usually too late). No more than half of the school or the looked-after children said they had any teaching on family life and relationships. It is hard to know what to make of this without some record of what the schools thought they delivered.

SUPPORT FROM SERVICES

Social workers

Only 4 per cent of the looked-after sample included social workers amongst the people they could trust. Only three young women in the pregnancy sample had positive relationships with social workers. Most had the usual litany of complaints that the social workers didn't listen, didn't listen to their opinions, didn't give honest accounts and explanations, couldn't be trusted, were difficult or impossible to contact, were not supportive, didn't stand up for them, were unreliable and sat in judgement on them.

These views clearly express the young women's feelings but the social workers' own accounts are needed to get a more balanced picture. Many quotes from the young people implied that the social workers did not meet their needs as quickly as they wanted. From the social workers' point of view what the young people saw as a good relationship often involved over-dependency, including constant phoning, and bypassing the foster carer. In some cases complaints echoed a common teenage complaint: 'Leave me alone but look after me.' It was often hard for services to help these girls and keep them involved with the help that was offered.

Assessment

There appeared to be little social work assessment of parenting capacity and girls clearly resisted this. Most of the pregnancy group were adamant that they didn't want any social services involvement with their babies. They had a strong desire to prove that they had the necessary skills on their own. Two who had been placed in mother-and-baby assessment units were indignant about it because they thought they were being watched. Those who lived in residential accommodation liked the support there better because it interfered less.

Accommodation

Local authorities have an obligation to house care leavers as a matter of priority, but the 11 authorities had no specific policies for pregnant young women or mothers. Arranging accommodation can be a major problem because of the frequent moves the young people make. Housing authorities often will not offer a second tenancy if someone had just abandoned one.

Provision varied from monitored and supported flats to mother-and-baby homes. Foster care was seldom used. Supported accommodation provided the benefits of company and avoided the tensions of communal living. For all forms of supported housing there were issues around who came in and out and how to accommodate boyfriends. Independence or quasi-independence seemed to bring an assumption that the young women could cope, for example, with handling money, to an extent that was beyond their capabilities.

Education

About one-third of the pregnancy sample had finished their schooling before the minimum age. Only one social worker saw it as her responsibility to help with continuing education. All sorts of approaches to education were used, including special facilities and home tutors, but the pressure of caring for the child and providing on-time and emotional resources produced a high failure rate, despite some notable successes.

After-care workers

After-care workers were viewed in a much more positive light. They dealt with housing and finance, and argued for help. They also gave emotional support. In some ways they were lucky. They were free of the hard decisions concerning the mother and baby, including child protection issues. If these come between the social worker and the young mother, the after-care worker is the one supporting the mother: a version of the bad fairy/good fairy scenario. On the other hand, after-care workers sometimes felt that the social workers dumped cases on them and withdrew into their child protection work.

Messages from the study
on teenage pregnancy

SEX EDUCATION

- Young people were not impressed by their sex education
- It was sporadic or missing for looked-after children
- No staff in any of the 11 authorities were aware of any policy on sex education

ATTITUDES TO SEX

The young people

- Had very conventional aspirations for work and family life
- Thought it was fine to begin sex at 14–15
- Social pressure for sex came more from the same gender
- Young people thought pregnancy occurred through invulnerability and carelessness
- All knew about contraception but were cavalier about its use

but

- The school sample was much more likely to say they would consider abortion

Looked-after young people

- Found early partnering and parenthood attractive
- Had a fatalistic attitude about their lives, including pregnancy
- Had pressures from adults to abort and friends to keep baby
- Felt overwhelmed by the variety of advice and opinions
- Keeping children often seemed the least worse option
- Were adamant that housing or to keep a partner were not behind the pregnancy
- Carers felt unable to give sex advice without parental permission

SERVICES

- Pregnant girls felt unsupported by services and birth mothers
- There was little social work assessment of the girls' parenting capacity

but

- Social workers often found them dependent and demanding
- Giving support was difficult

The parenting role of imprisoned fathers[3]

Background

At the time this study was done, an estimated 125,000 children were separated from their fathers because of imprisonment. Such children are commonly distressed, disturbed and confused by the event and their families put at financial disadvantage.

Prison service standing order no. 5 states that 'one of the roles of the prison service [is] to ensure that the socially harmful effects of an inmate's removal from normal life are as far as possible minimised…contacts are therefore encouraged especially between an inmate and his family…'. This is in accord with the welfare principle stressed in the Children Act and the insistence in the Convention on the Rights of the Child that children have the right to maintain contact with their parents in most situations of separation.

Unfortunately, criminal proceedings rarely take these principles adequately into account, even though the Woolf Report of 1991[4] recommended increased and extended visiting, home leave where possible and placement in an institution near home. In short, there has been a lack of strong and consistent policies to maintain family ties.

The study

This study explored the experiences of the fathers and their partners and children around contact. The focus was on the use and effectiveness of parenthood classes and ordinary and specialized family visiting schemes in keeping relationships alive. The researchers interviewed 181 men in 25 geographically spread establishments, including six young offender institutions. The men had served at least six months and were in the final two years of any longer sentence. In practice, about half had sentences of three years or more. Cases involving physical or sexual violence within the family were excluded. In those establishments that had special courses or arrangements, only those who had taken part in these were interviewed. There were also interviews with 127 partners and a small number of children (25).

As part of the agreement with the men necessary to get them to take part, direct comparisons between their accounts and those of their partners were ruled out. For this reason it is not possible to know whether the men's assertions about the changes brought about by classes are confirmed by their partners.

3   Boswell, G. and Wedge, P. *The Parenting Role of Imprisoned Fathers.* Referred to as 'the *Imprisoned Fathers* study' or 'the *Prison* study'.

4   Home Office (1991) *Report into Prison Disturbances April 1990 by the Right Honourable Lord Woolf and His Honour Judge Stephen Tumin.* Cmd. 1456. London: HMSO.

Effects of imprisonment on the children

It was clear from the partners' accounts that imprisonment was associated with problems with the children. For 22 per cent their behaviour became more difficult. Only 8 per cent were seen as not affected in any way. The problems mentioned were predominantly the ones the mothers most immediately had to cope with, such as misbehaviour and distress. Only 5 per cent saw children falling behind or having problems at school. This is likely to be a substantial under-estimate. Many children were tired, sad and tearful after visits.

The men's feelings about fathering

The men's judgements and hopes about their past, current and future parenting ranged from the unrealistically positive to a depressed negativity. The great majority had had hard or harsh parenting experiences of their own and wanted to emulate the good bits and avoid the bad. Over two-thirds of adult and young offenders said they felt guilty, helpless or 'gutted' about being a father in prison and about how hard this made it for the children's mother. The same proportion said they would go home and be with their children on discharge. When asked what they would do with the children their responses were somewhat general. Just over half simply wanted to be with them, while 25 per cent referred to activities such as playing with them, going for walks or taking holidays.

These responses were echoed in their views of what an ideal father is: he is loving, is not in prison and gives 'quality time'. Less than 10 per cent in adult or in youth institutions mentioned discipline, but 17 per cent referred to being a 'good listener' or a 'friend' and a further 17 per cent to being an 'economic provider'. Forty-three per cent of adults and 30 per cent of young offenders saw themselves as matching this ideal, while 49 per cent felt that nothing could be done to get them nearer to it. As the authors commented: 'These responses did not suggest that time in prison had been spent reflecting on ways in which inmates might have failed to match up to their ideal...'

Whether the hope of return to 'be with' the children is optimistic or otherwise can only be examined by follow-up studies. We cannot tell at the moment whether these responses were unrealistic, were the answers they thought the interviewers wanted or reflected a firm intention to change.

The provision and context of contact

All prisons had basic visiting arrangements and arrangements for contact by phone and letter. Some fathers nearing the end of their sentences were also allowed town or home visits. One in twelve institutions also had special children's or family visiting schemes. Most fathers in the study did maintain contact with the children and their partners felt a clear responsibility to make this happen.

BASIC VISITING

At a minimum, all drug-free prisoners are entitled to two visits of two hours within a four-week period. Up to three people are normally allowed to visit with a visiting order. Visiting is supervised and adults and children may be searched. In some prisons children cannot touch their fathers. Children do not understand why fathers cannot get up and play with them, fathers are bothered that they are not allowed to control or help their children, and there is a serious lack of facilities such as toys or crèches. In short, for many families the reality of ordinary visiting was depressingly awful.

Nevertheless, 80 per cent of adults and 60 per cent of young offenders used all types of visit available to them, although about half of the young offenders did not see their children, usually because they had never effectively parented them. About three-fifths of fathers had visits fortnightly or more often, two-thirds had phone contact several times a week, 88 per cent were sent or given photos, but only 13 per cent used audio or video tape. Twenty-eight per cent of men thought ordinary visits 'strengthened ties and relationships' but 30 per cent said that they were of no help at all to them as fathers.

THE VISITING SCHEMES

Visiting schemes tried to improve on the bleak experience of ordinary visiting. All eight currently existing schemes were included in the study. There were no schemes in young offender institutions. There were two basic types of scheme: *children's visits,* facilitated by voluntary agency staff (there were five of these, two of which were for fathers and children only), and two *family visits,* for inmates with sentences of over four years, of one half to a whole day, which might include lunch and walking in the grounds. There was also one *family learning scheme*: a fifteen-week programme of literacy support for fathers, partners and children. The schemes commonly provided toys, games and space for physical activities. Uniformed staff were always involved in some capacity and all schemes had some form of child care help from voluntary or charitable bodies.

Individual interviews with men in prisons with these visiting schemes suggested that the take-up rate was high: 80 per cent of adults and 60 per cent of young offenders in the sample used all types of visit and those who did not, in the main, had their children brought to see them anyway. However, in one prison where a group interview was conducted, only 10 per cent had used this particular children's visit scheme. Low use in this case was related to a lack of information about eligibility or to security concerns, especially around drug usage. Indeed, concern over drug conveyancing was a common reason for the closure of schemes.

There were far fewer barriers to fathering in children's and family visits. The greater freedom to do things with the children explained why children's and family visits were well regarded by prisoners, partners and children alike. Both inmates and partners continued to resent the inevitable intrusion of security and the consequent lack of privacy. There were also, paradoxically, downsides caused by the more relaxed context. Inmates feel generally good during visits but over half felt low and depressed afterwards and thought that their partners did too. Staff commented that the better atmosphere sometimes made goodbyes more distressing for the children.

THE PARENTHOOD COURSES

There were more parenthood classes than visiting schemes. These were common in young offender institutions and were in operation in 28 per cent of adult institutions in 1998. Run by the prison education service, they varied enormously in length, from a single session to a fifty-hour course. They could be predominantly practical, dealing, for instance, with cookery, baby care and budgeting, or they focused much more on relationships and child development. In addition to the fathers' positive responses, when partners were asked if they knew of anything that they thought had helped the man with his fathering, 77 per cent said 'nothing' but 12 per cent mentioned fatherhood courses (of which there were only eight in the sample of 25 prisons) and referred to improvements in both practical skills and knowledge about child development during the prison sentence itself. There have been moves to standardize the courses through the life skills programme.

At some times in their careers most young offenders had attended courses, but 57 per cent were currently in establishments that did not have them. Only a minority of adult prisoners had done so (29%), although a high proportion did when courses were available. Courses were clearly popular. Furthermore, 66 per cent of adults said that the courses changed the way they saw the job of parenting, as did 80 per cent of young offenders. They said that the courses had 'made them a better father' and taught them skills and something about child development. At the time the study evaluations based on inmates' views were the only ones available. No programmes had been externally evaluated. Thus it is not known whether the courses have an effect on parenting during visiting or after discharge.

Support for parenting

SUPPORT FROM KIN AND FRIENDS

The study noted who brought the children to see the prisoner. In the majority of cases this was the inmate's partner. In about 20 per cent of cases, children were brought by ex-partners and in two cases by siblings or friends, a significant amount of support from the wider network of family and friends. However, there were few data on the support given to partners because these data were not relevant to supporting the man's parenting role.

SUPPORT FROM PARTNERS

It is clear that partners (and the mothers of the children where these were different) took a serious and dedicated view about maintaining contact. Visiting opportunities were usually exploited to the maximum except where travelling difficulties or cost intervened (35%). Partners clearly valued the greater informality of special visiting schemes as well as their greater length – a considerable issue when visits involved substantial travelling. They also greatly valued telephone contact, as did the children. Indeed, partners saw all forms of contact as valuable.

SUPPORT SERVICES

The situation with regard to formal support for prisoners and their families was depressing. Forty-two per cent of adults and 30 per cent of young offenders had no contact with *any* voluntary or statutory agencies. For those that did, the home probation service was the most commonly cited. This applied to 38 per cent of adults and 59 per cent of young offenders respectively. Only 8 per cent of inmates had contact with social services departments, assisted visit schemes, counselling, help and advice lines or AA. Eighty-eight per cent of adult inmates and 84 per cent of young offenders knew of no other supportive agencies that could help them. None mentioned self-help groups.

In practice, there was a low expectation of help. A substantial minority of men (17%) wanted it that way. It is not clear whether this 'self-sufficiency' in parenting is a good sign of an intention to cope or a denial of difficulties and responsibilities.

SUPPORT FOR PARTNERS

Lack of contact with supportive agencies was apparent for partners as well. Sixty-four per cent had no links with any agency or organization. On the whole they did not know of any apart from the big agencies (social services, probation and social security). No-one mentioned prison-partner self-help groups. Nearly half had no links with any agencies that might help at discharge and 77 per cent could think of nothing that would help the prisoner in his fathering role apart from more or longer visits.

Messages from the study on imprisoned fathers

FAMILY LIFE

- Partners saw contact and visiting as a major responsibility
- Visiting schemes support partners in this
- Imprisonment made children's behaviour more difficult
- Children were also sad and depressed
- Over three-quarters of men hope/intend to return home to their children
- Contact was kept up through letters and phone calls as well as visits
- All available types of visiting were used

VISITING SCHEMES AND PARENTHOOD CLASSES

- Ordinary visiting was depressing and frustrating
- Children's or family visiting schemes were much preferred
- These were available in only a minority of institutions, and in *no* young offender ones
- Schemes were dependent on enthusiasm and vulnerable to security concerns
- About 30 per cent of adults and 80 per cent of young offenders attended parenthood classes

SERVICE LINKS

- Lack of contact with any helping agencies was striking
- Young offenders had *no* contact with any statutory or voluntary agencies
- There were low expectations of help and a majority of men wanted it that way

NEEDS

- Visiting schemes and parenthood classes need to be strengthened
- Prisons should appoint someone to be responsible for family ties
- Sentencing should take more account of children's needs for contact
- Strengthening family life through access to education and employment is necessary

Discussion

SUPPORTING PRISONERS' PARTNERS

Although this study was called *The Parenting Role of Imprisoned Fathers*, it is clear that the process of support involves helping those who enable children to go on having a relationship with their father when they are in prison. It was quite clear that the partners saw the job of maintaining a link with the fathers as a major responsibility, even though this took time, a lot of their resources and often caused temporary distress. Families want contact, and helping them have it in a form that is relaxed and 'family-like' is an essential part of the support they deserve.

EFFECTS OF SCHEMES AND COURSES

The study was not designed to see whether parenthood courses or children's or family visiting schemes made a difference to the quality of fathering shown by the men when they were in prison, nor whether they had any impact that survived the discharge. It was intended to illuminate the quality of the visiting experience seen from the viewpoints of the prisoner, partner and child. From this angle it is clear that the schemes were seen by all parties to strengthen ties and relationships and improve the quality of contact. Likewise, attendance at fatherhood courses improved knowledge and practical skills during sentence. The majority of men said they hoped to live near their children when they left and meant to do things with them. There is no reason to doubt their general intentions to avoid the bad parenting that they themselves had experienced and to repeat the good. Equally, there was sometimes a fatalism about whether anything could make a difference. Only follow-up studies can answer some of these questions.

It seems unlikely that the visiting schemes and courses can have a lasting input on their own. Indeed, some children do not want contact or are better off without it. Even when they do, sustaining parenting on discharge is almost bound to need support. Given this, the current level of help being given to prisoners' families and their knowledge of various statutory and voluntary sources of help was discouraging, as was the resistance of 17 per cent of inmates to the idea of help with parenting.

The true effectiveness of schemes will not be known until external evaluation is built in and follow-up studies conducted. However, this is a separate issue from providing improved conditions for visiting. Such provision is demanded by legislation and prison regulations, and providing it should not depend on demonstrating its 'effectiveness' in terms of improving parenting or strengthening family ties.

Parents who reject one of their children[5]

Background

The rejection of a child by his or her parents tests our feelings and beliefs about what parenting should be. Most parents have negative feelings towards their children from time to time but they keep these to themselves or deal with them rapidly. In a few cases these feelings lead on to physical maltreatment. In other cases the tangle of feelings and uncontrolled impulses result in sexual abuse. For others, the burden of caring, mental illness or the lack of personal or physical resources may result in neglectful parenting.

Rejecting parenting may include some or all of these kinds of maltreatment but it includes something else as well: the active singling out of individual children for harsh treatment, even to the extent that they are ejected from the family while their brothers and sisters remain at home. Rejection of this kind is an increasingly recognized phenomenon; its implications for the subsequent care and development of the children are profound and supportive interventions are particularly problematic.

To date there are no systematic ways of identifying the risk of rejection and no figures on the frequency of its occurrence. One retrospective survey of young people's reports gave a rate as high as 6 per cent but there are no figures from preventative or other services. For this reason rejection may only lead to intervention when it becomes extreme and when the adverse consequences for the children become inescapable.

Thus we are currently in the unenviable situation where we know it exists, we know how harmful it is, but we do not know how to spot it early on, we do not know how to differentiate it from problematic parenting when positive features and feelings are still present, and we know little about its origins.

The study

This study set out to try to establish whether potentially rejecting parenting could be noted by health visitors early on in the life of a child, what the population base rate for these problems was, what lay behind rejecting behaviour and whether, how and when persistent problems became addressed by services.

These ambitions were only partially realized because health visitors' worries over telling researchers who they thought were the rejecting parents prevented all but a handful of parents being interviewed. Another major issue for health visitors was whether their role might change from supporting to monitoring, and thus

---

5   Rushton, A., Dance, C. and O'Neill, T. *Parenting Different Children.* Referred to as 'the *Rejection* study' or 'the *Rejecting Parents* study'.

affect their relationship with the families. For these reasons the researchers had to rely on anonymized health visitor questionnaires on suspected cases, on child and adolescent mental health services (CAMHS) professionals' views on the nature of rejection and how to intervene in it, and on social service case file data on the identification of and intervention with instances of emotional abuse more broadly.

The health visitors' accounts

HOW COMMON IS REJECTION?

Questionnaires were returned by 104 health visitors. Full-time caseloads averaged about 300 families, a factor which itself limited the health visitors' potential role in monitoring rejection. All recognized the phenomenon of rejection, basing their judgements on parental criticism and blaming or on effects of the parent's behaviour on the child. A rough estimate based on these personal judgements gives a rate of about six cases per thousand families with young children. Although the health visitors felt they could spot rejection and have a remit to assess parenting, only 63 per cent felt well prepared for this. Moreover, they saw their role in abuse cases as the identification and referral of severe parenting problems, rather than in intervention. Two-thirds thought that counselling was part of their job but only about 15 per cent thought that parenting education was.

CHARACTERISTICS OF REJECTING FAMILIES

The families they identified had a lot of problems but not ones that distinguished them from those with parenting problems that did not include rejection. Contrary to what might have been expected, they were not young families and the proportion who were lone parents was not high. They tended to be very poor and socially isolated, and over half of the mothers had a history of mental health problems – mostly depression – but rejection also occurred in some 'well educated and financially comfortable' homes.

FORMAL SUPPORT

Contact with services

The families the health visitors picked out were already well known to services. Eighty-three per cent had been of concern to health visitors or social services for several years and about one-third of the mothers had broached the question of the child being cared for elsewhere. Child protection procedures had been started in 15 per cent of cases. Despite the fact that the families were well known to services, full family assessments had only taken place with 17 per cent of them and regular social work with 18 per cent.

The input from health visitors themselves was substantial, with over 70 per cent of families being visited at least monthly. But health visitors felt that they were often coping on their own. Two-fifths felt that they had insufficient access to the consultation and discussion opportunities they needed. They also thought that local resources to help parents were inadequate or were weakened by long waiting lists and the stigma of referral for 61 per cent of families.

Inter-agency working

Seventy-two per cent of the families had been referred on to or were involved with other agencies, nearly half with more than one. Social services were involved with nearly 50 per cent, CAMHS with 31 per cent, community child health with 30 per cent, and adult mental health services with 15 per cent. This apparently high involvement of services is deceptive. Most referrals were about social and circumstantial factors that had little to do with the rejected child. Only 25 per cent of contact with other agencies was specifically about parenting.

Health visitors' impressions of other agencies

Health visitors' feelings about contact with other agencies in the general course of their work were not good, except for parenting support services (64%). Less than half thought any of the other services they worked with to be very good. This was the case with social services (46%), with CAMHS (38%) and with adult mental health services (only 27%). CAMHS was most likely to be rated as inadequate overall.

When it came to dealing with emotional abuse their views were even less sanguine. As mentioned, they saw their role in this as primarily one of referring onwards. They thought the responses they got were particularly poor. Only 19 per cent rated social services as good. GPs did better, with 52 per cent responding well (we do not know what they actually did). Contact with social services was mostly to try to get assisted nursery places and family aides. In about half of referrals to social services (50%) and CAMHS (45%) the families were not seen beyond the assessment stage.

INFORMAL SUPPORT

Most striking was the health visitors' views on the families' lack of informal support. About half of the mothers had unsupportive partners. In a third of biological families and 47 per cent of reconstituted families current partners were seen as giving no support of any kind. The mothers tended not to have help from family and friends either. The wider family was seen as particularly unhelpful, giving emotional and practical support to fewer than one-third of the families and financial support to only 13 per cent. Reconstituted families got least support from families and friends. Lack of support from one informal source was often compounded by lack of support from another. Fifty-five per cent of mothers who had unsupportive partners were also unsupported by family and friends.

THE REJECTED CHILDREN

We have seen that there was nothing in the circumstances of the families that specifically explained the rejection of the children. Were the children themselves different in some way that might explain it? The answer was 'no'. There were no gender differences nor any differences on social or medical circumstances during pregnancy or birth compared with their non-rejected siblings. There were no obvious developmental differences according to the health visitors' accounts. They were a bit more likely to be overactive and restless (10% v. 2%) and their mothers were more likely to have had post-partum emotional problems (42% v. 25% siblings).

The parents in the eight interviewed families reported them as markedly more problematic in terms of eating, sleeping, irritability, toilet-training, activity, misery and clinging behaviour, but these problems might as easily have been the consequences or exaggerations of rejection as causes of it. Exaggeration seems an important part of this. Teachers rated the children and their siblings as more problematic than other children in their class but this applied to *all* the siblings, not just the rejected ones.

This interviewed group seemed to be within a 'rejecting spectrum' but not yet truly rejecting/ejecting families. Most of these parents did want to understand the children and relationships between the parents were reasonable. They were low warmth/high criticism parents with poor childhoods of their own. They described the rejected children as non-cuddly and colicky from birth, and later as hard to discipline, distractible and resistant to comfort or physical affection.

The impression is of things getting off to a bad start for one reason or another and not resolving, perhaps because the child was less rewarding, lowering the mother's fragile responsiveness and spiralling towards the risk of rejection. This danger was being held at bay for these children by the presence of at least one better relationship with an adult, which health visitors noted for 71 per cent of them (including their other parent).

What CAMHS professionals made of it

The survey of 53 professionals – practitioner/therapists, psychiatrists and clinical psychologists – showed that the phenomenon was familiar to them. Indeed, they estimated that serious concerns in relationship or singling out were present in 25 per cent of the cases they saw. These concerns seldom showed up in referrals, usually from social services, which were often very vague as to what was wrong apart from 'behaviour problems'.

REASONS FOR REJECTION

The clinicians had all sorts of views on what lay behind rejection, but this turned out to be a familiar list of factors associated with children's emotional and behavioural problems generally, rather than factors that differentiated rejection from other parenting problems. These included the parents' own childhood experiences, problems in their own relationships, the identification of the child with a former hated partner, economic and environmental stresses, reconstituted families, unreasonable expectations of the child, their own mental health problems (especially depression), traumatic birth experiences with the child and the interaction of parental stress with the child's temperament.

Explaining the psychological processes underlying rejection varied with the clinicians' theoretical perspective, but most included some notion of rejection having a 'function' for the parent's internal state or for problems in the family system. Thus the view tended to be that the child might be a projection of the parent's internal dramas, a symbol of some other person responsible for unhappiness, a barometer of the parents' own relationship, related to family secrets or an explanation for what was wrong with the family.

Other explanations were concerned with the history of the relationship between the parent and the child, including a lack of bonding due to traumatic birth experiences or extreme lack of temperamental fit. The picture seemed to be of a bad start for one reason or another, which led to seriously distorted perceptions of the child and a consequent worsening of the child's behaviour and of his or her relationship with the parents.

HELPING FAMILIES

It seemed clear that the children and the child–parent relationships were seriously disturbed by the time the families came to CAMHS or social services. As a consequence, no therapy seemed routinely successful. The clinicians found rejecting parents very hard to deal with emotionally. There was no consensus on whether you worked with the whole family or with individuals or, indeed, whether the clinic was the best place to do it.

THERAPEUTIC ISSUES

There were two main therapeutic issues. First, parents wanted therapists to collude with their view that the child needed sorting out and were quick to react to anything that seemed to shift some of the blame onto themselves. As a consequence, it was hard to engage with families if they perceived that the therapists

154 / SUPPORTING PARENTS

thought that they also needed to change. How do you make the setting safe and non-judgemental enough for problems to be acknowledged without seeming to collude in the parents' view of the child?

For these reasons, although clinicians could cite cases where therapy appeared to have helped, the prescriptions for intervention were not based on these cases but on more general ideas such as 'working alongside families'. Some thought very early work by health visitors better trained in these problems would help, especially if this improved the coordination of support for parenting. Family centres were mentioned as places where more user-friendly interventions might take place. Clinicians also felt that the positive aspects of the child's life outside the home should be strengthened, especially if the parents' attitudes were resistant to change. No one seemed to mention the end of the line; that is, at what point it is best to take the child from the family.

Social services' response to emotional abuse

The health visitors' data showed that they were unhappy with the response of social services to their referrals of rejecting families and that full assessments were the exception rather than the rule. The final part of this study looked at this issue as revealed by social services' case records. How do they deal with referrals? Do they identify emotional abuse – of which rejection is an extreme form – as a particular problem? If they do, what services do they put in place?

The researchers took a complete sample of referrals from two inner London boroughs over a three-month period – 647 children. There were child welfare concerns, following allegations of abuse, for 128 (20%) of them. Thirty-one concerned emotional abuse. The other 97 were accusations of other forms of maltreatment. Two-fifths of the families were headed by lone parents, one-half of the two-parent families experienced domestic violence and 42 per cent of families had mental health, drug or alcohol problems. About 22 per cent of these allegations of abuse were investigated and considered to be unfounded. Records were unclear on whether a needs assessment had taken place.

FAMILIES WITH EMOTIONAL ABUSE

There were no ethnic or age differences between the families referred because of emotional abuse and the rest of the child welfare cases, but the emotional abuse cases tended to be complex cases. They were more socially isolated and contained more domestic violence, substance abuse, financial difficulties and fathers' mental health problems, as well as other kinds of maltreatment. This mirrored the findings from the health visitors' questionnaires. Three-quarters of these families had had previous contact with social services, over half for parenting problems and nearly one-third for abuse investigations.

There was no reference on the files to any form of follow up of the referral in 12 per cent of welfare cases. Seventy per cent were followed up within a week but the response to emotional abuse referrals was slower than for other forms of abuse. This may have been because the families were well known to services anyway and follow up might have been assumed. It may also explain why follow up did not occur for 63 per cent of cases or was confined to extensive telephone contact. Those emotional abuse cases that were followed up remained open longer than those referred for other kinds of maltreatment. The researchers felt that this was due to the complexity of the cases rather than a response to emotional abuse *per se*.

ASSESSMENT AND PLANNING

Assessments – which included these telephone-only contacts – were predominantly incident-based (71%). That is, the follow up was used to decide whether the incident complained about had happened or was of sufficient severity to warrant further action. About one-third of the children were placed on the child protection register following these incidents but a genuine comprehensive risk assessment seemed to have been done in only a minority of these cases. Over the course of the following year the cases of ten families were closed and reopened.

The child was seen and an initial 'assessment' made in 88 per cent of referrals. The remaining 12 per cent tended to be cases dealt with by the police. Assessments were usually done to check the allegation, not to assess family needs. Doing this often involved getting information from GPs and schools but only one child received a full developmental assessment. Any information on the child was usually based on the parents' accounts. Ten families denied that there was anything wrong. The rest showed some recognition of the problem. The researchers constructed a summary rating of effective social work. On this scale 46 per cent of responses to referrals showed these to be hurriedly processed with no exploration and little social service or other intervention taken forward.

SUPPORT

Informal support

There was little information on file about support from family and friends, but the isolation of the families was often highlighted.

Formal support

About one-quarter of the emotional abuse families had substantial social work intervention. Nearly half (45%) had no more than one or two visits. Fifty-four per cent were offered additional services. Eight were referred on to CAMHS – often with very little accompanying assessment – but only three were 'accepted'.

Messages from the study
of parents who reject children

- Rejection is a serious and increasingly recognized phenomenon
- There are few data but it probably occurs in less than 1 per cent of families
- There is no way of identifying the risk at present
- Parents were often unwilling to accept help
- Families had many problems of social isolation and poor relationships

but

- They were not different from families with problems that did not reject

SERVICE RESPONSES

- All services recognize the problem

but

- Health visitors did not see assessment as part of their remit
- Social services concentrated on assessing reported incidents
- Systematic assessments of parenting and circumstances were unusual
- Developmental assessments of children were a rarity
- There was a lack of good information and liaison between agencies

CAMHS professionals acknowledged that

- Parents were challenging to work with
- Parents wanted to change the child rather than confront their own feelings
- Professionals could have complex responses to these parents

WHAT IS NEEDED

- Good holistic assessment of family problems
- Good inter-agency working and sharing of information

Community-based parenting services were preferred by social workers and advocated by CAMHS clinicians. They may be the best setting to encourage these parents to work on their parenting

Unfortunately, records did not say what happened to those rapidly passed on to other services. A year later 45 per cent of cases had been closed because relationships were said to have improved.

IDENTIFICATION OF REJECTION

Rejection, an extreme form of emotional abuse and the focus of this study, involves the differential singling out of children from their siblings. Rejection was not specifically identified in the case notes and therefore has to be inferred from the referral of single children from sibling groups. Strikingly, such children were significantly *less* likely to be accorded priority than those who were referred as sibling groups and none (*v.* 40%) of the sibling referrals had a structured assessment. This was partly explained by age (single referrals tended to be older) but response was also poorer for singly referred pre-schoolers.

The role of family centres in coordinating formal and informal support[6]

The purpose of this study was to do exactly what its title states: to examine the extent to which family centres could, would and should have a linking and coordinating role between families and services. But what is meant by 'coordination' in this context? Coordination can range from the power to command, or at least to put strong pressure on, other agencies to provide services, to a relatively powerless, if useful, facilitating role. No service providers can command services willy-nilly, but some, such as health, have more power than others to press for services.

The position of family centres as coordinators is at the facilitative end of this continuum. They have an approach that gives them an advantage when the need is for a holistic assessment of what families require. This is so because they take a more inclusive view of family needs than specialist services often do. For this reason they usually offer a wide range of services themselves and also act as a 'gateway' to other services, including community groups. The other way they can act as coordinators is through facilitating inter-agency working around particular families.

The study

In order to see whether they did operate in this way, the researchers collected the views of managers, workers and parents and also the views of staff from other agencies that had links with family centres. There were three phases to the study.

---

6   Tunstill, J., Aldgate, J. and Hughes, M. *Family Support at the Centre: Family Centres, Services and Networks.* Referred to as 'the *Family Centres* study'.

The first phase was a questionnaire survey of over 400 family centres in England (about 75 per cent of all the centres on the National Council of Voluntary Child Care Organizations network list at the time the study was done). In the second phase, 41 workers and 63 parents in 40 centres chosen to reflect both geography and diversity were interviewed and 112 workers in 25 agencies used by the centres gave thoughts via a questionnaire (the interview study). The third phase was a follow-up questionnaire survey of 344 centres one year later to explore themes found in phase two.

Origins and characteristics of family centres

The term 'family centres' covers a wide range of community-based services for supporting parents and families. These services are, in practice, diverse in funding and financial stability, size, the breadth or narrowness of purpose, restrictions on access and patterns of referral, both to the centre and by it. There are also big variations in the size of the catchment area and the location of the centres. Some are housed in social services area offices, some in houses, some in purpose buildings – sometimes within the grounds of primary schools – and some operate out of church halls. Some also operate off-site and do home-based visiting.

PHILOSOPHY

Centres saw themselves as concerned with the welfare of all young people and their families, although their work was mostly with families with pre-school children. Children's welfare was the main concern but parents were the main focus of activity. 'Partnership' with parents was a strongly emphasized value. Centres saw themselves – in contrast to their views on social services departments – as optimistic and positive, more concerned with people as individuals and a desire to effect positive change. They saw themselves as doing this through spending more time with families and getting to know them better, although the study has no data on whether this contrast was justified.

Centres wanted to be open-access, holistic services that gave support to families early on in the development of difficulties. In practice, centres funded by local authorities were often far from this ideal, tending to be closed-referral late-intervention services dealing mostly with children in need and child protection. Fifty-nine per cent of centres operated in this way. The desire to be a community-based resource was more likely to be retained by centres in the voluntary sector. It was unusual for any to offer a mix of preventative and crisis interventions, although most were able to retain some open access, even if this had referral criteria.

Centres saw themselves as developing special relationships with parents where support was offered, not imposed. They espoused casual dress and an open, honest and egalitarian approach in maintaining these relationships. The desire for early intervention and open access went along with maintaining a non-stigmatizing stance. Nevertheless, the tensions in their role because of the dominance of local authority funding remained, and they were likely to side with social services over child protection issues. These links with social services were a source of suspicion with families, especially when the centres were located on social services territory, but, nevertheless, 56 per cent of the interview sample of parents were neutral about other people knowing they attended the centre and 38 per cent positive.

Some centres liked to see themselves as operating at three levels of family support: prevention, intervention for families in need but not with child protection concerns, and child protection cases. The ideal was to 'hold' families so that they did not go up this hierarchy and the hope was that they went down it.

WHAT THEY DID

A typical list of centre activities might include assessments of needs, parenting interventions, emotional and practical 'support', therapies and family activities and resources, including information on other sources of help. Managers saw 'assessment' as a central element in the work of their centres because of their experience in child development, although, again, there were no data on whether staff were trained to assess parenting and family needs with families with multiple difficulties.

Parenting-related work

Eighty-seven per cent of centres provided services and activities for parents, including inputs on parenting skills in 57 per cent of cases. Thirty-six per cent provided therapeutic services. These were mostly family therapy interventions but also included a wide variety of other therapeutic approaches. Twenty-two per cent were running behaviour management and personal development services (31%). Nearly half had child care and crèche facilities (48%), 27 per cent ran advocacy services and 66 per cent had assembled a wide range of 'resources', including information on other services. In the national survey 42 per cent claimed to give general 'support'.

Contact

Forty-six per cent of centres – usually those funded by social services – did contact work. Some centres were ambivalent about this because it placed them in a supervisory or policing role and also because contact meetings could create tensions that upset workers and other users of the centre.

BREADTH OF PROVISION

Centres wanted a broad role but, as we have seen, their provision was mostly for families with pre-schoolers. Eighty-eight per cent of those in the parents' study had children of that age. The phase one survey showed that the centres had a low level of routine service for young parents, lone parents, children with special needs, ethnic minorities, fathers, specific therapies around substance abuse, women with depression, teenage girls and post-natal support.

Only about one-quarter of the interviewed parents thought that centres should do more for any of these special groups, apart from fathers. This extraordinary finding might have reflected a fear that they would lose services if these other groups got them, but it also went along with difficulties that staff experienced within the centres around the formation of exclusive cliques of parents.

This low level of provision is likely to be partly a reflection of the purpose for which most centres originally came into being. It also reflects the priorities of referral agencies, especially social services. If agencies do not want services for these neglected groups then it is unlikely that centres can or will develop them. It is, of course, striking that these services do not exist, given how common the list of needs groups are in any profile of parenting problems.

Funding

SOURCES OF FUNDING

Over two-thirds of centres (72%) were part of services funded by local authorities, 68 per cent being fully funded by them and a further 11 per cent partly so. Most of this funding came through social services. Only two centres were fully funded by children's organizations – Barnardo's, for example – and 22 per cent partly so. Over two-thirds (70%) of those not funded by local authorities had more than one source of income. There was a marked absence of the health sector as a sponsor or funder. The extent of funding varied from funding all the activities of the centre to supporting or paying for specific pieces of work.

CONSEQUENCES OF FUNDING

Funding had major consequences for the work and stability of centres. Those funded by local authorities were less likely to be open access and tended to be narrower in focus, with an increasing push towards child protection work. Funding from local authorities gave somewhat more stability but centres were still open to frequent changes. These came through changes in their funding agencies, such as the integration of social services departments with health or housing, or were brought about by new initiatives, such as Sure Start. The structure of local populations could change, reducing or increasing the need for a centre.

INSTABILITY

Instability, uncertainty and change were a feature of the lives of many centres. Crises and pressures in social services departments could trickle down to affect centres. Sixty-one per cent of centres reported changes in their services between the questionnaire survey and the follow up. These changes tended to reflect a move towards higher thresholds of eligibility and more crisis work. During this period also, 4 per cent of centres closed or were absorbed into other services.

Size, staffing and qualifications

The average number of staff in the centres was seven, with a range of one to 29. There were few men or ethnic minority staff at any level within them. Since the majority of centres developed from nurseries, it is not surprising that most of the qualified staff had nursery nursing at NNEB and NVQ level. Otherwise, staffing seems to have been dominated by those with social work qualifications and by 'family support workers', although no formal data on qualifications were presented. Staff also attended short-term training courses and group-work sessions. There was no information in the report on how many centres were headed by someone qualified in the assessment of serious family and parenting problems.

Referral and access criteria

All centres had some referral system based on definitions of priority and eligibility. Social services determined this to a large extent for the centres they funded, both the ones they ran and the ones run for them by the voluntary sector. Thirty-four per cent of centres took no open access referrals. Fifty-five per cent had some open access in addition to a closed referral system. The great majority of referrals to all centres were from social services – 31 per cent exclusively so. A broader range of referral sources only existed for centres that took both early and late referrals.

Only one-third could take referrals from families themselves. Even in areas with multi-agency referral teams, access could be subject to control by social services. This applied to the voluntary sector as well, especially through the mechanism of service agreements.

Thus, the majority of centres retained a mixed referral system; however, there was an ongoing tension between the pressure from referrers for centres to deal with families professionally identified as 'in need' or with major problems and the desire of the services to be open-access and community-based. The big advantage of the latter approach to referral was that coming to the centre was less associated with the stigma felt when social services were involved with nearly all the families. Nevertheless, the push was towards more specialization and services to families with intractable problems.

Decisions about who should have access were major determinants of what was happening in family centres, in terms of their service development, independent and collaborative service provision, and linking role. Some managers hankered after a system in which they became the referring agency, but that seems to be a dream when their funding came from the local authority.

Links with informal supports

FAMILIES

The great majority of centres had links with the families and friends of service users but only half had links with community groups. Links with families and friends seemed to happen case by case rather than arising as a matter of policy and effort. They were broader when centres offered more services and narrowed as the range of services lessened.

COMMUNITY GROUPS

Centres also had links with a wide range of community groups including action projects, residents' associations, children's projects, religious groups, family support and counselling organizations, and refugee groups. Again, these links tended to be reactive rather than proactive and tended to be narrow. There were no differences in this between local authority and voluntary sector centres. Narrow service provision went along with narrow informal links and broad provision with broad links. Community links were greater for centres involved in initiatives such as Sure Start. Nevertheless, links were often tenuous or sporadic, although they were stronger for voluntary sector centres.

Links with formal services

LINKS

The most common links were with social services, health visitors, general practitioners and education, but the number of links for each centre varied widely. One centre had no contact with other services. At the other extreme, one had contact with 15. In practice, however, the range was narrow. This was so regardless of whether the centre was funded by a local authority or the voluntary sector, broad or narrow in referral policy, or heavily involved in government initiatives or not at all. Not surprisingly, links were broader if the centre had an early- and a late-intervention role and if they themselves supplied a broader range of services.

Links with agencies operated at four levels: the centre as a referrer to other agencies, as a formal provider of services for other agencies, as a service partner providing services jointly or as a provider of informal links between workers. Eighty-three per cent provided services in association with other agencies, 52 per cent on behalf of others and 35 per cent in association with others but not on behalf of them. By far the biggest source of commissioned services was social services (47%).

At the individual level, relationships with other agencies were sometimes affected by vagueness about roles and responsibilities or even disagreements over assessments, in which the centres often saw themselves as possessing superior expertise. We do not have a direct comparison between these views and those of the linked agencies.

Apart from social services, links with health visitors and education formed the main contact with statutory agencies. Relationships with these were better than with social services, perhaps because they carried no funding implications. It was not clear to what extent the centres drew in these services on behalf of users – that is, acted as a 'coordinator' – and to what extent users were referred to them by these services. In addition, it was not clear whether these links were formal or arose case by case.

RELATIONSHIPS WITH SOCIAL SERVICES DEPARTMENTS

Strikingly, given the predominance of funding by local authorities, few managers (15%) mentioned their links with social services or that they were part of social services provision for children and families. There were complaints about social workers not working with the centre but off-loading clients. Centres wanted to maximize their autonomy and emphasize their expertise; social services preferred to see them as part of their service, to be used to meet social service needs.

Tension between social services and the voluntary sector could surface around service-level agreements, which the voluntaries felt sometimes pulled against their philosophies. The extent to which these affected their autonomy was very variable; but for some, tensions were felt around the push towards child protection cases and to meet Quality Protects and other targets.

LINKS WITH GOVERNMENT INITIATIVES

About half of the centres were involved with the Quality Protects initiative and in Early Years' Development and Childcare. Over half were involved or were planning to be involved with Sure Start, but only 18 per cent with Early Excellence. These involvements were more likely for those with open-access policies, a broad service range and broad links with informal and formal networks. Again, these links were not related to whether the centres were funded by social services or the voluntary sector or had broad or narrow referral sources. There were obvious benefits in these links but also tensions around competition for funding. The danger for centres was that any push for them to deal with 'children in need' might act as further pressure on them to specialize in intractable families.

Parents' use and views

Eighty-three parents in 28 family centres were interviewed. The parents were nearly all recruited by the centres and were volunteers. As the researchers point out, they were not a representative group. Their profile suggests that the sample was short on the most complex cases. They were mostly between 25 and 35 years of age. Seventy-eight per cent were 'white British'.

The majority of parents in the interview study were referred to the centres by social services (53%). They felt that they did not have much choice in the matter, although only 18 per cent were required to attend, in lieu of the children being taken into public care. Such attendance was likely to be time limited and to follow a referral for parenting problems. In practice, a whole variety of parenting needs arose from personal or social circumstances and life events. Lack of informal support figured large in parents' accounts of their lives.

The families were generally small, with an average of two children.[7] Sixty-three per cent lived in council or housing association dwellings, for 52 per cent main income was benefits, and the most common other stressor was in relationships with their partners (22%). Most were receiving help from about four formal services (including health visitors and GPs) and two community groups. Over two-fifths had no support from their families (40%) or friends (43%). What home and volunteer support they had was mostly arranged by the family centres. There was no association between the amount of support they were getting and the reason they were attending the centre or who referred them.

PARENTS' VIEWS OF THE CENTRES

Parents got more in the way of services from the centres than they anticipated but fewer social activities. They liked the fact that it was quick and easy to get a response to a problem from the centre and they valued the fact that the centre knew them and that they could drop in. They also liked the atmosphere of centres and the warmth and friendliness of staff. Only 36 per cent had things they did not like about the centres they went to. These were mostly about space, hours, openness of access, regularity of support, and help for older children and fathers.

Parents tended to want more of the same services, not different ones. They felt that what they got was better than they expected, except for assessments of their children's development, support for those with mental health problems and in the way of social activities. Like other parents in the studies across this initiative, they particularly liked key working arrangements.

7   Mean, median and mode.

PARENTS AND THE CENTRES' ORGANIZATION AND INPUTS

Although the philosophy of the centres was one of partnership with parents, in practice parents were not involved in decision making apart from over very minor things such as what to have for children's snacks or whom to invite to give talks. This was not just because centres did not include them. Many parents did not want that kind of involvement and, indeed, it might have been a problem, given the tendency for cliques to form.

Centres varied in how much they thought they should help parents become friends. Should they promote it or simply let it develop as the parents' self-esteem improved? Friendships tended to interfere with work with the parents because they spent too much time chatting. Friendships also fed into the development of cliques that could be hostile to newcomers or interfere with the work of the centre. Nevertheless, 88 per cent did make friends, without the help of the staff. Some even met outside the centre and gave practical support and information and shared problems.

Centres were clearly a link to other community resources and often kept information related to these, as well as on other services and benefits. The completeness of this varied very greatly from centre to centre, but 59 per cent of users said they had been helped not just with information but in making contact with these resources.

There was a need to identify the end of the centre's involvement with a family, even though this went against an open-access philosophy. For some parents, the centre became the 'family' support they otherwise lacked. Some were even reported to have considered having more children in order to retain it.

Centres as coordinators

The account so far shows that the centres operate primarily as resources for social services departments who exert a pressure towards the centres being a service for severe parenting problems and child protection. This, of course, was not the only way centres operated. Some retained a much more community-based and open-access approach. Acting as a resource for social services need not necessarily mean that centres are at the mercy of local authority policies on what they provide or whether they take a role in coordinating support to families. Indeed, they could act in a way similar to that of key workers.

But were they ever a single gateway? Centres strongly felt that they *could* be so, although this was usually couched as a role on a case-by-case basis rather than as a general remit. In most cases it was not in their hands to determine who the service coordinator was. A slightly less powerful but still important role would be to act as the coordinator of a range of services within an overall package organized by another provider; for example, by setting up a 'family forum' discussion group. In one example this included education, health, mental health, learning disability services and services for drug abuse. This cannot disguise the fact that some professionals thought that such groups were seen as especially dreary and a waste of time.

A less powerful position can be useful because the centre has no personal agenda as far as the content and process of meetings is concerned. Although mainstream social services may be in a better position to take an overview, family centres should be able to act as a gateway to an appropriate mix of coordinated services, avoiding duplication.

DOES IT HAPPEN THAT WAY?

Although there were good examples of centres working in this way – for example, managers meeting together to share experiences – they tended to be case based and the arrangements to be very fluid, involving frequent changes in the network group and many *ad hoc* arrangements.

Networking with other agencies was often even more fluid and *ad hoc* and had the added complexity of the different concerns and perspectives of the various agencies. Time and resources were a problem for everyone so that networking could be selective and pragmatic. It was not surprising, therefore, that networking arrangements were easily destabilized for a variety of reasons. These could include changes in the structure of the managing organizations, professional boundary issues, fluctuations in the interest shown by different health visitors or community police officers, the fading of personal links, or opposition to this kind of role from mainstream social services.

In short, networking seemed *ad hoc* and made from a very weak and vulnerable position.

WHAT DID PROFESSIONALS IN OTHER AGENCIES THINK?

The questionnaire responses from other professionals were from the health, mental health, social services and education sectors, but predominantly from the health sector. They described their links to the centres in very general ways: to meet needs of families, to meet organizational needs, for local planning and for professional contact outside the context of particular cases. Most tellingly, however, they saw the family centres as a resource for them, not themselves as a resource for the family centres, although they described quite a lot of two-way flow and joint working. Otherwise they saw plenty of barriers, often involving finance but also around differing agency philosophies, agendas and boundaries, as well as a lack of formal systems for communication.

Nevertheless, 58 per cent thought family centres had a coordinating role, although definitions varied. What they described as 'coordination' was more in the realm of promoting good inter-agency practice than a responsibility for coordination. Others thought that social services should have this role.

The other agencies liked a lot of things about the family centres, their varied and flexible service, their specialist programmes of work and their holistic approach. They also liked their capacity to be non-stigmatizing, in contrast to social services involvement. They saw them especially as providing assessments of the needs of families, containment and the provision of quality day care. The big plus for the centres was the time they had to develop relationships with users and in this way to provide an ongoing kind of informal support. Eighty-seven per cent of the staff from other agencies thought that links with centres were successful for their clients, although it is not known whether this led to improvements in the problems for which they were referred, or just containment of them.

COULD THEY HAVE A COORDINATING ROLE?

Advantages of family centres

The special position of family centres in delivering services lies in their community image, in both their location and their philosophy, despite the push towards becoming a service for families with complex and intractable problems. As part of this, their desire to assess families holistically and to provide a range of linked services means that they start from a different place to specialist health, educational and social services.

Managers thought centres *could* coordinate clusters of services for individual families. Indeed, in the phase three survey 86 per cent thought they *did* have a coordinating role. This view was common to centres funded by social services as well as independently run ones. But this coordination seemed to involve liaison, assessment, administration and acting as gateways. All this activity was facilitating but not based on any authority acknowledged by other services. It seemed to involve holding the ring, providing information and pointing people towards other services. Probably because of this, some managers were against centres taking on a coordinating role, especially if this meant taking on responsibility without authority to command services.

Professionals in other agencies also thought that centres could have a role, but again this seemed to be in activities such as bringing all professionals together to develop integrated services, not as a coordinator in the sense of them taking a central role.

Barriers to the coordinating role

The foregoing discussion points to the potential of family centres as facilitators in the coordination of services for families but not as coordinators in a more formal sense without the agreement of more powerful agencies. The sources of funding and support are against this. Social services see the centres that they fund as part of their service and themselves as the coordinators – whether they handle this well or not. The pressure is for centres to become specialist agencies dealing with intractable family problems, even though they themselves fight against the loss of their autonomy and open-access philosophy. For centres in the voluntary sector, closely specified service-level agreements limit the coordinating role because they define what the centres do and limit the time for these wider activities.

Discussion

DIVERSITY AND COORDINATION

This study emphasizes the diversity of family centres in size, focus, funding, location and their relationships to mainstream services and to family and community support. For these reasons alone a neat summary of their potential as coordinators is impossible. Significantly, the report does not give examples of any centres effectively managing to fill this role. Family centres are also a constantly changing form of service provision. It might seem from the barriers to a coordination role that their philosophy and way of working are on the wane because of top-down pressures.

THE PHILOSOPHY WINS

This may be true for individual centres, which can come and go, be absorbed into social services provision or meet other fates. But, from another perspective, family centres have won the argument for the style of provision of many services to families. The idea that these should be delivered through a non-stigmatizing community resource that has under its roof a whole variety of help for families on health, education and parenting is the central idea behind Sure Start and related initiatives.

Indeed, many family centres are now being absorbed into this programme. Fifty-four of the centres in this study were within Sure Start catchment areas and nearly all of these had been affected by funding changes associated with that initiative. Centres generally took a positive view of these developments, despite some envy over the resources the Sure Start centres received. Family centres did not fear a takeover but it would seem inevitable that many will be absorbed into this programme if it proves successful and enduring.

Messages from the study of family centres

- Partnership with parents provides a strong value of working positively and in partnership
- Centres are very diverse in size, focus, funding and location
- 72 per cent were part of local-authority-funded services
- Funding issues often made the future of centres uncertain
- 57 per cent of centres provided direct input on parenting skills
- Centres wanted to be open access and holistic

but

- Were often pushed towards closed-referral work with child protection cases

RELATIONSHIPS WITH USERS OF THE CENTRES

- Parents got more services than they expected but fewer social activities
- Users had poor informal support
- Centres worried about issues of dependency
- Users resisted expanding the service to others

LINKS WITH OTHER SERVICES AND AGENCIES

- Other agencies liked the centres' flexibility and holistic approach
- 87 per cent thought that referrals to centres helped their clients
- Centres felt they could be a single gateway to services
- They did promote good inter-agency work

but

- The range of service links tended to be narrow
- Coordination was mostly case-based
- Networking arrangements were fluid and easily destabilized

The family centre approach to a non-stigmatizing, community-based resource for families, with health, education and parenting held under one roof, is advocated as a model in many studies in the initiative

170 / SUPPORTING PARENTS

What do these studies tell us about supporting parents who may be hard to help?

This chapter has been concerned with parents whom society may see as undeserving of support, although, in fact, they are amongst those most in need of effective interventions and policies, if the burden they can place on services is to be reduced. Support for them is, indeed, in short supply, but this is not entirely the fault of services.

Informal support

The parents are notably short of help from their own families. The pregnant looked-after teenagers had poor relationships with their own mothers, who tended to look to them for support rather than giving it to them. The imprisoned fathers – while loyally visited by their wives and partners – seemed very short of support in other ways. The emotionally abusing parents in the *Rejection* study also had very poor relationships with their own families and little support from anyone within their social circle. Relationships between the couples in these studies were often fragile, quarrelsome or violent. The data speak of the poverty of relationships for many of these parents. Those attending *family centres* were strikingly unwilling to see services extended to other groups of needy parents.

Relationships with services

Contact and relationships with services also painted a rather depressing picture. The *pregnant teenage girls* were hostile to social services involvement with them and their babies, although they wanted support from them, providing it was given on their terms. The *imprisoned fathers* had good intentions about their parenting and liked the better opportunities for 'normal' contact with their children that visiting schemes gave. Equally, a high proportion thought that there were no services that could help them or from which they would want to take advice. The rejecting parents, although well known to services, were likely to deny the incidents that led to referral. Those seen at CAMHS clinics were likely to continue to want the child to be seen as the problem. The family centres also had concerns about parents who became dependent on them for support. This concern was associated with worries about how to manage time-limited interventions and how to end a piece of work. In short, these were often difficult families to 'support' and work with.

Input from services

This difficulty – or perceived difficulty – was associated with fragmented services and with some suggestion of buck-passing. In some cases there was a simple failure to do what the service was supposed to do. Sex education for the teenagers –

although a responsibility for social services – was almost entirely lacking. Indeed, few of the authorities in the study had any policy on the matter. Most did not know how many pregnant teenagers they were looking after. *Prisons* were supposed to encourage family contact and extend family visiting schemes and home contacts. But these aspirations were vitiated by the lack of schemes, the grim circumstances of ordinary visits and the limitations seen as necessary because of security – especially drug – concerns. The *emotionally abusing* parents were passed on from health visitors to social services and sometimes from social services to CAMHS, but no service had a very high opinion of another and referrals often led to no clear action. In this study the picture was of under-resourced services protecting themselves by setting high thresholds for their intervention or circumscribing the limits of their responsibility.

Information

Parents often knew little about services that might be available to them. This was particularly so for the prisoners and their partners, who mentioned little beyond social services and probation and never mentioned support groups. We do not know what the other groups of parents knew about services open to them. Some family centres worked hard to collect such information for their own areas, but we do not know how often this led to services being taken up. The suggestion was that it was most likely when the centres organized it.

In other ways the lack of information was notable. Social services case notes seldom included letters from the services to which they had referred parents. Referral letters to CAMHS about *rejecting* parents often contained no assessment of the problem as seen by the referrer. Systematic assessments of parenting by health visitors or social workers were lacking. Indeed, health visitors did not see this as part of their role. Social workers concentrated on the reported incident. Only about 3 per cent of emotionally abused children received a full developmental assessment on referral, and there was no evidence that this had been done previously.

Ways forward

The health visitors and social workers of the emotionally abusing parents liked the responses they got from community-based parenting services best, although whether these were effective in modifying parenting problems was not known. The use of these non-stigmatizing services was seen as a way into these families by the CAMHS clinicians and the social workers. For this reason they show an obviously preferred way forward.

As has been noted, families with multiple needs are often difficult to support. This is the case not only because of the frequent poverty of their circumstances but also because of their own difficulties in relationships, usually arising from the way in which they themselves were parented. For this reason, most parents in the *Teenage Pregnancy, Imprisoned Fathers* and *Rejecting Parents* studies will have lacked good models of parenting. It is, therefore, interesting that for the latter health visitors and social services most liked community inputs dealing with parenting issues.

We have no idea from these studies if these services 'made a difference' to parenting, nor how likely it was for parents to go to them. It was certainly very hard to get the teenage parents to attend any kind of service around parenting on a regular basis. Many of the *emotionally abusing* parents also thought that nothing was wrong with them and the problems lay in the child. Getting them to stick with parenting courses would be hard. Nevertheless, it is encouraging that many parents, including the *imprisoned fathers*, like input on parenting. Parenting courses were very popular in prison and youth offender facilities.

Family centre-based community resources were seen by the traditional formal services as a way of providing non-stigmatizing inputs. This is a very important element in engaging parents with complex needs. Engagement is the first requirement of an effective service for parents and parenting. In this respect family centres have won the argument for their style of delivering many services to families. This is the central idea behind Sure Start and related initiatives.

The dangers are that the balance between complex and more ordinary parenting needs will either be pushed towards the complex end of the spectrum because of funding issues, or that those with ordinary parenting needs will begin to shun the centres if the balance tilts too much towards the complex end.

Messages from the studies on parents who may be hard to work with

THE FAMILIES

- The families often have many overlapping problems
- Poor relationships with family and friends are common
- Relationships in the home are often fragile and may be violent

RELATIONSHIPS WITH SERVICES

- Parents are often pessimistic about services and suspicious of or even hostile to them
- Relationships can either involve excessive dependence or independence

In return services

- May assess needs poorly or in a very narrow way
- Can become fragmented and uncoordinated
- Can pass the buck to each other
- May fail to meet responsibilities
- Can be poor in their communication with parents and each other

WORKING WITH THESE PARENTS

- Some parents are hard to engage and work with
- Good coordinated assessment and joint working are essential
- Non-stigmatizing community-based services such as family centres were seen as a way forward

Part 3
Cross-Cutting Themes

Chapter 8

Summary and Cross-Cutting Themes

In this chapter we pull together those findings and ideas about supporting parents that go across the studies. Of course, these themes do not appear in every study, but they all appear in projects that are diverse in focus and methodology. Each study also has findings that are specific to their own topic area. These specifics are not repeated here. Rather, we concentrate on the more general messages. Given the diversity of this initiative there are a surprisingly large number of these.

Entitlements and effects

Before doing this it is useful to introduce an important distinction to help orientate our discussion of the findings; that is, the distinction between conclusions drawn on the basis of *entitlements* (or *rights* in an everyday sense) and those made on the basis of *effects*. The main thrust of the initiative was towards the latter. The idea was to discover ways of supporting parenting that 'made a difference' by promoting better parenting. Policy is rightly directed towards making this kind of a difference in demonstrable ways. The studies were able to come to conclusions on this with variable amounts of success, given the inevitable limitations in sampling and design.

However, much of what they have to say about giving help to parents does not depend on a demonstration that giving help makes some kind of improvement in parenting. Listening to parents' concerns, taking their views seriously, treating them as partners in solving problems with their children, giving them useful information, paying attention to the realities of their lives rather than the agendas of particular services: all these things, which are reflected in the findings from many of the studies, are a matter of the right and proper way to treat people. We do not need a demonstration that these behaviours promote better parenting in order to change our approach to service delivery to take them into account. There is evidence from some of the studies that families engage better with services if they are treated in this way, but they ought to be able to expect such responses even if there are not any demonstrable 'effects' of them.

Limitations of the initiative

The initiative encompassed a wide range of parenting circumstances and supports and more than fulfilled the intentions of its originators to broaden the field of research in children's social care. Even so, it was not able to cover all the angles. The studies mostly focused on informal and formal supports to individual families or groups of families and on how these related to the needs they had around their parenting. In doing this they touched on many key areas of current policy. There were, however, no studies on the effects of broad policy initiatives around financial supports for parents, such as tax credits, or initiatives designed to help parents into work. The reason for this is simple: these policies were not in effect at the time this initiative started. However, such approaches seem very important given the evidence from many of the studies on the marked social disadvantage of many families as well as parents' strong desire to be in charge of solving their parenting problems.

The second set of limitations involved questions of the design of the studies. The majority are cross-sectional or 'snapshot' studies. Only three (*SPOKES*, *Supporting Fostering* and *Fostering Adolescents*) had a follow-up element. Follow-up designs are essential if we want to be sure that supports are *predictive* of parenting and children's outcomes. The *New Forest* study was also based on a follow-up design, but its measures of parenting were based on parents' retrospective accounts collected at the time of the follow-up only. Follow-up designs are much more powerful in deciding what leads to what; that is, deciding on 'the direction of effects'. Only one study – the *SPOKES* project – tried directly to change parenting and to see what effect those changes had on children's behaviour one year later.

The 'snapshot' design used by most of the studies is very useful for pointing up the issues faced by parents and the way that these connect to many aspects of their lives, but it is harder to decide from studies using these designs exactly how 'support' relates to parenting.

Finally, although all the studies have parents' views on the problems facing them as parents, few have detailed assessments of parenting or parenting problems or of support as seen from the point of view of someone else. The *Supporting Fostering* study was able to use social workers' ratings of parenting and the *SPOKES* project had videotaped observations, but data from these have not yet been presented. In short, there is a reliance on the parents' accounts of parenting and support which makes it harder to disentangle the relationships between the two. To put it in the modern jargon, there is often a lack of 'triangulation'. Of course, having detailed accounts from parents on their parenting issues and on the help they need with these has a considerable pay-off in pointing to what formal services need to address.

Conceptual issues

In Chapter 2 we considered the question of what we mean by 'support' and 'parenting'. It is important to be clear what we mean by both of these if we are to frame policies and change practice in order to support parents.

What is support?

'Support' is a very general term. It can be both wide-ranging and vague. It's easy to respond to a problem by saying that we should 'put in more support' without being at all clear on what we mean by that or what we want to achieve. The word itself implies something that is helpful, so we can be fooled into thinking we are doing some good simply by giving something we label 'support'. This can range from saying 'never mind' to providing a very specific service. The danger in using 'support' as an umbrella term is that it can become devalued as an idea.

Support involves both a giver and a receiver. Their views on what is needed may not be the same. Support is sometimes not there when we want it, is not what we want or is inappropriate or intrusive. We may blame what goes wrong on a lack of support even if this is not justified. We may claim that we did something without the help of others, even if this is not so. If we offer support we may be rebuffed. We may include under 'support' something counter to the views of the persons we are trying to help. We may even decide that something needs to be done against one person's wishes in order to support the needs of another. Much child-care policy is based on this 'welfare principle'.

Support is complex to assess, to get right and to deliver, especially for parenting, because of the balance between the neglect of family problems and intrusion into family life, not to mention ideas of what satisfactory parenting is, how and when this needs support and who should decide that.

CLASSIFICATIONS OF SUPPORT

In the academic jargon services are usually referred to as 'formal support' and support from the family or friends as 'informal' support. Not surprisingly, community groups or organizations often sit in the middle of this classification and their support is called 'semi-formal'. This is a useful way of dividing up support, by whom it is delivered and where parents might look for it.

It is also common for these different sources of support to be seen as having different characteristics and supporting somewhat different things. For example, formal services are generally seen to provide a kind of specialist help beyond the skills and resources of the informal 'network' – another piece of jargon meaning relatives, friends and neighbours. The informal network is seen to give comfort and emotional support and to help with day-to-day practicalities in a way that is not generally expected from formal services.

As a generalization this is, of course, true but, as we shall see later, is also an over-simplification because the quality of the relationship between the giver and receiver of support is a critical element in making some action 'supportive'. This relationship aspect will become clear as we discuss what parents tell us about the ways in which they like support to be offered. This emphasizes the point that understanding 'support' includes understanding how being given support makes people feel. Put the other way round, it makes nonsense of the everyday meaning of 'support' to call services and interventions 'supports' if they do not fulfil the normal notion of 'supportive behaviour'.

What is parenting?

Three key points were made in the discussion of parenting. The first was that parenting in a modern industrial society includes a formidable range of tasks and responsibilities. For parents to pull these off requires sufficient resources and social supports, that can be drawn on to help them. Single parents, for example, are at an automatic disadvantage in this, as are couples who do not get on or who cannot work together harmoniously.

The second point was the importance of the 'ecological' perspective. What this perspective emphasizes is that 'parenting' – what parents actually *do* with and for their children – arises from a very wide variety of influences. Some of these derive from parents' own genetic characteristics, others from the consequences of their experiences of being parented and others from their current mental and physical health. The translation of these individual differences into 'parenting problems' is strongly influenced by the circumstances in which they are trying to look after their children. These range from those social and structural forces, such as labour market changes, to the quality of relationships with partners, relatives and friends.

The ecological perspective forces us to recognize the complicated and often reciprocal relationships between all the influences on parenting. Parents can do little about some of these – labour market changes, for example. Others are more dependent on the parents' own current capacities and personal resources. Influences on parenting do not just go in one direction. Our own behaviour influences our relationships as well as the other way round. It follows from this that the best ways of supporting parenting may be far from obvious. Is it better to work on what parents do with their children – how they parent – or should we first deal with personal problems or circumstances that may be causing the parenting difficulties?

The final point was that formal services themselves should be seen as *part* of the ecology of parenting, not just as something trying to influence it. Services have to take the ecological view as well. If this is not done then tackling one problem – say adult mental health difficulties – may be ineffective, because tackling that problem should mean tackling related ones, such as poverty or the children's behaviour. The

Cross-cutting themes 1: Concepts of support and parenting

THE IDEA OF 'SUPPORT'

- If we use 'support' as a non-specific and umbrella term, the idea becomes devalued
- Receivers and givers of support may differ in their views on what is given and what good it has done

THE CONCEPT OF PARENTING

- In modern societies parenting is complex and hard to do
- Parenting – what parents do with their children – arises from many influences
- The ecological perspective points up the complexity of the relationships between these influences and the difficulty in understanding the direction of effects
- Formal services are part of this ecology, not just influences on it
- Families were committed to maintaining their independence
- All parents wanted to feel in control in dealing with parenting problems
- Parents first wanted information to help them solve problems and then specialist advice
- Research on the effects of supportive interventions – i.e. on 'what works' – needs more specific attempts to understand the *direction of effects* through well evaluated trials of different approaches

benefits of inter-agency working are now usually part of discussions on the delivery of services, but inter-agency working needs to be part of an effort to understand the whole of the parenting ecology – not just a desire to see agencies work together better.

VARIETIES OF PARENTING

Although these general considerations about parenting and its ecology hold for all the parents in these studies, the research also highlights the range of different circumstances and parenting conditions to which these general considerations apply. At one extreme are the parents of the *technology-dependent* children, whose lives are taken over by the needs of their children to the extent that the boundaries between parenting and nursing become blurred, their homes often become extensions of the clinic and parenting becomes professionalized. Then there are the foster carers in the *Supporting Fostering* and the *Adolescent Fostering* studies, who know that their care of the children is likely to be temporary but who need to deploy all the features of positive parenting that are features of parenting generally. One group of parents are working under the stress of an uncertain illness trajectory, the others under the circumstances of caring when the length of their commitment is also uncertain. At the other extreme, there are the *emotionally abusing* or *rejecting* parents who seem not to want to care for one of their children at all, or to blame him or her for all the family's ills.

Support from family and friends

Responsibility and balance

Support from relatives, friends and neighbours depends on our sense of responsibility to help each other and on our sense that the give and take of help and support is reasonably balanced. These things are part of the idea of what a personal relationship is. So we give comfort and advice and do the practical day-to-day things that help each other get by. Family and friends are able to anticipate and adapt to needs in a very flexible and responsive way. We usually know how our families and friends feel and what is on their minds or is making life difficult for them at that moment.

Balance and independence

If this balance is hard to maintain then we may feel a loss of independence or, indeed, open the way to interference and intrusion. It is probably for these reasons that the most common forms of support in the *Poor Environments* study were those that could be 'traded'; that is, those that were easy to give and were interchangeable, such as child care, sharing chores, comforting and giving advice, rather than those things that we might have to give back in the same way, such as money or care during times of sickness. Even with close family, where a kind of trade in support might be less calculated, the receiving of support still sometimes involves a trade with independence.

Special needs

The more complex and specialized the parents' needs were, the less likely it was that their families and friends could give what would otherwise be normal day-to-day support. This was especially apparent for the parents of disabled children in the *South Asian Families* and *Technology-Dependent* studies. In both studies even babysitting or taking the children out required skills that were beyond the competence of relatives. Further, these parents' own resources were stretched to the extent that they could not take part in the normal give and take that usually characterizes these relationships. In the *Disabled Parents* study, services made assumptions about the capacity of the informal network, especially partners, to take on the burden of caring without any discussion of whether this was so or not.

Independence

The families in the *Poor Environments* study were very committed to maintaining their independence. Those most vulnerable to losing their independence – those who saw themselves as most in need – were the most apprehensive about accepting support from family and friends. They feared that asking for help was a sign that they could not cope and that accepting help would weaken the independence of the family. The issue of independence and a need to establish their new families seemed to turn the *step-families* inward onto their own resources and away from formal or informal support. The *New Forest* parents with mental health problems were dissatisfied with the practical support they got from friends and turned to GPs and health visitors for emotional support.

Family and friends as a source of stress

Families and friends are not necessarily supportive. They can themselves be what is on our mind or giving us trouble. The *Poor Environments* study brought out the difficulties and balances in these relationships as well as their positive aspects. This was true also for the foster carers in the *Supporting Fostering* and the *Adolescent Fostering* studies. Support predominated over stress, but a third or more of carers in both studies experienced criticism from family, friends and neighbours.

Indeed, family and friends were especially a source of stress for the parents with the most problems. The *pregnant looked-after teenagers* had poor relationships with their own mothers, who tended to look to them for support rather than giving it to them. The *imprisoned fathers* – whilst loyally visited by their wives and partners – seemed very short of family support in other ways. The emotionally abusing parents in the *Rejection* study also had very poor relationships with their own families and little support from anyone within their social circle.

The *disabled* parents and the parents in the *South Asian families* not only experienced the limitations on support that arose because of their special needs. They often faced incomprehension or hostility from their families as well, because the families did not understand their problems, or even blamed them for them.

Support begins at home

It was clear from many studies that relationships at home were a critical part of parents' support 'networks'. This was true both for positive effects of support and the harm done by its absence or, even more, by discord and hostility between parents.

The foster carers in both of the *fostering* studies put their partners first amongst those who helped them; the *South Asian* parents leant on each other for comfort and decision making; the parents in the *Technology-Dependent* study had to work in a highly coordinated way; and the *imprisoned fathers* relied on the tenacity of their partners in maintaining contact with their children. This in-house support involved children as well. This was an important source of help for the *disabled* parents, the *South Asian* families and the *fosterers of adolescents*.

Conversely, a lack of support at home was stressful. The negative impact of fostering on relationships in the immediate family was an influence on placement disruptions in the *fostering* studies, the *pregnant teenagers* did not want the children's fathers around, while the parents in the *Rejection* study had relationships that were often fragile, quarrelsome or violent.

Cross-cutting themes 2: Informal support

- Support from family and friends involves feeling responsible for each other and feeling that help is reasonably balanced
- Support within the home is very important and the first port of call
- Family and friends are often a source of stress as well as support
- Policy makers can do little, short of providing payments, to mobilize informal sources of support; families do this better themselves
- Parents who got support from informal sources were more likely to get it from formal ones as well
- Informal and formal sources generally did not replace one another because they deal with different things

but

- emotional support is important in *all* supportive relationships; some parents relied on services for emotional support

---

Semi-formal support

The rest of this chapter deals with the balance between informal and formal sources of support, with parents' responses to services and with what the studies have to say about delivering support. Lodged between the informal and formal systems are the semi-formal organizations. These deserve some attention both because of their important role in the ecology of support but also because of what they tell us about the ways in which parents use the supports available to them.

Semi-formal sources of support include all those community and self-help organizations that cater for particular needs or give support and advice for specific problems. They include community-based organizations, such as baby and toddler groups and toy libraries, as well as groups serving more specialized needs, such as those supporting lone parents or people with mental health problems. Some groups may be organized by formal support organizations but be run by their members. Foster carers' groups are an example of this.

Community groups

The *Poor Environments* study was the only one with data on parents' attitudes to and use of community groups. It was clear that parents used these on a 'take it or leave it' basis, depending on how well they fitted with their current needs. Use was also low on a day-to-day basis, but 40 per cent of families had used such resources in the previous three years, overwhelmingly for child care or for children's activities. Use of these groups was not related to any measures of need except for children's special health problems. Strikingly, use was *less* common amongst those who saw themselves as most in need. Rather, use of these groups was associated with relatively *higher* family incomes.

It would be wrong to conclude that these community supports were unimportant, simply because regular use of them was generally low. Rather, the pattern of occasional use points up their value in increasing the flexibility of provision available to parents. This is what a high proportion of parents wanted: support that was there for them and could be activated when they needed it. On the other hand, it seemed that parents needed sufficient energy and resources before they were able to add this to the supports they used.

These resources are important, are inexpensive since they rely on a substantial amount of goodwill from their staff, and need relatively low financial inputs. They try to deal with all sorts of family and community issues and deserve all the support they can get. But, although they meet specific parenting needs – mostly around child care and socializing – they are not used by the most needy families, but by those who already have a range of resources to draw on.

Specialist and users' groups

The use of and positive reactions to specialist support groups was most in evidence in the fostering studies. Both studies showed that meeting other carers was a very important source of emotional support and advice. About half of the carers in the *Adolescents* study went to the groups that were available, as did about two-thirds of the carers in the *Supporting Fostering* study. Over 70 per cent of carers in both studies also had personal contact with other carers, such contact often arising through the organized groups. As in a number of the other studies, support begat support. Thus the carers of the adolescents who were satisfied with their social workers had more contact with other carers. Similarly, the carers in the *Supporting Fostering* study who went to groups regularly were more likely to have other carers to call on informally. These contacts were a very important source of information and advice.

Support groups were thought of less positively and used less by other parents. Cultural and language barriers affected the use of support groups by the *South Asian* parents with disabled children. Groups were generally not available – or not known to be available – to these families. Only 19 per cent belonged to a support group and these generally did not find them helpful. They used them as sources of information, for contact with people with similar problems (a reason for 91 per cent of those who used a support group), or for contact with parents with similar cultural and religious affiliations.

The situation with regard to formal support for *prisoners* and their families was depressing. Forty-two per cent of adults and 30 per cent of young offenders and 64 per cent of all partners had no contact with *any* voluntary or statutory agencies and none mentioned self-help groups.

The relationship between informal and formal supports

One of the questions the initiative intended to answer was the relationship between support from family and friends and support from services. The questions asked were whether these complement each other or deal with different aspects of parenting, whether one makes up for lacks in the other and whether the informal network can be mobilized to enable better parenting.

Mobilizing support from kin and friends

Policy makers have been interested in whether family and friends are an under-used source of support, especially in child care or fostering. These studies do not have direct evidence on this. It is clear from the *Poor Environments* study that family and friends *are* heavily used to help in day-to-day parenting but there appears to be little scope for mobilizing them – except, perhaps, through financial incentives. Parents and their social circles are themselves the natural and most effective organizers of their support. If they are not doing this already it is unlikely that they can be encouraged to do it, because help from kin and friends depends so strongly on the quality of relationships. Moreover, the resources of families and friends in poor neighbourhoods or with complex problems are themselves likely to be stretched practically and emotionally.

Finally, parents who felt unsupported even when they were actually getting quite a lot of help tended to have problems about which the informal system could not be expected to do much; for example, long-term health problems, high levels of current family difficulties, financial problems and children with health and behaviour difficulties.

'To them that hath...'

A common finding across many of the studies was that parents who got support from services tended to get it from family and friends as well. This was true in the *Poor Environments* study. There were relatively high and relative low consumers overall. The *South Asian* parents were more aware of services if they had better informal and semi-formal support. They also had a wider range of services if someone in the household was employed. Those who spoke English got more services. In the *foster care* studies getting on well with social workers went along with more input from them, with better connections with other services and with higher use of foster carers' support groups.

The *Supporting Fostering* study team draw the rather pessimistic conclusion that the direction of these associations was that more skilled foster carers attracted more support, rather than that support leading to better parenting. That is, some parents are better at attracting support than others. Of course, this does not mean that support has no effects, an issue we take up later. It does mean, however, that those who seem less able to attract support from family and friends may be less able to attract it from services as well. This is an important message for services.

Looking for emotional support

Although family and friends and formal services do not supply what families lack from each of them, families were likely to look to formal services for emotional as well as practical support. Heavy users of services in the *Poor Environments* study did this, as did the parents of *technology-dependent* children, the *Asian* parents and depressed parents in the *New Forest* study. For some services this need of users for emotional support could begin to look like dependency, a concern noted by the social workers looking after the pregnant teenagers and some family centre staff.

Support from formal services

The initiative was set up to look at issues of support that went far wider than the provision of formal services but, inevitably, a substantial number of the lessons to be learned are lessons for services themselves. But the focus on the wider context of support had many lessons about what families think of services and want from them, and how these fit into their lives.

Parents' overall reactions to services

This section deals mostly with the criticisms parents had about services and the ways they would like them to change. In setting these out it is easy to come to the conclusion that the picture is one of general dissatisfaction, but that was far from the case. It is a useful corrective to begin with their positive responses and work through to the less positive ones. This will be followed by more specific critiques.

The parents in the *Poor Environments* study were usually positive about the help they received. Indeed, those who were frequent users of services often felt less ambivalent about drawing on their help than they did with their families and friends. The parents in the *New Forest* study also had positive things to say. Parents with mental health problems were more satisfied with the help they got from services than they were with the help from friends. Parents with children with behaviour problems saw health visitors as having an important and valued role in giving good information and in giving emotional support. Over half the carers in the *Supporting Fostering* study and over 70 per cent in the *Adolescent Fostering* study thought that their link workers gave them good support. On the whole, despite their criticisms, carers got on well with their social workers and made allowances for their shortcomings.

On the other hand, not all studies reported these positive relationships. The *step-parents* appeared to keep themselves aloof from services even though half of them had problems in family relationships, children's behaviour and legal issues that they said they would like help with. In practice, their overall level of contact with formal services, private agencies or self-help and voluntary groups was lower than that in two-parent birth families in a comparable sample from the general population.

The *South Asian* parents' experiences were also less positive. Uptake of general health and welfare services was generally low. Their views of services for the child's disability were poor. It took too long to get them organized (87%), they did not know what services were available (82%) or where to get information (81%), they had to fight to get services (75%) and often had services reduced or withdrawn (74%).

The *pregnant looked-after teenagers* were especially negative. Only 4 per cent included social workers amongst the people they could trust. Most had a long litany of complaints that social workers didn't listen, didn't listen to their opinions, didn't give honest accounts and explanations, couldn't be trusted, were difficult or impossible to contact, were not supportive, didn't stand up for them, were unreliable and sat in judgement on them.

From the social workers' point of view what the young people saw as a good relationship often involved over-dependency, including constant phoning and bypassing the foster carer. It was often hard for services to help these girls and keep them involved with the help that was offered. The teenagers liked their after-care workers much better because they dealt with housing and finance, argued for help and gave emotional support. These workers were free of the hard decisions concerning the mother and baby, including child protection issues.

The data on support for the *imprisoned fathers* and their families were the most depressing. As mentioned, 42 per cent of adults and 30 per cent of young offenders had no contact with any voluntary or statutory agencies. Only 8 per cent of inmates had contact with social services departments, assisted visit schemes, counselling, help and advice lines or AA. Eighty-eight per cent of adult inmates and 84 per cent of young offenders knew of no other supportive agencies that could help them. None mentioned self-help groups. Within this, however, family visiting schemes were positively regarded because they provided a 'family-like' atmosphere for prisoners, their partners and their children to meet, despite the felt intrusion of the inevitable security supervision.

More positively, the parents attending the *family centres* got *more* in the way of services from the centres than they anticipated. They liked the fact that it was quick and easy to get a response to a problem and they valued the fact that the centre knew them. They also liked the atmosphere, the warmth and friendliness of staff and the fact that they could just drop in. Indeed, they wanted more of the same services, not different ones. Their criticisms involved practicalities like opening hours, but they also pointed up shortcomings such as inadequate assessments of their children's development, inadequate support if they had mental health problems, and too few social activities.

What parents wanted services to be like

What parents wanted from formal services was very consistent across all the studies that asked the question. The parents in the *Poor Environments* study liked services best that were practical and professional, took their views on their needs seriously, listened to them and were emotionally supportive as well as practically helpful. In short, parents wanted services to treat them like adults and to see them as partners in solving their problems.

The carers in the *Supporting Fostering* study were quite clear what they wanted from social workers. They wanted them to be there for them, respectful of their views, considerate, supportive (that is, warm, approving and ready to listen) and practical. This meant sorting out finance and transport, arranging professional services, working with the birth family, working with the child, enabling the carer to work with the child and supporting the carer. In nearly all these things the link/family placement workers were seen much more favourably, perhaps because the social workers had a more conflicted role – as they did for the *pregnant teenagers*.

The carers in the *Adolescent Fostering* study echoed these sentiments and added some things of their own. They wanted people who listen in a supportive way, help them unravel an issue and give practical support, such as arranging child care. They liked workers who could see both sides of an issue and were impartial. For them, the key element was availability and responsiveness, especially as evidenced by answering phone calls.

The question of responsiveness was especially important for the parents of the children in the *Technology-Dependent* study, a characteristic they got if they were lucky enough to have link workers. Here the use of mobile phones was a particularly important element. This kind of service link gave emotional as well as practical support and helped the parents organize and argue for other services and supplies.

Specific elements in parents' views on services and support

PARENTS IN CONTROL

Whether they were talking about their relationships with their families or their relationships with services, an abiding message from all the parents in these studies was that they wanted to feel in control when they were trying to solve parenting problems. Regardless of whether they were drawing on the help of family and friends, or using the expertise of specialist services, they did not want their parenting decisions to be taken out of their hands. It is important for all those providing support to understand how strong this feeling is, even in circumstances where parenting is clearly problematic, as with the rejecting parents. This need to feel in control was most clearly articulated in the quote from the *Poor Environments* study at the end of Chapter 4: 'Support means that you are still in charge…' It was also reflected in these parents' desire to receive information on parenting issues first through leaflets or videos and then, if necessary, from home visits. They wanted to solve problems for themselves. This need was apparent in many studies. In all three of the projects on disabilities the parents worked hard to provide their children with the experiences, rewards and positive parenting which parents generally try to give.

The need for control was reflected in a more negative way in the step-parents' wariness of formal services while they were still establishing their families, in the pregnant teenagers' rejection of social work 'interference' in their parenting or in some of the imprisoned fathers' resistance to the idea of support. It was, perhaps, strongest in the denials of a substantial proportion of the emotionally abusing parents – who were well known to social services – that anything was wrong.

It seems clear that as parenting problems become more complex, so the capacity of parents to manage all these tasks becomes more and more tested and formal services need to take on some of this task. But the need to feel in control is not necessarily diminished by this, although it frequently was, as the parents' reactions to services showed. Support is too easily determined by service agendas; for example,

South Asian parents felt they had little control over service supports, were 'slotted in', often inappropriately or unreliably, or that the support offered did not have the expertise to cope with the child.

PARENTS AS EXPERTS

Another way of thinking about parents' need to feel in control – and their frequent sense that they are not – is to begin by presuming that they are experts in their own family needs. At a minimum their expertise needs to be acknowledged and their views on their problems taken seriously. Experience may in the end prove otherwise – for example, when rejecting parents want to locate all their family problems in one child – but it is the right place to begin.

Three studies highlight particular issues around parental expertise: the *Technology-Dependent* study and the two *foster care* studies. In the first of these parents began as novices in the specialized care of their children but soon became not only the people who delivered specialist procedures but also the best judges of their children's special needs. This expertise was not a problem for specialist nurses but was for community services more generally, such that parents who could assess needs accurately felt particularly frustrated when their assessments were ignored. Service professionals need to recognize the change in their role from *providers* of care to *enablers* of care and to recognize parents as part of the team caring for the child, as many of the studies in this initiative illustrate.

PARENTS AS PART OF THE 'TEAM AROUND THE CHILD'

The *foster carers* felt that social workers wanted them to approach fostering as 'professionals' but were unwilling to treat them as 'part of a team' caring for the child. This ambiguity may arise because foster carers are both part of a service and recipients of a service, but it may also arise because of professional snobbishness or a tendency to blame carers for failure. If social services expect carers to be 'professional' they should treat them like professionals. Fewer than half of the carers in the *Adolescents* study felt that they were part of the team caring for a child or young person. Thinking about inter-agency working should include the carers.

Support as a relationship

We have pressed the point that all support involves good relationships. The parents in the *Poor Environments* study wanted services to be efficient and to be expert, but they also wanted them to be respectful and to take their views seriously. Respectfulness is the way in which services can deal with the imbalance inherent in the relationship. Balance and equality cannot come through the parents giving something back to the service, but it can come by treating them as partners in problem solving.

Support from any source should not make parents feel vulnerable, small or obligated. If 'support' does not have these features it is, simply, not 'supportive'.

Attention to this kind of balanced relationship becomes more critical the greater and more complex the needs; but it also becomes harder for services to keep in mind the more they concentrate on their technical expertise, as they did with the parents in the *Technology-Dependent* study, or on the power imbalances inherent in the system, most dramatically the case in the relationship between prison authorities and *prisoners* and their families. For the *disabled* parents, support from services was used to make up for limitations in what family and friends could give. Because of these limitations they relied on services for information, comfort and support. Services clearly need to provide emotional as well as practical support.

Support as a process

It was clear from many of the studies that supports from services is not just a question of giving help in a piecemeal way. The effectiveness of support and its ability to maintain the relationship elements that are so important are improved if support is seen as a process. If relationships are right from the start, then parents feel better about the help they are getting and are more likely to stay engaged with the service.

For the *South Asian* parents the support process started with how, when, where and what they were told about their child's disability. Telling the parents in a supportive way helped them accept the disability; acceptance by them made it easier to get understanding and support from kin and friends; this helped parents become more aware of and more confident about services. But mobilizing services needed the active engagement of services themselves, through good language support and a collaborative relationship between parents and professionals. Good service supports reinforce the collaborative relationships and help identify unmet needs and improve parental health.

The importance of getting the relationship right at the beginning was clear for the *disabled* parents as well. Ambiguities in roles and responsibilities were a problem for the parents in the *Technology-Dependent* study. For them the question of whether they would care for their children at home was not well negotiated. The *looked-after teenage* parents were panicked and depressed at the news of their pregnancies, but social services had no clear policies on how to help and support them. The girls' parents pressed for terminations and their peers for them to keep the baby. In the end, doing nothing seemed the easiest course, but the girls' regard for social workers and their subsequent willingness to have them involved in their parenting was very low.

The *SPOKES* project worked hard to get things off to a good start with very careful approaches to parents, work on tailoring the parenting programme in a way that would appeal to parents, home visits to learn about the family pressures that might affect their attendance and the choice of schools as the non-threatening venue for the work.

The delivery of family visiting to *prisoners* and the services for *rejecting* parents were the hardest to get right. The former were beset with problems around security and the supply of drugs and the latter with issues around child protection.

Cross-cutting themes 3: Support and services

- *Parents should first be seen as experts* in their own parenting problems, even when their views may need to be changed – as amongst the parents who are difficult to support
- *Support is a relationship* that requires respect and partnership
- *Support is also a process* – services need to get off on the right foot and be aware of and responsive to changing needs
- Parents and foster parents were generally positive about services

but

- Views were less positive in the studies of disability, especially those of the Asian parents because of poor attention to language and culture
- Some negative views of services may involve unreasonable demand or dependency. Users' views, *on their own*, may not always be a reliable guide to improving services

Parents wanted services
- To be practical
- To be professional
- To take their views seriously
- To listen to them and be emotionally supportive
- To treat them as partners or part of the 'team around the child'

Link and key workers were more successful at this

Cooperation between services

'Inter-agency working' is currently much discussed and the subject of many policy initiatives and service reorganizations. It is hoped that these will, indeed, deliver services that are more responsive to parents' needs and will be able to view these in a more 'holistic' way. Much of this activity post-dates the studies in this initiative, but not by much. This initiative does not provide many good examples of effective inter-agency working. Rather, the more common picture is of services protecting their boundaries and their expertise, both because of issues around professional identity and in order to conserve resources or deal with funding problems.

Boundary setting

A number of examples of boundary setting can be given. All three of the *disability* studies show specialist services concentrating on the disability in a narrow way rather than linking with others to provide a more comprehensive package of services. The needs of the *disabled* parents as parents were not taken into account in planning. For the parents of *technology-dependent* children, arranging short-term care and obtaining equipment was often difficult because of disputes between hospital trusts, community trusts and GPs over who should pay for these services. These problems were resolved in areas where care packages were jointly and equally funded by health and local authorities but, in general, short-term care suffered from a lack of strategic planning, and post-discharge multi-disciplinary meetings to plan care were rare.

In the *Rejection* study coordination between services was poor. Health visitors and social workers did not have positive views of each other. Social workers found child and adolescent mental health services (CAMHS) unhelpful and made very few referrals to adult mental health services. There was a picture of services protecting themselves by setting high thresholds for their intervention or circumscribing the limits of their responsibility.

Service rigidities

The question of boundary setting was part of a wider picture of service rigidities. Some of these arose from policy more generally but some arose through the relationships between services themselves. Policies and services had difficulty in responding to fluctuations in need. This was apparent in the application of benefit rules to fluctuating illnesses for the *disabled* parents. Fluctuations also made it harder for parents to have and keep jobs and to fit these in with the benefit rules.

Short breaks

Rigidities in service provision were a particular issue with respect to short breaks (respite care) for parents in the *disability* and *fostering* studies. Short breaks are very important to parents and carers who are under pressure, but providing them was complicated by inter-agency squabbles over funding, the lack of skilled carers and, in the case of the *South Asian* parents, a lack of culturally appropriate provision. Moreover, short breaks should ideally allow parents to fulfil normal family obligations such as going to weddings and funerals, but this kind of flexibility was absent. There is a need for flexibility in arrangements, including drop-in centres open at evenings and weekends and in-home care to allow parents to go out or for the children to take part in activities outside the home. Lack of appropriate short-term breaks was also a major issue for the parents of the *technology-dependent* children.

Short breaks are a support that parents dealing with complex tasks should be able to expect in order to make their lives more tolerable, not as a response to crisis. That they were sometimes the latter is shown in the *Supporting Fostering* study where the provision of breaks was associated with poorer outcomes. This, of course, was almost certainly because breaks were a marker for more problems, especially anti-social behaviour in adolescence, and were used to try to sustain placements that were in difficulties.

Information

The issue of information crops up in so many studies that it deserves a section of its own. The giving of good information is a key to helping parents solve problems and is part of the process of support for parents. Information between agencies is a good reflection of the quality of their cooperation and the extent to which they are providing coordinated services and tailoring these to needs on the basis of comprehensive assessments.

Information to parents

As we have pointed out, parents wanted information so that they could understand the problems that they were facing in order to work out ways of solving them on their own or working with services to solve them. This issue was critical for the carers in the *Adolescent Fostering* and *Supporting Fostering* studies, who needed information on the young people's lives and problems before the placement was made. The young people needed information in return. They wanted to know something about the people who were going to look after them. Lack of both kinds of information predicted poorer outcomes.

The parents in the *Poor Environments* study wanted videos and leaflets. Providing information on services was an important function of family centres. The *South*

Asian parents wanted information on their child's disability in their own language and in terms they could understand. Ideally, they also wanted this told to them by someone who understood the disability and spoke their own language so that their questions could be answered. They wanted this not just when they heard about the disability but also as their experience of parenting developed and their children's needs changed. They knew little about the services open to them.

Teenagers in the *Teenage Pregnancy* study generally felt that sex education in schools came too late and did not tell them what they wanted to know. Sex education for the looked-after young people was sporadic and depended on the vagaries of their school experiences. Many missed out completely. No local authority in the study had any policy on sexual instruction, even though they have a statutory responsibility to provide it.

Parents often knew little about services that might be available to them. This was particularly so for the prisoners and their partners, who mentioned little beyond social services and probation and never mentioned support groups. Some *family centres* worked hard to collect such information for their own areas, but we do not know how often this led to services being taken up. The suggestion was that it was most likely when the centres organized it.

Information between services

The flow of information between services was not a focus of any of the studies, but where data were collected the lack of information from one service to another was notable. In the *Rejecting Parents* study social services case notes seldom included copies of their social workers' formulation of problems or letters back from services giving an opinion or course of action. Referral letters to CAMHS about rejecting parents often contained no assessment of the problem as seen by the referrer.

Delivering support

The broad conclusion of many researchers was that family needs should be addressed 'holistically', not piecemeal. By this they meant that services should not concentrate on their narrow area of expertise and ignore the broader family context of parents' problems. So often a parenting problem went along with social disadvantage, mental health problems, difficulties in intimate relationships and sometimes with disabilities in the parents or children as well. Parenting problems are often a consequence of these overlapping difficulties and it makes little sense to deal with one while ignoring the others. Sometimes, of course, the children's own behaviour and problems contribute to the parents' unhappiness or poor relationships, but dealing with the behaviour on its own is unlikely to solve these problems.

The poor flow of information between services points to the lack of a holistic approach. This was not a universal picture but better coordination of services often depended on a particularly energetic consultant here or a particularly effective social worker there. There was seldom a built-in mechanism for assessment and coordination. Even with the *emotionally abusing/rejecting* parents, systematic assessments of parenting by health visitors or social workers were lacking. Indeed, health visitors did not see this as part of their role. Social workers concentrated on the reported incident. Only about 3 per cent of emotionally abused children received a full developmental assessment on referral, and there was no evidence that this had been done previously.

Assessment of needs

The assessment of needs, and by whom and how it should be done, is top of the list of ways to improve coordination and delivery of services. Parents of disabled children, for example, should have their own health needs met and the space to have their own social lives and pursue their own interests. *South Asian* parents' mental health was poor but parents did not use mental health services. None of the *disability* studies was able to show that services paid particular attention to support around parenting itself, apart from care in the context of the child's disability or concern over the parenting of disabled parents. There was no evidence of help with parenting approaches or with relationships.

Beginnings of better planning were seen for the families of *technology-dependent* children, where there was strategic planning and post-discharge multi-disciplinary meetings to plan care and agree funding. But these were rare. GPs and nurses could even be unsure about who was responsible for the children when they returned home and communication between hospital and community services was often poor.

For potentially *rejecting* parents, assessments need to begin early and be part of the process of support. The health visitors are a natural starting point for this. Assessments should include family resources; the relationships between the parents and the children, including attachment problems; the parents' own childhood experiences; parental mental health, especially post-natal depression; the children's emotional distress and poor self-image; parental warmth and criticism; and the willingness of parents to accept help. Information on the children should not just rely on the parents' accounts. For *disabled* parents the assessments should include what is needed to help them to continue to parent.

The new integrated children's system provides a valuable model for systematic assessments of this kind but, without a willingness of services to cooperate in agreeing the assessments and delivering the services, the assessments on their own will not be sufficient.

Link and key workers

This review of inter-agency working is not encouraging. Did the studies point to any obvious mechanisms for delivering services that met needs more holistically? It seems appropriate to begin with things that seemed to work better, at least from the parents' point of view. As far as they were concerned link or key workers were easily the most favoured of the methods of coordination on offer.

As the *Poor Environments* study highlighted, parents usually act as their own key worker: they collect information, make decisions on action, seek out services, argue for the help they need and try to fit this in with their lives. But being supported requires a lot of activity on the part of parents. Support does not just arrive, it has to be sought and organized as well. In this the parents, and especially the children's mothers, are the prime coordinators of support and services for the parenting task.

But there are many occasions where the task becomes too complicated and onerous and where someone else with some professional leverage needs to help find out what support is available and battle for it. The list of those who were positive about the link worker role is long: parents in all three *disability* studies; foster carers in the *Supporting Fostering* and *Adolescent Fostering* studies; and the *pregnant looked-after teenagers*, who liked the practical role taken by after-care workers.

WHAT DID THEY LIKE ABOUT THEM?

The *foster carers* rated key or link workers highly because they did what the carers wanted social workers to do: they respected their views, and were considerate, warm, approving, ready to listen and practical. Equally important, they were available and answered calls. In short, they were 'there for them'. The foster carers of the adolescents used their link workers for day-to-day support as well as for organizing and arguing for services. Indeed, link workers came top of these carers' lists of those who were both available and useful.

The parents of the *technology-dependent* children also found that services delivered best when they were coordinated by a key worker who could help deal with the complexities of getting supplies and support. Again, these workers were available through their mobile phones, a highly valued means of contact.

The value of linking was seen in other ways as well. A notable source of help for the *South Asian* parents was their children's schools. These were sources of information, emotional support and help with getting other services.

In short, link workers were able to combine the flexibility and relationship qualities of family and friends with professional knowledge and expertise and a greater power to argue for services. When this role was working well parents felt that the link workers knew them and understood their problems as a family. Of course, this was not always the case. Some link workers were not effective in their jobs. Moreover, outside of social services, the use of link workers was still the exception. There seems no doubt, however, that the link worker role provides a demonstrably effective way of supporting parents.

In this context, as pointed out in Chapter 2, it should be noted that *the great majority of parents function as their own key worker:* they analyse and diagnose problems, decide on actions, make contact with appropriate sources of support, try to tell their supports what their needs are and try to resist handing control to others or incurring obligations that cannot be reciprocated.

Families who are hard to work with

This summary of cross-cutting themes would not be complete without some discussion of supporting parents who are hard to work with. Three studies dealt with support for parents who have complex and suspicious relationships with services, and often with their own families and friends as well: the *looked-after pregnant teenagers*, the *imprisoned fathers* and the *emotionally abusing* or *rejecting* parents. These parents were somewhat provokingly grouped as 'undeserving' parents in order to highlight the ways in which public and service responses can affect the support offered to them.

In terms of the ecology of parenting all three groups tend to especially unsupportive contexts for parenting. The adults were often poorly parented themselves and had experienced few models of good parenting, their social disadvantage is very high, their personal relationships are negative and fragile and their relationships with family and friends are often weak and unsupportive. They are often, indeed, difficult families to help, even with the best of intentions. The *pregnant teenagers* thought that they knew how to parent and did not want social workers helping them; the *imprisoned fathers* often thought they were close to the ideal of what a parent should be, and sometimes wanted to keep help at arm's length; the *rejecting* parents frequently denied the incidents which led to their recent referral and were hard to engage in interventions designed to help their parenting. The CAMHS professionals stress how hard these families were to engage and how easy it was for them as professionals to have negative feelings about them.

Service responses reflected this negativity. Social services had no policies for dealing with the *pregnant teenagers* and, indeed, often did not know how many of the children they were looking after were in this state. Social workers had difficulty in dealing with what seemed like over-dependency and demandingness. What the teenagers saw as good support was, from the social workers' point of view, dependent on their willingness to be constantly available and to meet needs on demand. The *prisons* generally failed to meet the requirements to facilitate and strengthen family ties. Family visiting was not the responsibility of anyone in the establishments and visiting schemes were not common. Where such schemes existed they were supervised because of concerns over the transfer of drugs and were frequently closed for these reasons. The *rejecting* parents were well known to social services and contact was quite frequent, but this seemed to be based on incident not needs, and developmental assessments of children were a rarity. Even the *family centres*, which frequently tried to work with parents with complex problems, were aware that they needed to limit the length of their interventions and to resist becoming the parents' main source of support.

The difficulty in supporting these parents was associated with fragmented services and with some suggestion of buck-passing. In some cases there was a simple failure to do what the service was supposed to do. Sex education for the *looked-after teenagers* – although a responsibility for social services – was almost entirely lacking. Indeed, few of the authorities in the study had any policy on the matter. *Prisons* were supposed to encourage family contact and extend family visiting schemes and home contacts. But these aspirations were vitiated by the lack of schemes, the grim circumstances of ordinary visits and the limitations seen as necessary because of security – especially drug – concerns. The *emotionally abusing* parents were passed on from health visitors to social services and sometimes from social services to child or adult mental health services, but no service had a very high opinion of another and referrals often led to no clear action. In this study the picture was of under-resourced services protecting themselves by setting high thresholds for their intervention or circumscribing the limits of their responsibility.

Support in the community

Were there any pointers as to how support for these parents and, indeed, others with complex problems might be more effectively delivered? For the *imprisoned fathers* and their families, of course, the solution lies in better efforts to develop visiting schemes and parenting courses that are helpful to them and their families. The equally difficult task of giving support to their partners around their children's behaviour and development was not addressed in this study, but the lack of connection with support groups and the partners' view that the imprisonment did not affect the children's education are matters to ponder. The researchers suggested the adaptation of American models of integrated formal and informal support in which academics, professionals, lay people and prisoners and their families have campaigned to support the relationship between the child and the imprisoned parent.

Many studies advocate developing supports on a 'non-stigmatizing' basis, on the grounds that parents who are difficult to engage are least likely voluntarily to respond to help from social services, CAMHS clinics or other bodies who they fear are 'spying' on their parenting. There is no clear evidence from these studies that such approaches would be more successful in engaging parents but there are suggestions that this might be so.

Social workers and health visitors in the *Rejecting Parents* study were most positive about the responses and the help they got from community-based parenting programmes; the parents attending the *family centres* were surprised that they got more than they expected in the way of services and like the atmosphere and style of the centres; the *SPOKES* project went out of its way to set itself up as a community project and to avoid the dangers of seeming 'official'. Engaging parents in planning the programme was successful, as was the effort at understanding their lives and agenda. Moreover, the project showed not only that parents of children with behaviour problems could be engaged in this way – even when they themselves did not see their children as problematic – but that parenting styles and children's behaviour could be changed.

But some caveats need to be introduced into this positive picture. First, neither the *Family Centres* study of parents' views nor the *SPOKES* project is clear about the parents they were *not* able to engage. Similarly, the *Rejection* study had no informa-

Cross cutting themes 4: Inter-agency working

INTER-AGENCY WORKING

- There were few good examples of effective inter-agency working or cooperation between services
- Cooperation often depended on energetic individuals rather than structures
- Services tended to protect their boundaries and restrict their responses to their own areas of expertise
- Professional anxieties and funding issues often seemed to be part of this

HOLISTIC SERVICES

- The studies highlight the *overlapping needs* of many families, with poverty and hardship a frequent element
- *Support should be delivered holistically*, not piecemeal
- This requires *good assessment, cooperation* and *information* between services and to parents
- Good assessments of family needs were notably lacking for the majority of parents
- *Support in non-stigmatizing settings* like family centres was advocated as a response to many parenting problems, although the studies had no information on the effectiveness of these

tion on how successful the referral of families to community parenting resources was, either in terms of attendance or of effects.

A further issue for supports located in the community – which in many ways can provide holistic assessments and services – is the pressure towards specialization in more complex and intractable family problems. If this is the case, it is likely to limit the use of *family centres* by those with more day-to-day issues and also turn the centres into the 'stigmatized' services that the parents with many problems are anxious to avoid. As they stand, however, centres were not in a position to coordinate services in a formal way, although they played an important facilitating role by bringing services together to discuss coordination and even the needs of individual families.

Clearly, the current policy push to increase the number of community-based holistic services receives much support from the studies in this initiative.

Does support make a difference?

In Chapter 2 we queried the assumption that support – especially 'putting in' support – actually did make a difference to parenting and, if it did, how this came about. It is necessary to return to this question at the end of this overview.

Does parenting make a difference to outcomes?

First we should ask whether parenting makes a difference to outcomes; that is, does it make a difference to children's development, to the breakdown of foster placements or whatever? This question may seem unnecessary, given the wealth of research that tells us that it does, at least where the extremes of poor parenting are concerned. On the other hand, it is important to see what these studies tell us about differences in parenting in a more usual range. We often have strong ideas about the impact of relatively small differences in parenting on 'outcomes', but at what level do we need to intervene?

The *New Forest* study had interesting findings on this. A variety of parenting styles were identified, including a relaxed and somewhat indulgent style, one that was somewhat negligent and lacking in warmth, one that was involved with the children but maintained firm boundaries and a style that was predominantly hostile and aggressive. These parenting styles generally seemed little related to children's behaviour, although involved and effective parenting that went along with consistency between parents was associated with the disappearance of children's behaviour problems between the ages of three and eight. The only style associated with persistent psychological problems in the children was the hostile and aggressive one. This parenting style was identifiable early in the child's life and is, of course, redolent of the behaviour of the parents in the *Rejection* study.

The conclusion from these findings was that a wide range of techniques are used within ordinary parenting without increasing the risk of behaviour problems. The researchers concluded that services to improve parenting should be targeted on those with markedly hostile and disengaged parenting.

The effectiveness of certain parenting styles in encouraging better outcomes was apparent in the foster care studies as well. Effective parenting in the *Supporting Fostering* study involved sensitivity, boundary setting, supervision and child-centredness. This style of parenting went along with lower breakdown rates and more positive ratings of the success of the placement by social workers and carers. Moreover, this study was able to introduce one additional critical test. The researchers were able to show that this style of parenting had an effect even when the children's level of problems was taken into account. It was not simply that parenting looked better when children were easier. Rather, better parenting *predicted* better outcomes. The *Adolescent Fostering* study added one refinement to this. For the adolescents, sensitivity in parenting involved the carers' ability to adapt to the emotional rather than the chronological age of the young person.

Finally, the *SPOKES* project provided a convincing demonstration that parenting approaches can be changed and that these changes lead to a significant reduction in behaviour problems. The features of parenting that the programme sought to develop were precisely those that were effective in the foster care studies. Moreover, the follow-up design and the random allocation of parents to the programme or to an everyday support comparison group ensured that the findings were not due to something else besides the programme.

Does support make a difference to parenting?

A thornier question to answer is whether support makes a difference to parenting. The *SPOKES* project shows that a carefully thought-out intervention can do so; but does the more usual kind of support that parents receive also have this effect? Certainly there is plenty of evidence that parenting problems go along with a lack of support, but we have raised the question of how we understand the direction of these effects.

Apart from the *SPOKES* project, most other studies looked at support making an assumption not only that support would make parenting less stressful but also that support would translate into parenting behaviour; few, however, had direct measures of parenting. The *Poor Environments* study provided an extended analysis on the relationship between support and the parents' sense that they were coping, but without looking at whether support actually modified the way they parented.

Did support make a difference to parents' sense that they were coping? The associations between coping and support were complex. Those who were not coping clearly wanted more support but so did a third of those who were coping. In practice, those who felt they were coping were actually getting less support than those who were not. This was true both for support from family and friends and from services.

Because of its follow-up design the *Supporting Fostering* study was able to test whether support was associated with more positive parenting styles. It was clear that it was but it was also clear that parenting style was a relative stable characteristic of parents. Some carers simply seemed better at the task than others. Both this study and the *Adolescent Fostering* study showed that parenting could be destabilized by all sorts of family stresses as well as by a lack of 'fit' between carers and children.

Most kinds of support were valued by carers, made them feel better about what they were doing and helped them sort out day-to-day issues. On the other hand, there was a lack of evidence that social work support made a difference to parenting styles or to placement breakdowns. If anything, more support was given to those who were more effective carers. It seemed that the more successful carers got on better with their social workers and got more help from them, rather than the other way round.

These fostering studies also highlighted another issue in looking at the effects of specialist support on outcomes. Both studies conclude that more focused and specialized work is necessary if support is to help these children. On the other hand, as is often the case, these studies were unable to show that specialist services had any effect on outcomes – with the possible exception of educational psychologists – probably because most specialist support was going to the most troubled children. Different research designs are necessary before we can be sure of the effectiveness or otherwise of specialist inputs.

Conclusion

At the beginning of this chapter we drew a distinction between the implication of the projects depending on whether we are considering the ways in which parents should expect to be treated ('rights') and whether support of particular kinds is effective in helping parents with their problems. It is worth emphasizing this distinction again. The studies were very effective in pointing out how parents saw support and what they wanted from it. These are very clear messages for services. Taking serious note of these views is not only a matter of entitlement, it is also likely that doing so will make it easier to engage even more parents with the most complex parenting problems in services intended to help them.

It seems reasonable to assume that services that make parenting less stressful will have an effect on what parents do with and for their children and that, in the majority of cases, they can safely be given the information and encouragement to work out their problems in their own way. Nearly all parents want to do this, but many have more complex problems that need specialist input. Specialist services, however, should have in mind the objective of helping parents problem solve and working with them to allow them to do so. The complexities of inter-agency workings and the battles between agencies over professional boundaries and funding are not matters that ought to complicate the parenting task.

On the other hand, the studies suggest that we are far from the point at which needs are assessed holistically and in partnership. We are often still at the point when the objectives of 'support' are poorly defined and the effectiveness of it untested. These studies have sufficient evidence to show that parents can be helped directly with their parenting, but also that the ecology of parenting and the direction of influences within it are exceedingly complex. This suggests that future research efforts need to work on the idea of 'evidence-based services' and to do this through studies whose designs are adequate to test the effectiveness of different interventions. On top of all this, we need to keep social disadvantage clearly in our sights. So many of the studies show the overlap between parenting problems and poverty and disadvantage. This needs to be addressed both as a matter of 'rights' and as a key to positive 'effects'.

The Researchers' Summaries of their Studies

Department of Health Research Overviews always give space for the researchers to summarize their projects in their own way and to bring out the messages that they think are important. This appendix has only been lightly edited in order to produce summaries of reasonably equal length and to provide consistency in headings and typefaces. Extended accounts of methods and sampling are not included here as these are given in the main text.

The order of these summaries follows the order of the presentation of the studies in the main body of the overview text.

Parenting in Poor Environments: Stress, Support and Coping

Deborah Ghate and Neal Hazel
Policy Research Bureau

This study of parents living in materially disadvantaged neighbourhoods was designed to explore, from parents' own perspectives, the stresses they faced in the course of their daily lives at different levels of the 'ecology' of parenting (individual, family and community); the extent to which different kinds of support were available and used by parents; and the impact of stress and support on coping with parenting. Overall, we wanted to discover what parents want from social support, and how better support for parents in poor communities can be mobilized.

The study

The study had two components:

- It comprised the first ever representative national interview survey of 1754 parents, randomly sampled from areas of the country objectively defined as 'poor parenting environments', using a scale[1] specially developed for the study. The areas represented in the study were drawn from the top 30 per cent of the national distribution of disadvantaged areas.

- It included a qualitative follow-up study of 40 parents in especially disadvantaged circumstances (e.g. parents on extremely low incomes; parents with health problems or disabilities; lone parents etc.).

---

1   The Poor Parenting Environments Index (PPE-Index).

Findings
KEY PROBLEMS FOR PARENTS IN POOR ENVIRONMENTS

At the individual level

Parents living in poor environments were in considerably worse physical and mental health than other adults of the same age in the general population. Forty per cent had a long-term physical health problem or disability, compared to 27 per cent in the wider population. Parents in poor environments were three times as likely to have high scores on a measure indicating mental health problems as adults in the wider population.[2] Parental physical and mental health problems were highly interrelated, and were also likely to go along with poor child physical health, and having a behaviourally or emotionally 'difficult' child.[3] Interestingly, however, children in the study were not in substantially worse physical or mental health than other children in the wider population. Overall, 15 per cent of children were rated as 'difficult' or challenging to parent by the researchers, having an abnormal or clinical-range score on a standardized parent self-report measure – only slightly more than would be expected according to recent wider population studies.

At the family and household level

Key stresses arose from the widespread occurrence of very low incomes, high unemployment, and high levels of anxiety about finance. The average equivalized household income was £7000. Only one in six households had an income at the national average level, and 50 per cent had no adult in paid work. On a list of 'basic necessities', two-thirds of the sample (62%) could not afford at least one item.

Two in five of all parents (41%) reported a serious problem with the quality of their housing. This figure rose to just over half of all private tenants (53%) and local authority tenants (51%).

Lone parents were struggling more than parents with partners on almost all counts and were much less likely than parents with partners to say they were 'coping' with parenting. However, parents who had an 'unsupportive' partner had the same (low) rates of coping as lone parents. Large families (with three or more children) were hit by the 'double whammy' of having more expenses and smaller equivalized household incomes.

At the community and environmental level

There was a 'hierarchy of risk' in terms of the likelihood of reporting problems in the local neighbourhood. The poorer the neighbourhood on the PPE-Index, the dirtier and more degraded the environment, as well as having more social problems like crime and anti-social behaviour. Environmental problems (e.g. dog fouling) were reported to impact on parents more than social problems.

2   Rutter, M., Tizard, J. and Whitmore, K. (1970) *Education, Health and Behaviour.* London: Longmans.

3   Bates, J.E., Freeland, C.B. and Lounsbury, M.L. (1979) 'Measurement of infant difficultness.' *Child Development 50,* 794–803; Goodman, R. (1994) 'A modified version of the Rutter Parent Questionnaire including extra items on children's strengths.' *Journal of Child Psychology and Psychiatry 35,* 1483–1494; Goodman, R. (1997) 'The Strengths and Difficulties Questionnaire: a research note.' *Journal of Child Psychology and Psychiatry 38,* 581–586; Richman, N., Stevenson, J. and Graham, P. (1982). *Preschool to School: A Behavioural Study.* London: Academic Press.

Overall

Once poverty was controlled for, five key factors predicted problems in *'coping' with parenting* (as self-assessed by parents themselves):

- having a 'difficult' child
- having a high Malaise score (i.e. having poor mental health)
- having a high score on our 'Current Problems Questionnaire' that measured a wide range of family and household problems
- having a large family
- being a lone parent.

Parents' problems were overlapping, multiple and cumulative, so that if they had problems in one area they almost certainly had problems in other areas of their life, compounding parenting difficulties. The more problems, the less likely they were to be 'coping' with parenting. Evidence suggested that the 'key need groups' in the study were:

1. parents living in the poorest neighbourhoods
2. parents on lowest incomes
3. lone parents
4. parents with mental health problems
5. parents with problems in other areas of their lives (e.g. debt, domestic violence)
6. parents with 'difficult' children
7. parents with accommodation problems
8. parents with large families.

FINDINGS ABOUT SERVICES TO PARENTS IN POOR ENVIRONMENTS

Different types of support tend to cater to different needs of parents:

- informal support from family and friends more often addresses emotional and practical needs
- semi-formal support (e.g. mother and toddler groups) predominantly addresses the social needs of children and parents
- formal support (statutory and professional services) addresses need for expert and emergency/crisis help and advice.

Any one type (e.g. informal) cannot necessarily compensate for a shortfall in another (e.g. formal). There were signs that services, both semi-formal and formal, were reaching parents with higher levels of need. However, there were substantial gaps in awareness of services – even in 'universal' services such as health visiting. One in ten parents thought there were no semi-formal services in their local area, and one in sixteen (6%) thought there were no formal services. Three in ten parents (32%) said they had never had a visit from a health visitor.

Main themes in terms of what parents wanted from semi-formal and formal services were:

1. increased accessibility (e.g. reduced waiting lists, longer opening hours)
2. expansion of facilities in existing services (e.g. more staff on duty)
3. improvements in staff quality and training (e.g. more understanding staff)
4. an expanded profile of users
5. supporting written information for parents.

On this last point, there was a large information deficit reported by parents, with parents feeling that they wanted to know more about different aspects of parenting (especially discipline and child behaviour). Overall, two-thirds of parents wanted more information about some dimension of parenting or child care.

Parents were acutely aware that asking for and accepting social support can also have 'downsides'. Concerns about 'negative support', including the fear of interference and a potential loss of privacy or control over one's life, may be a barrier to seeking help, both at the informal level and the level of seeking help from formal services.

Parents were generally happy with support if they had received it, but were particularly critical of formal services for not listening to them or valuing their skills as parents. They sometimes saw formal support as too prescriptive and irrelevant to their real needs. Parents indicated that professionals' support agendas did not always correspond to their own.

Messages for policy and practice

- Poverty is at the root of most problems. Parents in poor environments don't see themselves as having 'problems with parenting' as much as having problems with poverty. Parents reported that, overall, tackling material poverty and deficits in family resources was their prime concern and that poverty was the cause of many of their problems. However, improvements in other areas will benefit parents in poor environments. For example, improving the physical quality of the neighbourhood is a priority for parents.

- As different types of support address different needs, diversity of support is essential to meet a diversity of need in this group.

- Services need to realize the multiple and overlapping needs of parents that may compound each other. This suggests the need for an holistic assessment of need at first contact with services, and multi-agency solutions.

- There is a need for more comprehensive child care support, both to allow parents to work, and to give 'respite' at stressful times.

- There is a need to improve and create local activities for children in poor neighbourhoods, particularly for older children.

- Services directed at improving the quality of adult relationships in families under strain would help parents cope.

- Enhancing semi-formal services (e.g. mother and toddler groups) could also help enhance informal support networks, because of the predominantly 'social' reasons that parents gave for accessing semi-formal services.

- Services should be careful to ensure that parents feel 'in control' of what happens to them and their family – fear of loss of autonomy as a result of involving services in family life was a strong theme.

- There is an urgent need to tackle the poor public image of many family support services, which seems to be a barrier to seeking support. This particularly applies to social services and some health services, and mostly relates to parents' fears of interference and loss of control.

- However, services should ensure that they are addressing parents' self-defined needs if they are to keep parents on board and maximize the benefits from intervention. This means that any attempt to make a service more 'approachable' must also be accompanied by clear practical outcomes related to parents' concerns – working on image and accessibility alone is unlikely to be enough.

- Because formal services tend to be used as back-up support in crisis situations, these services should be designed to allow at least some access to parents when they *need* to access them – rather than being unavailable, wait-listed and often slow to respond in every way.

- Parents were, on the whole, remarkably resourceful and resilient in the face of multiple problems, and harboured a strong sense of pride in their neighbourhoods. We did not find widespread evidence of social fragmentation or a sense of community disintegration. For example, only around half of parents wanted to move to another area, and over three-quarters said their community was 'generally friendly'. Only 7 per cent said they knew none of their neighbours by name. This existing sense of community could be built upon. Perhaps, at a community level, those who identify themselves as coping better with parenting could be mobilized to help those coping less well.

A Study of Stepchildren and Step-parenting

Marjorie Smith, Jeremy Robertson, Jo Dixon, Margaret Quigley and Emma Whitehead

Thomas Coram Research Unit, Institute of Education, University of London

(Note: This study was not originally commissioned as part of the Supporting Parents initiative, but was added to it after commissioning because of the relevance of its content.)

Despite an increase in the number of stepfamilies – 8 per cent of families at any one time with children contain stepchildren – there is little empirical information on how successful stepfamilies function, and increasing evidence of the failure of some of them to function well, although there is great variation. It could be hypothesized that the successful stepfamilies are so because they are like successful biological families, but the evidence, such as there is, is that this is not so. It has been said that, currently, 'there are almost no guidelines as to how a stepfamily should behave and therefore each family has to negotiate their roles anew in a virtually ad hoc way, often during periods of considerable stress' (Robinson 1992, p.63).[4]

This study set out to investigate how 'ordinary' stepfamilies behave, and how they function. The three main aims of the study were:

1. to investigate how children in stepfamilies were parented, and whether this differed markedly from parenting in original families

2. to investigate the process of formation and functioning in different types of stepfamily, to see which variables or which models of stepfamily were associated with a good outcome for children

3. to investigate children's views of stepfamily life and relationships in a stepfamily.

For the purpose of this research a stepfamily was defined as a household with a family unit of at least one child, and two cohabiting adults (whether legally married or not), only one of whom was the child's biological parent, and where the other, who was not, was not part of the household at the time of the child's birth.

---

4 Robinson, M. (1992) 'Making sense of stepfamilies: a guide for practitioners when applying the Children Act 1989 to steprelationships.' In B. Dimmock (ed) *A Step in Both Directions: The Impact of the Children Act 1989 on Stepfamilies.* London: The National Stepfamily Association.

The study

The study was a cross-sectional investigation in a representative community sample of nearly 200 new stepfamilies. It was conducted in two parts. In the first stage ('Changes in Children's Lives') a large-scale screening exercise in London was used to identify a representative sample of eligible new stepfamilies, and the second stage was an in-depth interview study of these families. Ten thousand questionnaires were returned and 434 families fitting the research criteria were found. Half of these participated in the study, in which the parent, step-parent and up to two children within the age range were interviewed separately, at home.

Findings

Changes in children's lives

It was evident that it was normal for children to experience changes in their lives or home circumstances – nine out of ten children had experienced at least one significant change in the previous three or four years. On average, children experienced nearly three changes during this period. More than a quarter of children had experienced the death of a grandparent in the previous three or four years, and 16 per cent the death of someone else close to them. Nearly one in every six children had experienced a parental separation or divorce in the previous three or four years. In general, both parents' and teachers' ratings of child behaviour were associated with the number of changes children had experienced, with more changes associated with worse behaviour.

Becoming a stepfamily

Over nine out of ten of the identified stepfamilies were stepfather families – that is, with a mother and her children, and a stepfather. There was evidence that mothers now in stepfamilies differed in several ways that predated the current stepfamily, from mothers, with children of equivalent age, not in stepfamilies. For example, women in stepfamilies were likely to have been significantly younger when they had their first child, and they were much more likely than women in two-parent families to have a history of depression.

For nearly a third of stepfathers, the stepfamily relationship was their first experience of a cohabiting relationship, and over half had no previous experience of children or of parenting. More than half the children now in stepfamilies did not know their future step-parent at all, or well, before they became part of the household, and only about half the stepfamilies had ever discussed any aspects of the step-parent's behaviour towards children in the household. Only about one in ten families had made any practical arrangements such as changes in financial arrangements before cohabitation and, with the exception of household expenses, most had never done so.

Identification as a stepfamily

Over three-quarters of stepfamilies never identified themselves as such. Stepfamilies where the step-parent had no children of his or her own were most likely to do so, and those with new 'shared' children least likely to do so.

Relationships within stepfamilies

The quality of parent/child relationships in stepfamilies and two-parent families did not differ. Although the majority of children described themselves as having good relationships with their step-parent, there was more variability in step-parent/child relationships, and children were more likely to have poor relationships with step-parents than with parents. About half the step-parents described their relationship with their stepchild as good. The quality of relationships between adults in this group of new stepfamilies was better, on average, than in the comparison group of two-parent families.

Parenting and family life

In general there were more similarities than differences in parenting between stepfamilies and non-stepfamilies, although stepfathers were significantly less involved than were fathers in two-parent families in care-taking activities with the children. Most notable were differences in punishment and control in stepfamilies. Mothers in stepfamilies were significantly less likely than mothers in two-parent families to have smacked the child, and smacked less frequently. Differences between stepfathers and fathers in two-parent families followed the same pattern, but were even more marked. In a small group of stepfamilies the step-parent did not exert any control or discipline over the child.

Contact with non-resident parents

Children in nearly three-quarters of families had had some contact with their non-resident parent in the previous year, although practical arrangements relating to contact were often identified as a cause of problems. In nearly half the families, children were in regular and frequent contact with their non-resident parent. Children in nearly two-thirds of families continued to have contact with members of their non-resident parent's extended family. This was most often their grandparents, but also uncles and aunts.

Support needs of stepfamilies

Half the parents in stepfamilies identified problems or issues that they would have liked help with. Many of these problems appeared to relate either directly or indirectly to the stepfamily status – for example, problems relating to relationships within the household, or legal problems. Despite this, stepfamilies reported less contact with statutory services than non-stepfamilies, and tended not to seek help from any source.

Outcomes for children in stepfamilies

Outcomes for children, measured by means of a standardized assessment of children's health, behaviour and functioning, were most strongly associated with the quality of relationships within the household. The associations were strongest with the quality of the parent/child relationship, and the quality of the parent/step-parent relationship. There was little or no evidence of an association between child outcomes and variables relating to the type or current status of the stepfamily, the history of the stepfamily, or variables relating to the contact with the child's non-resident parent. The presence of a new half-sibling in the household was, however, associated with slightly poorer outcomes for children.

Children's views of life in stepfamilies

Only a quarter of the children interviewed knew what a stepfamily was. Most children gave vague or limited explanations, and a quarter had no idea. Only one in five children thought of their families as stepfamilies. Despite this, children tended to have rather inclusive views of 'family', and most included both their non-resident parent and their step-parent as part of their family. Most children explained their step-parent in terms of the step-parent's relationship with their parent, rather than in terms of any relatedness to themselves.

For a significant group of children the stepfamily had come into existence without any warning. Nearly one in five children had no prior knowledge of the step-parent becoming part of the household, and fewer than one in ten of the children felt they had been party to the decision.

There was a strong association between step-parent involvement in the family and household, and the step-parent/child relationship. Children who described their step-parent as more involved were also more likely to describe having a good relationship with their step-parent.

Messages for policy and practice

- Although not necessarily good for children, coping with change is part of the normal experience of childhood. In most cases, parents will bear the brunt of helping children to cope with changes, but there will be occasions when either because of the nature of the changes, or other stresses or pressures on the parents, they will need help and support in supporting their children. Teachers and GPs may be used by parents in such circumstances, but it is not clear that these professionals always feel it is part of their role to provide support. Other parents may use telephone helplines, but there are indications of a need for some form of 'drop-in' centre where parents can go, without referral or waiting lists, for advice and support on problems affecting their children. Family centres may go some way to providing this support, but only a small sector of the community is likely to have access to a centre, and not all those who do would use them.

- The evidence from this study was that what was important for child well-being were factors in the 'here and now'. Past family history, structural variables relating to the stepfamily, potential mental health vulnerabilities in their parent, and even the relationship with their non-resident parent were all insignificant, compared with the dominant influence on child well-being of relationship variables in the current stepfamily household. The indications are that supporting the adults' relationship and the parent/child relationship would have the same impact in a stepfamily as it would in a non-stepfamily.

- Stepfamilies appear to be a largely 'unseen' population who, for a variety of reasons, do not see themselves, or wish to be viewed, as stepfamilies. There were indications of greater vulnerabilities within stepfamilies, particularly in relation to parents' mental health histories. Compounding the greater vulnerability in stepfamilies was the finding that mothers in stepfamilies were less likely than mothers in two-parent families to have contact with support services, despite the fact that many had babies or young children, and would have been expected to have some statutory contact with professionals such as health visitors. At the same time, parents in stepfamilies were unlikely to seek help from any source, despite half of them identifying 'needs' or problems that they would have liked help with. This suggests that parents in stepfamilies try to contain problems for as long as they can. The fact that children from stepfamilies are over-represented in many negative statistics, such as young runaways, child abuse or looked-after children, suggests that this tactic is not always successful. It does also suggest that issues of stigma or perceived stigma, and the lack of an open access, pre-crisis support service, are still issues that need to be addressed in order to provide effective support for all those in parenting situations.

A Normative Study of Children's Injuries

Marjorie Smith, Janet Boddy, Sue Hall, Caroline Morse, Cheryl Pitt and Maggie Reid
Thomas Coram Research Unit, Institute of Education, University of London

(Note: This study was added to the Supporting Parents initiative after commissioning because of the relevance of its content.)

There is little information on the normal pattern of minor injuries to children or what causes them, or on the way in which parental supervision, the organization of the home and other parenting variables relate to incidents of minor injury. Information on day-to-day injuries is relevant to investigations of possible child abuse or neglectful parenting, and detailed information about the context in which injuries occur is important in prevention. Detailed information may also help explain differences in the rates of more serious injuries that are associated with variables such as social class, maternal age, marital status and family stress.

The main aims of the study were:

- to identify and provide a profile of the normative experience of injuries at different ages in childhood

- to investigate the association between particular contexts or activities and identifiable patterns of injury to children

- to investigate the association of different levels of parental supervision and the safety of the home environment to minor injuries to children.

The study

The research involved a randomly selected community sample of nearly 700 families with children from birth to eight years of age, drawn from General Practitioner lists in a number of different locations selected to include inner and outer city areas as well as non-metropolitan areas.

Parents completed a detailed 'incident diary', covering nine days, recording all the incidents when the child appeared to have hurt themselves, and information on any resulting injuries, including minor soft tissue damage. Parents were also asked to check on a daily basis for any other visible injuries on the child, and record these. At the end of the nine-day diary recording period, the mother was interviewed at home about the family, including parenting, supervision and safety practices, and the child's history of more serious injuries.

Findings

Minor injuries were very common

Children sustained an average of nearly seven minor injuries during the nine-day diary completion period. Babies and one-year-old children had fewer injuries, with the peak age for the number of injuries at two years. At this age children were getting an average of one injury a day. Not all incidents gave rise to a visible injury – over a third of incidents, most commonly those described as bumps or bangs, and injuries to the head did not. Parents were not aware of the incidents that caused over two-thirds of the injuries they observed. Some of these injuries would have occurred while the child was not with the parent, for example when they were at school, but this was certainly not the case for all injuries, especially those in young children.

Most injuries where the cause was known were caused by bumping into things (most commonly furniture) or falling or tripping over, mostly in the home. Over half of all the minor injuries recorded were trivial – for example, small bruises or surface scratches that did not bleed significantly. Only 5 per cent of minor injuries were classified as 'significant' (for example, a large blue/black bruise on the forehead of a two-year-old child; or a puncture wound to the lip caused by a tooth, in a seven-year-old girl), and 1 per cent as more serious (for example, a deep cut on the thigh of a six-year-old child).

Patterns of normal injuries

Clear patterns of 'normal' injuries were evident. For example, the large majority of injuries were either cuts or bruises, or both. Over the diary completion period, over 80 per cent of children had at least one cut or scratch, and three-quarters sustained at least one bruise. Other types of injury (such as burns, crush injuries etc.) were relatively uncommon. Over half of all injuries were to the legs, mostly to the knee or the shin. A fifth of all injuries were to the head.

Normal patterns of injury were related to the age of the child, with the average numbers of cuts and bruises varying with the age (but not with gender). Age-related patterns of bruises and cuts followed similar trajectories, with both appearing to peak at the age of two. For children aged less than a year, the majority of injuries were to their heads, but this proportion declined with age. By the age of two, and thereafter, the largest proportion of injuries was to the legs.

Relationship with the child's history of more serious injuries

Mothers were asked about the child's history of more serious injuries necessitating hospital attendance. Nearly half had had, at some point in their lives, an injury serious enough to warrant going to an Accident and Emergency department, and about 15 per cent had been more than once. Not surprisingly, since questions related to lifetime history, older children were more likely than younger children to have been to hospital as a result of an injury. The injuries that caused hospital visits were most commonly lacerations or cuts, or head injuries.

As hypothesized, there was a significant association between the number of minor injuries and the child's history of more serious ones, with children who had had one or more hospital visits as a result of an injury experiencing more minor injuries during the diary completion period. This association remained when child age and maternal ethnicity – associated with fewer hospital visits – were taken into account.

Relationships between minor and more serious injuries and other variables

In the main, however, there were relatively few associations between either minor, or more serious, injuries and social or other family variables. Although boys were more likely to have sustained a serious injury and to have been taken to hospital as a result (which is in line with previous research), there were no gender-associated differences in minor injuries, with the exception of minor head injuries, which boys were more likely to sustain. There were few associations between social disadvantage and hospital attendance for more serious injuries. Indeed, measures of disadvantage were associated with *fewer* recorded injuries. The more advantaged mothers recorded a higher rate of minor injuries in their children. Multivariate analysis indicated that maternal ethnicity was a key variable in the number of injuries recorded.

It seems probable these unexpected associations were the result of a number of factors, such as the complexity of the research instrument (the incident diary), and lower levels of suspicion or anxiety about their parenting being under scrutiny in better educated parents in two-parent families. It is also possible that the social differences were partly attributable to seasonal and area differences, which were themselves socially associated, and that there *were* more minor injuries in more advantaged children, who tended to have larger areas of play space, and whose parents were more likely to have been completing injury diaries during the summer months. This is supported by the validity study of the research instrument, in which similar differences were observed by the research health visitor validating parents' diary responses. The impact of these potential biases remains to be explored further.

A similar picture emerged in relation to parenting and family and child characteristics – there were relatively few associations, and those that there were, were generally weak. For example, there was little relationship between child characteristics and minor injuries, although children described by their mothers as clumsy, fussy, naughty or difficult to control had experienced more minor injuries. Similarly, child behaviour was only very weakly associated with minor injuries, with these being less likely for children with 'tics', whereas children rated higher on conduct disorder items were slightly more likely to have had an injury requiring hospital attendance. There was no evidence of an association between minor or more serious injuries and the quality of the mother/child or father/child relationship, maternal mental health, or the recent history of negative life events. There was no apparent relationship between parental supervision and the frequency of minor injuries, and an unexpected positive relationship between the use of safety equipment and the frequency of minor injuries – that is, children in homes with more safety equipment were more likely to sustain minor injuries. Since the presence and use of safety equipment was associated with advantaging social variables, it is likely that this was an artefact of the inverse social biases that were apparent in relation to the reporting of injuries.

There was, however, a pattern in the relationships between parental punitiveness, punitive attitudes, frequency of physical punishment, more disharmonious marriages, higher scores on the measure of parenting stress, and higher rates of verbal aggression outside the family, with more minor (and in most cases, also more serious) injuries. This provides some tentative evidence that lower thresholds for tolerance of parenting stress and general irritability and aggression in parents are implicated in minor injury causation (and probably in parental punitiveness too).

Safety practices in the home, and parental anxieties and fears about harm to their children

There was evidence of unsafe parenting for a significant minority of parents in relation to some aspects of safety in the home, such as the storage of hazardous substances. Most mothers said they kept medicines 'out of reach', but only a very small proportion (3%) kept them in a locked cabinet, or a cabinet with a safety latch. Over a fifth of parents kept medicines in a drawer, or on a sideboard or other accessible place. This proportion was higher for the storage of cleaning products such as bleach, and in over half the homes in which it was applicable, alcoholic spirits were accessible to children.

Despite this, levels of maternal anxiety about potential harm to their children were high. Mothers were most anxious about very rare causes of harm to their children, and least anxious about the most common causes, with the exception of traffic. Maternal anxiety tended to be associated with slightly fewer minor injuries to children, and more robustly with a history of more serious injuries. Mothers of children who had had an injury necessitating a hospital visit had lower levels of maternal anxiety. The least anxious mothers were those whose children had had two or more hospital visits.

Messages for policy and practice

- Minor injuries were everyday experiences for young children, and should be viewed as part of normal child development.

- It was quite normal for parents not to know how most minor injuries to their children were caused.

- Since the number of minor injuries was associated with the probability of more serious injuries, it seems sensible to support and educate parents to try to reduce minor injuries, with a view to reducing the risk of more serious injuries.

- There was a clear and identifiable pattern of the normal experience of injuries at different ages, in terms of the types of injuries sustained, and where on the body they were found. There was considerable variation between children in the number of injuries, but little variation in the pattern. Exceptions to the normal pattern merit investigation and exploration.

- Children of stressed, harassed mothers were at risk of more injuries, and also more likely to be physically or punitively punished. There are clear implications relating to the benefits of parenting support in families where the parent is stressed or finding it difficult to cope, in terms of reducing both minor injuries and punitive behaviour towards children.

- There was evidence of unsafe practices in many homes with young children, for example, in relation to the storage of hazardous substances, and hazards around the house.

- There was also evidence of considerable anxiety in parents about the risk of harm to their children, but in general this was directed at unlikely causes of harm to children, and parents were least anxious about the more likely causes of harm to their children. Parental education was indicated to reduce misdirected anxiety, and to educate parents about the more likely causes of injury – both minor and more serious – to their children.

Effective Strategies for Parents with Young Children with Behaviour Problems

Jim Stevenson, Edmund Sonuga-Barke, Margaret Thompson, Deborah Cornah, Alex Rayner, Charlotte Sizer and Gill Taylor

Centre for Research into Psychological Development, University of Southampton

(Note: This summary was adapted by the overview author from a summary presented at the Supporting Parents Initiative Conference, Dartington Hall, 2001.)

The study

The study was based on a sample of originally 1047 children on whom data had been obtained at the time of their third birthday. A sub-group of 560 were contacted again at the time of their eighth birthday and their behaviour assessed on the basis of parental report using the modified version of the child behaviour checklist.[5] On the basis of these two assessments children were placed into one of four groups:

1. those without behaviour problems at either age (no problem group N=320)

2. those with behaviour problems at both ages (problem group N=53)

3. those who showed behaviour problems at three but not at eight years of age (offset group N=85)

5   Achenbach, T.M. (1991). *Manual for the Child Behavior Checklist / 4–18 and 1991 Child Behavior Profile.* Burlington: University of Vermont.

4. those who did not show behavioural problems at three but did so at eight years of age (onset group N=102).

For this project the children in the problem group (N=53) were matched for gender, social class and temperament scores at the age of three with children in the offset group. Children in the no problem and onset groups were matched with children in the problem group for the same factors except for their behaviour score at three years. This gave a total sample of 212 children, of which 128 (60%) were male.

The families in these groups were contacted again when the children were aged ten. Parents were interviewed about their child's behaviour and the ways in which they had responded to it and a number of standardized questionnaires were administered. The interview included a section concerning support from friends, family, GPs and health visitors in relation to emotional, informational, physical and material needs. Each aspect of support was rated for usage, satisfaction and availability.

The analysis of the support data centred on the differences between sources of support and the parents' appraisal of their value and the association between current behavioural status of the child and maternal mental state.

Findings

The analysis highlighted five key messages concerning support:

- Parents turn to friends and neighbours for emotional and physical support.

- Parents turn to family for material and physical support.

- Parents use and value emotional and informational support from health visitors.

- This use and value of emotional and informational support from health visitors is even more marked in parents with children showing behaviour problems.

- Mothers who are depressed use their GP and health visitors for support but they are much less satisfied with support from GPs than support from health visitors.

The SPOKES Project: Supporting Parents on Kids' Education

Stephen Scott
Institute of Psychiatry, King's College, London, and the Maudsley Hospital
Kathy Sylva
Department of Educational Studies, University of Oxford

One objective of supporting parents is to enable them to develop a nurturing, stimulating relationship with their child, so they help the child's emotional and intellectual well-being develop. The question arises how this is best done. This project sought to implement and evaluate a programme directly to support improvements in the quality of the parent–child relationship, rather than address the indirect factors that can stress it.

Parenting difficulties often lead on to behavioural problems in the children and to school failure. Without effective intervention, these problems can lead to theft, violence, alcoholism, drug dependence, anti-social personality disorder and parenting and other problems, including unemployment and dependence on benefits. One recent UK study showed that, by the time they are 28 years old, individuals who were anti-social as children cost society ten times more than children who were not. There is therefore a need for effective early intervention in behaviour and school problems.

The study

NATURE OF PROJECT

To address the need for effective early intervention this project operated early, when the children were five and six years old. It carried out an innovative community-based intervention to support parents in managing the two sets of child difficulties for which they most frequently seek help, namely behaviour and learning. Key questions were whether the programme could easily be held in an everyday life venue (the primary school), whether a substantial proportion of parents with children at risk would enrol in the courses and whether the children would show improvement.

PARENT SUPPORT PROGRAMME

The intervention package was delivered in eight primary schools over three school terms. In term one there was a basic 12-week parenting course addressing the parent–child relationship and how to handle difficult child behaviour using videotapes and home interviews. In term two there was a newly devised ten-week reading programme, and in term three a six-week combined course that dealt with communication and problem solving with the child, and had a top-up element for literacy.

SAMPLE

Strengths and Difficulties Questionnaires (SDQs) were completed on 733 reception and year one children by teachers, representing 99.5 per cent of those in their classes. Parents of 433 children returned SDQs, a rate of 61 per cent, of which 394 were correctly filled in and usable. About one-third (34%) of the children seemed at risk of social exclusion through a high level of anti-social behaviour. Half of the children were randomly allocated to the parent support programme. The other half were offered an advice helpline.

ATTENDANCE BY PARENTS ALLOCATED TO THE INTERVENTION

Personal development programme (term 1): mean attendance 7 out of 12 sessions. Literacy programme (term 2): mean attendance 6 out of 10 sessions.
Combined programme (term 3): mean attendance 4 out of 6 sessions.

Findings

CHILD BEHAVIOUR

Anti-social behaviour

There was a significant effect in favour of the intervention group on the main outcome, the parental interview. The effect size was 0.51 standard deviations, substantial for a prevention trial. The reduction in anti-social behaviour corresponded to an improvement from being within the worst 15 per cent of anti-social children to being outside the most anti-social 35 per cent. The effect size for hyperactivity was also significant, 0.43. Hyperactivity is an important independent risk factor for social exclusion.

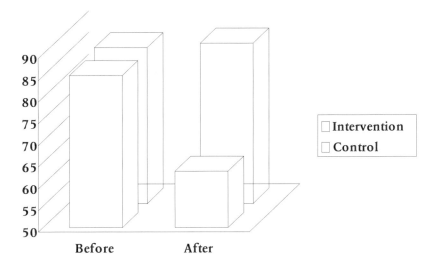

Figure A1.1 Antisocial behaviour percentile
50th = average for age; 90th = only 10% of children worse

Parent-defined problems

Problems parents reported included arguing, disobedience, fighting, whining, spitefulness, jealousy etc. The intervention group showed a significant improvement compared to the controls, with an effect size of 0.64.

Eyberg Child Behaviour Inventory

The Intensity Score, which is a measure of the frequency of difficult behaviours, reduced significantly more in the intervention group, with an effect size of 0.28.

PARENT SATISFACTION

Ninety-three per cent of parents said they were well or extremely satisfied with the programme.

CHILD LITERACY

The intervention group gained seven months in reading skills, an effect size of 0.43. This result held up unchanged after multiple regression correction for age and gender. Race, parent education, parent income, and child age and gender did not affect degree of change in the intervention group compared to the control group, suggesting that the programme is robust and suited to disadvantaged populations.

DISCUSSION OF THE FINDINGS

This study showed that a programme to support parents was effective in substantially improving child outcomes on two crucial aspects of child development: social behaviour and reading. Parent satisfaction was very high. The programme was successfully delivered in an everyday community setting, the local primary school, which contributed to its being seen as non-stigmatizing and part of normal life. Over two-thirds of parents of children at risk of social exclusion took part in the programme, a good rate of take up for such a time commitment, especially as parents did not usually perceive that their children had a problem that needed intervention. Parents attended on average at least half of the sessions offered, a reasonable attendance in light of their other commitments. This is the first study in the world to combine a general parenting programme with a parent-led literacy development programme for children. The effect sizes of both the behaviour change and the reading improvement were good.

A relatively large sample was studied, representative of families under stress with children at risk of social exclusion. Assessments using reliable and valid instruments were carried out blind to the group the parents were in wherever possible. The analysis covered all those parents on whom there was information, not just those who attended.

Messages for policy and practice

Intervention studies are crucial but all too rare

There have been thousands of studies of parenting difficulties but very few on what interventions make a difference to families' lives and functioning. This matters since several family support practices have been shown to be ineffective. Commissioners of services are increasingly demanding demonstration of effectiveness and cost-effectiveness, and policy makers and the general public want to know that services are delivering key outcomes. This major study provides much-needed evidence about the usefulness of an intervention that could be widely used.

First study of its kind in Europe

This is the first demonstration ever in the UK and Europe to show that a preventative programme can improve not only child social behaviour, but also child reading ability. Until this study, nobody knew whether a reasonable proportion of parents with children in need, but not actively seeking a clinical service, would take up a parenting course, nor whether it would be effective.

Size of impact of the programme on children's lives

The reduction in anti-social behaviour moved the children from a high risk of later social exclusion to within the normal range. If these improvements are maintained they should translate in far fewer exclusions from school, continued better parenting and better relationships at home, and much less delinquent and criminal behaviour.

Replicability of the SPOKES programme under 'real-life' conditions

This programme should be relatively easily transferable into regular practice, where comparable effects should be achieved. This would almost certainly be cost-effective, due to the very high long-term cost of childhood anti-social behaviour and the effectiveness of the intervention.

Factors that made the intervention effective

- Choosing an appropriate parenting programme, including a literacy element.
- Pitching the programme as universally applicable for any parent who wanted to do the best by their child.

- Taking considerable trouble to make a close and enduring relationship with the schools.
- Supervising group leaders weekly to maintain a high standard of intervention.

Ways to improve the programme

- A home visit prior to starting the group would help reluctant parents to take part.
- Explicitly asking to see the child's father could increase the number attending.
- Holding the groups in the evenings would make the groups accessible for parents who work.
- Offering some home-based sessions would help parents who are faltering.
- Holding some 'live' sessions with the child present would hone parents' skills.

RELEVANCE TO GOVERNMENT PROGRAMMES

Child protection

The study offers an evidence-based preventative intervention for families in difficulties; with suitable training, social workers could use it to reduce emotional and physical child abuse.

Child and adolescent mental health services

This trial shows that preventative work can be carried out successfully, and in a community setting that is not stigmatizing. Many of the skills for such programmes are currently found mainly within CAMHS.

Forensic services

By the later teens most cases of severe anti-social behaviour are all but untreatable. This study shows that early prevention is feasible.

Anti-social behaviour in schools

Anti-social behaviour in schools is a major concern and there is a strong drive to improve reading. This study shows a way forward.

Early prevention of crime

Child anti-social behaviour, poor reading and harsh parenting are three of the strongest risk factors for future criminality, and all are improved by this programme.

Social exclusion

There is a strong drive to prevent social exclusion by all measures possible, including supporting parents and reducing child poverty. This programme targets the same objectives effectively.

Further steps

There could be a case for setting up a small national centre for training other professionals from a range of disciplines.

Supporting Foster Placements

Ian Sinclair, Ian Gibbs and Kate Wilson[6]
Social Work Research and Development Unit, University of York

(Note: This account was edited from the SWRDU website.)

The study

In this study we looked at what foster children, carers and social workers thought about foster placements and about why they were more or less successful. To do this we surveyed 600 placements and got detailed information on 476[7] of them at two points in time, roughly a year apart. The information came from postal questionnaires to carers, social workers and family placement social workers (*The Placement Survey*). In addition, 151 older children in these placements responded to a brief questionnaire asking about their experience of fostering and what they wanted from it (*The Foster Child Study*). Finally, we carried out 24 detailed case studies, which were intended to both check and deepen our conclusions. We could then see how what these told us fitted with our statistical information. This covered what happened to the children, which placements broke down, which were seen as successful, and how far children who remained in the placements changed.

Findings

WHAT THE CHILDREN TOLD US

The foster children did not all want the same things but they did have some common needs. Some of these related to a need for a normal family life, although some wanted to be part of the family more than others. Typical 'wants' were:

- the care, concern and encouragement others get from their families
- to feel they belonged and were not the 'odd one out'
- fair treatment – not to be picked on or treated too strictly
- to get on with all in the placement, including other children
- not to have their family or school turned into a branch office of social services
- as much pocket money etc. as other children
- to be able to ask their foster carers for permission to stay with friends
- respect for their individuality and their concerns.

6   Now at the School of Sociology and Social Policy, University of Nottingham.

7   Numbers vary depending on the question asked.

Another key issue related to contact with their own families. Most wanted to have a say in:

- the kind of contact they had (e.g. some wanted telephone contact)
- who they had contact with (not necessarily everyone)
- the amount of support they had when contact occurred (from none to a lot)
- as few conflicts of loyalty between carers and family as possible.

Most fostered children wanted a say in their career in care. They are placed and moved by others and this can lead to feelings of insecurity and of being powerless. Most wanted:

- respect for their wishes to be adopted, fostered or returned home
- a say in who fosters them
- less frequent moves
- moves when placements were not working out
- ability to stay after 18 if they wanted
- efficient planning and review
- good information on plans for their future and on their own past
- regular contact on their own with social workers (not all wanted this).

Most of the children who replied to us were committed to their placements. More than two-thirds wanted to stay until they were 18 and nearly half (44%) wanted to stay longer than this. The great majority said they were happy where they were. It did not seem that children who were not happy were less likely to reply since those who did reply were no less likely to have a placement breakdown than those who did not.

WHAT HAPPENED TO THE CHILDREN?

Although the children wanted stability they did not often get it. Very long stays in placements were uncommon. Fewer than one in eight had been in the same placement for longer than four years. Many experienced a kind of 'serial parenting' with different families. This was because of:

- policies working towards return home – on average those aged 16 or over had had at least four episodes 'in care' punctuated by returns home
- adoption breakdowns – one in nine of the children had been living with adoptive parents but the arrangements had broken down
- placement breakdowns – at the start of the study social workers said that six out of ten of the children had had placements that had ended earlier than intended
- authority policy – one authority, for example, was very reluctant to keep children over 16 with foster carers.

Four out of ten of the children were no longer fostered a year after we first got information on them. Where they went depended on age. The main destinations were: their families (all ages), adoption (for younger children), residential care (for teenagers) and independent living (for older teenagers). Many of these moves were intended, but between a fifth and a quarter of the placements had 'broken down' over the 14 months. Just under half (46%) of our sample were with the same foster carers and a minority (about 1 in 20) had been adopted by them – a step that was sometimes resisted by the authorities. The foster children seemed to want more permanent placements than they got. More carers seemed to want to adopt their foster children than actually do so.

WHAT MADE FOR EFFECTIVE PLACEMENTS?

In our study we looked at 'success' in different ways. We looked at breakdowns and we looked at whether carers, social workers and family placement social workers felt that the placement had gone well. Each of these said that seven out of ten placements had gone very well as far as the child was concerned. Fewer than one in ten said that they had not gone too well. In the remaining cases they said things had gone as well as could be expected.

We also looked at whether children who remained in the same placement had improved on certain psychological measures. However, psychological change seemed difficult to bring about. Disturbed behaviour did seem to improve at the beginning of a placement but changed little over the year the children were followed up. The same was true of problems over giving and receiving affection. The children might be contained and loved in their placements but they remained vulnerable nonetheless. The 'chemistry' or 'fit' between the child and the carer was very important, but the best of carers could fail with some children and the most difficult children could succeed in some families. Shortage of placements and the difficulty of predicting 'who would get on' made this 'matching' difficult to arrange.

Breakdown, success and change, if it occurred, all depended on:

- the children – children who wanted to be fostered, who had attractive or appealing personalities, and who did not display very difficult behaviour were more likely to succeed
- the carers – carers were more likely to succeed if social workers saw them as warm and encouraging, having clear expectations and a family committed to fostering, and not being 'thrown' by difficult behaviour
- the relationship between carer and child – success was more likely where the carer was fond of the child and saw her or him in a good light
- the influence of the birth family – outcomes were better for abused children when at least one person was forbidden contact with them (this was not so when a child had not been abused)
- placements – they were more likely to succeed when children wanted to be in them.

Some of what we found was not what we had expected. We did not find that outcomes were on average better or worse in placements with relatives, where the child was placed with brothers or sisters, where there were other unrelated foster children or where the carer had resident children of her own. Similarly we did not find that children became more disturbed because they changed placements. It was rather that children who were already disturbed were more likely to have many placements.

The research did not support 'rules of thumb' for making placements (e.g. children should always be placed with their brothers and sisters).

WHAT SKILLS DO CARERS NEED?

The success of foster care depends heavily on the qualities of the foster carers. Some of these qualities – their commitment, 'stickability' and capacity to care for children, but willingness to give them up when needs be – are not normally called 'skills' but are important characteristics, as is the ability to be comfortable with the way children express their needs to be safe and loved. Some children want closeness and warmth, others want a more distant relationship. Carers also need to encourage children and help them to feel worthwhile, and also to handle difficult behaviour in a way that does not make the child feel insecure, unloved or worthless. They need to be able to deal with the child's birth family, avoiding as far as possible a conflict of loyalties. Finally they have to be able to elicit help from their own family, their social workers, the school and so on.

Placements quite often break down because of a downward spiral in which one thing going wrong leads to another. Carers need to be able to 'ride out' difficulties – not react to them in such a way as to make matters worse. Difficulties in any one of these areas – for example, in handling behaviour – can lead to problems in others and hence to a downward spiral and breakdown.

DID OTHER PROFESSIONALS HELP?

To our disappointment we could not show that support from social workers, family placement social workers, other foster carers or social services made successful placements more likely. Special help (psychotherapy, contact with psychiatrists etc.) was linked to poor outcomes, probably because it was triggered by a worsening situation rather than because it caused it. There were two exceptions to this rule. Aggressive children who had had special help using a 'behavioural approach' were said by carers to become less aggressive and children who had seen an educational psychologist were less likely to have a placement breakdown, perhaps because this improved school attendance or because referrals to educational psychologists were more likely if everyone was determined to keep the child in the placement.

Messages for policy and practice

This research provides a snapshot of foster care, its success and the problems it faces. Some of these problems call for money and determination. A lot is now known about the kind of support that carers need. The question is whether there is the will to provide it. Other problems call for clear thinking, careful debate and the careful testing of solutions suggested by carers and social workers. Among the key questions are:

- What kinds of fostering should there be?
- How far should carers be allowed to adopt?
- How far should they be encouraged to care after a young person is 18?
- Is sufficient account taken of children's placement choices?
- Difficult behaviour leads to less successful placements but could more use be made of behavioural methods?
- Successful carers give a picture of good practice. Is it possible to use this practice wisdom as the basis for training other carers?
- Is enough distinction made between those family contacts that are desired and helpful and those that are neither?
- Do local authorities take a sufficiently flexible attitude to adoptions by carers?
- Is sufficient financial and other support available to allow children to stay beyond 18 if they want to or to encourage ongoing contact when children do move on?
- Is there enough scope for professional discretion over placement decisions and enough attention given to the wishes and rights of those involved?

The Fostering Task with Adolescents

Elaine Farmer, Sue Moyers and Jo Lipscombe
School for Policy Studies, University of Bristol

There is little information about what makes some carers particularly successful in looking after young people or which services make a real difference. This research therefore examined how supports for foster carers and their parenting approaches relate to outcomes for adolescents.

The study

In this one-year prospective study 68 young people aged 11 to 17 were selected when they entered a new foster placement that was intended to be medium to long term. The reasons for admission had to include concerns about their current behaviour and/or emotional well-being. The young people's case files were reviewed to obtain background information about their backgrounds and care histories. Interviews were conducted with the young people, their foster carers and social workers at the beginning of the placement and again 12 months later or at the point of placement ending if this occurred earlier. Standardized measures were also used.

Two types of outcome were considered. The first was placement breakdown. The second was the quality or success of the placement. 'Successful' placements were those that were going well or had had a planned positive ending by the one-year follow-up (47%). Those rated 'poor' were those that had disrupted or showed evidence of severe difficulty (53%).

Findings

FORMAL SUPPORT SERVICES

Pre-placement

Placements disrupted more often when social workers had not been open about the extent of the young people's difficulties and had given inadequate information about schooling, plans for their education and long-term care. Foster carers were able to deal with some very difficult behaviour, provided that they knew what they were taking on, and if social workers responded to their requests for help. The young people too wanted to know more about the foster families before they moved. Most had not felt sufficiently involved in pre-placement decisions.

Placements were also more likely to break down if the carers' gender preference had been overridden. These preferences were generally based on well-founded concerns about the effect, for example, of placing a teenage girl in a household of boys.

Placing young people of a similar age to those in the foster family did not create difficulties, but placements were at an increased risk of disruption when foster carers had a birth child between two and five years younger than the fostered young person, probably because these children were more vulnerable to problematic or violent behaviour by the fostered adolescents.

During the placement

Two forms of support were helpful. First, foster carer groups were important to half the carers and might have been more used if 'child-sitting' had been provided and the carers allowed 'to have a moan'. Second, family placement workers provided consistent high quality support. Generic services were less effective. Foster care was rarely prioritized by busy children's social workers or general out-of-hours services, although out-of-hours services run by the family placement service were seen as much more supportive than emergency duty teams. Deficits in these generic services led to carers feeling poorly supported overall. Support was experienced rather like a net: it was only as strong as its weakest point. All these elements needed to be in place if foster carers were to feel adequately supported. For this reason, moves to strengthen one part of the service (for example, the out-of-hours service) at the expense of another (for example, family placement workers) are likely to lead to considerable carer dissatisfaction.

Problems with the service given by the young people's social workers included difficulties in contacting them (70% of carers) and low levels of visiting (21% saw the child and 37% the carers less often than monthly). These were significantly related to carers feeling poorly supported, as were unresolved contact issues. Foster carers were upset when the specialist help they thought the child needed was not forthcoming. A lack of support from the young people's social workers was related to poorer outcomes. The opposite was also true: there were significantly more successful placements when social work support was good. But partnership was often not achieved. About half of the carers felt that their views were usually taken seriously. Fewer than half felt that they were an important member of the team looking after the young person.

Counselling for the teenagers made carers feel better supported and placements were more successful when young people reported that they were receiving it.

INFORMAL SUPPORTS

Support did not always match the needs of carers. Placements were significantly more successful when carers had support from family members, friends or local professionals, such as doctors and teachers. In addition, carers who received a lot of support from their own children – including adult children in or outside the home – had fewer disruptions. Carers' children's role in supporting placements is often unacknowledged. The carers' own children at home wanted their views to be listened to and their difficulties heard. But the young people's social workers were more likely to visit foster carers who had *good* support from these sources. Family placement workers and social workers need to know about carers' informal support and help from local professionals so that they can identify those who lack support.

THE YOUNG PEOPLE'S RELATIONSHIPS WITH OTHER CHILDREN

Young people who had a negative impact on the other children in the home had poorer outcomes. Carers could deal with difficult behaviour unless it affected other children – including other fostered children. If it did they would seek to end the placement. This process emerged as time went on – it was not apparent at the beginning.

EDUCATION

Low confidence in schoolwork was related to disruption and low confidence in relationships at school to lower success rates. Conversely, young people with skills and interests were more likely to have successful placements.

YOUNG PEOPLE'S BEHAVIOUR AND CHARACTERISTICS

A history of aggressive behaviour or of no previous attachments to an adult predicted disruption, and hyperactivity and conduct problems in the placement predicted poor outcomes.

PARENTING SKILLS

Strain and parenting skills

Many of the foster carers faced the arrival of a newly placed young person when they were already under pressure from stressful life events such as bereavements, family changes and poor relationships, illnesses and accidents, financial worries and recent placement breakdowns. Two-fifths had experienced four or more of these in the six months before the placement. The extent of strain before as well as during the placement was significantly related to poorer outcomes. Carers under strain responded less sensitively to the young people, disliked them more often and were less warm to them.

The contribution of parenting skills to outcomes

Four parenting approaches apparent at the first interviews predicted outcomes. There were fewer disruptions when:

- foster carers were able to respond to the young person's 'emotional age' if this was considerably younger than their chronological age, reflecting an understanding that many looked-after young people are emotionally immature and may at the beginning need the opportunity for play and nurture appropriate to a much younger child

- the young people were able to talk about their past histories, requiring time to be made for the teenagers to share difficult issues and the capacity on the part of carers to hear painful past events. Disruption occurred also less frequently when young people had access to other people in whom they could confide.

There were more successful placements when:

- foster carers had encouraged the young people to learn life skills that would help them when they left care such as budgeting, cooking and filling in forms

- the carers monitored the activities of the young people when they were not at home. This required skill and a wider view of the foster care role. It was especially important for young people who were unable to keep themselves safe or out of trouble when away from the family.

THE DIFFICULTIES OF SINGLE CARERS

One-third of those fostering were single carers. They were more disadvantaged than couple carers in a variety of ways. They received less training, lower levels of local authority services and less support from local professionals, though they had weaker family support. Support from their friends was therefore particularly important. Fewer single carers actively facilitated the young people's education or attended the foster carer groups because of lack of child-minding facilities, pressure on their time and a feeling that the groups were not serving their needs.

CONTACT

Almost two-thirds of the young people had contact with a family member that was detrimental to their placement and a third of those with contact had none that was beneficial to them. Thirteen per cent had no contact with anyone, generally because of an adoption breakdown, because their parents had died or in the aftermath of an allegation of sexual abuse.

Difficulties with contact were significantly related to higher disruption rates, either directly or because difficulties in the relationship between the young people and their parents influenced disruption. These difficulties included repeated rejection by parents, unreliability in visiting and exposure to high-risk situations. The young people often returned from contact extremely upset and sometimes disturbed or violent.

There was little change in the quality of the young people's contact during the follow-up and remained poor for over half (57%) one year after placement. In a few cases social workers had taken action to improve contact, usually by reducing the frequency but improving the quality or by involving another family member, such as a grandparent or aunt, who could provide attention and nurture. Young people who had contact with their maternal grandparents had more successful placements, partly because grandparents often ensured that contact with other family members occurred and because they themselves provided helpful relationships for the young people. The widespread idea that adolescents can manage their own contact was not borne out in the study.

Messages for policy and practice
TRAINING FOR CARERS

Outcomes are likely to be improved if training includes:

- helping foster carers to respond to young people's emotional age
- dealing with contact issues and talking abut relationships with their families
- talking to young people about their past
- monitoring adolescents' activities outside the home.

Other training gaps identified by the carers included: working with withdrawn, depressed and suicidal young people; the management of deliberate self-harm; dealing with young people who sexually abuse others; and managing violent behaviour.

Training and clarification of roles and responsibilities is also important concerning:

- sexual health and sexuality – two-fifths of the carers did not discuss this with the young people even though many were poorly informed about normal sexual development, sexual health and contraception
- involvement with schools – half of the carers had little involvement with schools, and 20 had no contact with the young people's school teachers
- developing life skills – two-fifths of the carers did little to encourage the young people develop life skills such as budgeting, cooking meals and form filling
- sensitivity to gender differences in worries – carers were less sensitive to the needs and anxieties of girls than boys. A small number of girls told us of worries and unhappiness in their placements that carers did not know about.

INFORMATION

Foster carers should be given full and honest information about the young people even in placements made at short notice, and young people want more prior information about the foster families.

SUPPORT FROM SERVICES

Good support reduces the strains on foster carers and leads to better outcomes. In particular:

- Strain is reduced if the young person's social worker is regularly and reliably available, if social work has continuity and if carers' views are taken seriously. Given the high pressures on children's social workers, improvements to the service they provide will require organizational change that allows specialization or major task reallocation, or both.

- Out-of-hours services run by the family placement service are much more useful than those run by emergency duty teams.

- Substantial packages of support, including specialist help, are needed for carers who take young people who are hyperactive or have conduct problems.

- Stresses on carers *before* each placement is made affect the success of the placement. Foster carers already under strain should be asked to care for less challenging adolescents, or be given increased support or breaks between placements.

- The support needs of single carers need careful exploration. Some supplementary services might well benefit lone foster carers and the young people they look after.

- Foster carers' own children are both important supports and factors in breakdown if the placement adversely affects them. This issue therefore needs careful monitoring and review.

- Counselling and other specialist help is important in its own right and in the maintenance of placements. Foster carers' requests for such help for the young people should always be taken seriously.

- More proactive work is required on contact with family members, especially in helping young people to cope with continuing parental rejection, ambivalence or unreliability, and in encouraging the involvement of relatives who can offer them more positive relationships.

- Local authorities need to organize more extensive packages of support if placements are to survive. These might include shared care between two foster families, dedicated respite care, buying in the services of specialist helpers or purchasing therapeutic counselling.

Supporting Parents Caring for a Technology-Dependent Child

Susan Kirk and Caroline Glendinning
National Primary Care Research and Development Centre, University of Manchester

Medical advances have enabled increasing numbers of babies born prematurely or with severe impairments to survive, and have improved the prognosis for children with serious illnesses such as cystic fibrosis and cancer. Some of these children depend on complex medical devices and therapies such as ventilators and artificial feeding. Most technology-dependent children now live at home, with their parents providing substantial levels of nursing care. However, until this study was conducted between 1997 and 1999, in the UK we knew very little about their experiences and support needs.

This qualitative study aimed to explore parents' experiences of caring for their child at home; to identify problems and good practice in the purchasing, delivery and coordination of services; and to assess the appropriateness and adequacy of support.

The study

Families were recruited through regional children's hospitals. We interviewed 21 families caring at home for a technology-dependent child and three families before and after hospital discharge. Families were purposively selected to ensure that the sample incorporated a range of technologies, a range in the lengths of time that children had been at home and a range of nursing support services in the home (for example, areas with and without community children's nursing (CCN) teams). Four lone parent families participated in the study and one family in the sample was from a minority ethnic group. Eleven of the children were girls and 13 were boys. At the time of interviewing 12 children were aged under five, six were aged between five and eleven and five were aged between 12 and 18 years. Thirteen of the children had been technology-dependent since birth. Eight of the children had no siblings.

Parents interviewed in the study provided the names of all the professionals supporting them in the home care of their child. From this sampling frame, 38 professionals were interviewed in depth about their experiences and views. Purposive sampling ensured that the sample reflected a range of different professional groups and organizations, a range in the technologies of the children professionals were supporting, a range in the geographical areas where the professionals worked (both near to and far from specialist centres), and a range of service configurations (areas with and without CCN teams). In addition three health authority purchasers and three nurses with a hospital discharge planning role were interviewed about their experiences of planning and organizing services for this group of children.

Findings

Parents' experiences of caring

In addition to everyday parenting activities, parents were providing most of their child's nursing care, which was often complex and involved the provision of clinical procedures. This care not only carried risks but could also cause their child pain and distress. Parents felt that the emotional aspects for them of providing this care for their own children was often overlooked by professionals, who instead concentrated on their technical competency. Parents felt that they had little choice but to take on responsibility for their child's medical and nursing care if they were to be cared for outside the hospital.

Family life was dominated by the child's needs. Homes were transformed by medical equipment and supplies, and privacy was compromised by the presence of professionals and support workers. It was difficult for parents to have a break from caring as their child's specialized needs often meant that family members and friends were unable to babysit for them. The cumbersome equipment and the need to provide procedures in the home restricted family activities.

Parents' sleep was disrupted by machine alarms, the need to provide treatments or if their child required constant vigilance. The additional costs of the child's care, coupled with reduced incomes if parents had to give up work, could cause financial problems.

Relationships between parents and professionals

Parents and community professionals felt that it had been assumed (rather than negotiated) before discharge that parents would be willing to provide the nursing care for their children at home. However, once home, parents became more assertive in setting the boundary between what they saw as parental and professional roles.

Parents were experts in their child's care, possessing significant knowledge of their child's condition, treatment and equipment. They also developed knowledge in caring for their child as an individual and were able to detect subtle changes in their child's condition that could indicate a deterioration. Parents' expertise led them to challenge professionals' advice and sometimes refuse to comply with treatments if they were incompatible with their own perceptions of their child's needs. Parents felt that sometimes their expertise was not recognized by professionals. Only a minority of community-based professionals expressed feeling threatened by parents' greater specialized knowledge, although some may have avoided contact with parents for this reason.

Parents respected professionals who were honest about their lack of specialized knowledge and did not have expectations that general practitioners, health visitors or district nurses would possess this type of knowledge.

Parents and professionals identified similar types of activities as being supportive. Emotional support was important in terms of parents having access to an approachable and accessible professional who knew the family. Knowing that there was such a professional able to help them if needed was seen as enhancing their capacity to cope. Nurse specialists working from regional centres often fulfilled this role. Parents also valued continuity of relationships. Instrumental support was important – practical help in applying for benefits, accessing services and advocacy.

Information was an important means of enhancing parents' sense of control. However, information giving was often poor, with parents receiving inadequate, inappropriate and contradictory information.

Inter-agency and inter-professional working

Few families received adequate, well-coordinated services. Poor communication between hospital, community health and social services was common. Services were poorly planned and coordinated, which resulted in families feeling at times overloaded by visits and appointments, unclear about the roles and responsibilities of the different professionals, and relied upon to pass information between professionals and to coordinate the services they received.

Obtaining a break from caring was difficult as their child's specialized needs meant that local services were inappropriate. Families preferred home-based support and many had home support workers employed to care for their child's specific needs. However, disputes between health authorities and local authorities over funding such services were common and could delay discharge. There were variations in the amount of home support families received, which appeared to relate to local policies rather than family need. Funding for support workers to enable children to attend mainstream nurseries and schools could be a further source of inter-agency disagreement.

Disputes were also common between hospitals, community trusts and GPs over the funding of equipment, supplies and medication in the home. A wide range of professionals and organizations could be involved in the supply of equipment; many families were receiving supplies from several different sources. Those receiving supplies from commercial companies found this to be more reliable and efficient than the health service. Problems in the supply of equipment were a source of considerable stress for parents and some were forced to return to regional centres for help when supplies were needed urgently. Community nurses also found it difficult organizing specialist equipment for children with unpredictable needs and were critical of the lack of time they were given by hospitals to obtain equipment and supplies before children were discharged home.

Messages for policy and practice

- Service development has not kept pace with medical advances and the discharge of children with complex health care needs into the community. Appropriate short-term care and home support services are lacking and the funding and supply of equipment and medications is fragmented and poorly organized.
- The fragmentation of services could be reduced by health and local authorities pooling budgets, delegating commissioning to a single 'lead' agency or integrating services within a single organization.
- Families would benefit from having a designated service coordinator and from the regular planning and evaluation of services.
- Professionals need to ensure that:

- families' information needs are regularly assessed and that they facilitate their access to information
- there is an accessible, reliable and approachable professional who knows the family who can provide advice and emotional support
- they work in partnership with families – negotiating roles and recognizing parents' expertise.

Supporting South Asian Families with a Child with Severe Disabilities

Chris Hatton, Yasmeen Akram, Robina Shah, Janet Robertson and Eric Emerson
Institute for Health Research, Lancaster University[8]

The study

This study aimed to provide a comprehensive picture of the lives of UK South Asian families[9] with a child with severe disabilities. The project also included structured interviews conducted with 136 parents, sampled across five local authority areas, and semi-structured interviews at two time points with 26 parents to provide qualitative information on the lives of families. All interviews were conducted in the first language of the participant.

Almost all the main carers interviewed were mothers.[10] Most families were Pakistani (70%), with substantial numbers of Bangladeshi (11%) and Indian (17%) interviewees. The vast majority of interviewees were Muslim (93%), the remainder being Hindu (4%) or Sikh (3%). Twelve per cent of families were headed by lone parents and 21 per cent had more than one child with a disability. Most main carers were born outside the UK, but had spent many years in the UK and cared for the family full time. Just under half the participants could speak, read or write English, with parents reporting a wide variety of spoken and written languages.

Findings

Resources

Parents reported pervasive material disadvantage. Household income was low (median £100–£199 weekly), unemployment was high (55% of households had no-one in full-time employment), and the patchy uptake of benefits was insufficient to meet the extra costs of caring for their child. Housing was often unsuitable for the needs of the child, particularly in terms of space and safety issues. Adaptations to housing were rare, often delayed, and sometimes insensitive to the cultural needs of the family. In all, the range of unmet needs reported by parents was extremely high, substantially higher than those reported in comparable UK research.

---

8   This work began at the Hester Adrian Research Centre, University of Manchester.

9   The term 'South Asian' is used to refer to populations originating from India, Pakistan, Bangladesh, and families largely originating from India who had lived in Africa for a substantial period of time.

10 Because almost all participants were parents of the child with severe disabilities, the term 'parent' rather than 'carer' is used throughout, in line with the preferences of participants.

The child with disabilities

The age range of the children was wide, with slightly more boys than girls. Most children needed substantial support across a range of self-care skills, household tasks and spoken communication. Most parents said their children were fairly happy, sociable and affectionate, but over 80 per cent reported problems with eating, toileting and bedtime routines, and their child throwing things, yelling, screaming and throwing tantrums. Around half of parents felt their child had made progress in the past six months, with most adjusting their expectations to the skills and progress of their child, enabling the family to celebrate the child's achievements.

Disclosure

Most children were diagnosed as having a disability by four years of age. Disclosure was mostly conducted by a medical professional in English. Around half of the parents said they understood what they were told then and most received good support from partners and the disclosing professional. Post-disclosure support was, however, lacking. Parents saw the following as essential to make disclosure satisfactory: it should be prompt, made in their language and with the partner present; emotionally supportive; and with clear and practical information linked to services.

Information

Most parents reported having enough information about the disability, but fewer had enough about services for the child or for themselves. Parents preferred to have information face-to-face from a professional and in their own language. Parents using English were more likely to have enough information. Although most parents needed an interpreter, fewer than half had been provided with one. Interpreters were highly valued, allowing parents to speak confidentially rather than through family or friends.

Informal support

Most informal practical and emotional support came from within the household, especially from partners. Absent or unsupportive partners could cause practical difficulties and emotional distress. Practical support from children was also helpful, although parents were concerned about the impact of caring responsibilities on them. Few parents received support from extended families, partly because family members lived too far away or were unable to provide support. Even when received this support was often seen as unhelpful.

Formal support

Parents were aware of generic health, welfare and special education services, but much less aware of other specialist disability services. Indian parents and parents who used English reported greater awareness and uptake. Major problems in accessing services included uncollaborative professionals, communication barriers and fighting for support, resulting in frustration and a lack of confidence in services.

Less than a third of parents (28%) had a keyworker, although social workers and health visitors sometimes took this role. Keyworkers were almost always seen as invaluable in raising parents' awareness of benefits and services, organizing integrated packages of care, and giving emotional support.

Almost all the children were in special schools, which were seen as being good for the child, as giving respite to parents and as being responsive to their concerns – often the only reliable place to get information and support. However, very few schools provided for the language, cultural or religious needs of the children, and parents were concerned about the availability and quality of speech therapy and physiotherapy.

Few parents had considered or discussed future plans for the child. Those with a child about to leave school felt considerable uncertainty and confusion about the post-education service supports available. Parents who had been in contact with adult services were concerned about the cultural and religious appropriateness of the services offered.

Few parents were aware of or used respite care services for their child. Almost all that were available were in respite units managed by social services. These services were generally highly valued and responsive to the child's cultural needs, but were insufficient to meet the parents' needs.

Few parents knew of or took part in family support groups. Those that did valued the information and emotional support they got, although attendance was not associated with increased service support.

Family social life

Parents, especially those from Pakistan, reported many restrictions on their social activities, including nights out and weekends away. Restrictions were greater if the child needed constant supervision and if the family was headed by a single parent. Reliable informal and formal supports outside school hours helped parents have an active social life.

The social life of the child was similarly restricted, with the vast majority having no involvement with friends or organized activities. Social life was particularly restricted if the extended family and the general public held negative attitudes towards the child.

Parental health

Compared with national data, these parents had a whole range of physical health problems. This was reflected in increased use of GP and hospital services. Rates of distress (74%), depression (40%) and anxiety (27%) were up to ten times higher than comparative UK populations. Pakistani parents were particularly likely to report anxiety and depression. Despite these high rates, no parents had used any psychological services in the past year. Parents made explicit links between caring for their child with disabilities, particularly without support, and physical and mental health problems.

FACTORS ASSOCIATED WITH POSITIVE FAMILY OUTCOMES

Several factors were central in promoting positive outcomes for families:

- First, the disclosure process was crucial. A well-conducted disclosure helped parents accept their child's disability and helped mobilize formal support services and the uptake of benefits. Parental acceptance increased acceptance and support by extended family and friends. More able and socially responsive children, with fewer problem behaviours, made informal support more likely.

- Second, informal support, information from support groups and greater parental acceptance and understanding helped parents be aware of and mobilize formal services, although this was also helped by language support, a trusted keyworker and a collaborative relationship between parents and professionals.

- Third, culturally sensitive services reinforced collaborative relationships between parents and professionals, put parents in contact with support groups, reduced the unmet needs of families and helped improve the physical health of parents. Informal supports and parent support groups helped improve the social life of the child and the family, especially when the child was socially responsive.

- Finally, informal and formal supports working together and an active family social life helped to reduce parents' depression. Their distress and anxiety was more likely to be relieved if the family's needs were being met, the parents had fewer health problems and the child was easier to supervise.

Messages for policy and practice

Three current policy initiatives are directly relevant to South Asian families with a child with severe disabilities: the National Carers Strategy; the Quality Protects Initiative; and Valuing People. Priorities in these initiatives include the following.

Improving the material circumstances of families

A striking feature was the material disadvantage of the families. Although improving the uptake of benefits would have helped many of them, many said that benefits did not cover the costs of caring for their child. Additional priorities include suitable housing and the provision of aids and adaptations based on thorough assessments of family needs.

Improving information given to families

Policy rightly emphasizes the importance of information. These families wanted this given to them face-to-face in their own language. They are unlikely to use sources such as NHS Direct. Good information requires a well-conducted disclosure process, ongoing keyworker support and the encouragement of family support groups if it is to increase parents' acceptance and understanding of their child's condition.

Assessments of family needs

These parents rarely had the fast, comprehensive and regular assessments of needs stressed in current policy. Consequently service supports were absent, patchy, uncoordinated or unhelpful. Assessments must be in the preferred language of the parents, be relevant to their circumstances, be quickly followed by action, and be regularly updated. 'Colour-blindness' and ethnic and religious stereotyping are detrimental to the identification of individual needs.

Coordinated packages of care

Comprehensive and coordinated packages of care were extremely rare, despite the often desperate needs of parents for services. Except for special education, family support services were rare and often seen as so unhelpful that they were discontinued. Coordinated care packages that meet families' needs and provide 'family-centred' support require much greater creativity by agencies.

Meeting language, cultural and religious needs

Few services met the language, cultural and religious needs of these South Asian families, including appropriate diet, celebration of religious festivals and same-sex carers for intimate personal care tasks. The recruitment of South Asian staff throughout mainstream services and the expansion of specialist interpreters trained to deal with disability issues should be a priority. Parents preferred integrated services that routinely meet users' cultural and religious needs, rather than ethnically separate services.

Choice, control and consultation

There was very little evidence that families were consulted about services, or that parents had choice or control over the services they got. Meaningful consultation involves encouraging parent support groups, and being responsive to parents' suggestions. 'Person-centred' planning assessment processes, along with greater flexibility and creativity in developing packages of care, could help families gain more control over family support services.

Meeting the needs of the child with disabilities

Current policies aim to maximize the child's educational achievements, encourage them to be fit and healthy, and ensure that they lead a normal life. Parents valued special education services highly and mostly felt their child was making progress, despite their needs and problem behaviours, but some teaching in the family language of the child and reliable and helpful speech therapy and physiotherapy were priorities for parents. The extreme social isolation of the children should be seen as a support priority. The severity of the children's needs affects parents' informal support and mental health and thus intensive early interventions could have a broader impact upon the family system.

Meeting the needs of parents

The National Carers Strategy emphasizes the need to help parents live a full life, be in paid employment if they want, keep their physical and mental health, and integrate into local communities. The parents in this study were clearly a priority group for all these objectives. Flexible, reliable, sufficient and culturally appropriate short-term care services are crucial for meeting these objectives, as are reliable schemes during school holidays where current support is absent or largely unhelpful. Many parents also suggested the idea of drop-in centres, where children could be left out of school hours.

Improving parents' physical and mental health was closely tied to improving supports for the whole family. However, no parents had help with mental health problems, despite their high use of GP and hospital services. Given the extremely high rates of distress, anxiety and depression, this issue should be addressed urgently.

Inclusion

Current policy stresses the social inclusion of families with a child with disabilities, with education services shifting from special schooling to the integration of children with disabilities into mainstream education. Parents supported integrated services but were also highly appreciative of special schools, which provided a reliable, high quality service, and also often served as the parents' only point of access to other parents and to information about other services. Any moves towards mainstreaming children with severe disabilities need to ensure that effective alternatives exist in terms of supporting and providing information to parents.

Transition to adulthood

While transition plans are a current policy, no parents of adolescents were aware of a plan and they were very anxious and uncertain about post-education services. Greater consistency between child and adult services is also needed. Some parents reported that adult services did not meet the cultural or religious needs of their child.

Joined-up thinking

These parents repeatedly emphasized that services should meet the needs of the whole family. Their circumstances should make parents like them a priority for other policy initiatives such as the National Service Frameworks for Children and for Mental Health, and for the Children's Fund. Policy makers and commissioners need to coordinate resources from this array of policy initiatives to meet the needs of families. Such 'joined-up thinking' is necessary if the often desperate circumstances and lives of South Asian families with a child with severe disabilities are to be transformed.

Parenting and Disability: The Role of Formal and Informal Networks

Richard Olsen
Nuffield Community Care Studies Unit, University of Leicester
Harriet Clarke
Institute of Applied Social Studies, University of Birmingham (formerly Nuffield Community Care Studies Unit, University of Leicester)

The study
BACKGROUND

This study looked at the experiences of disabled parents, as well as their partners and children. The research was largely conducted with families living in England, most of whom lived in the Midlands. It originated in two distinct but related concerns. First, despite some campaigning and awareness-raising activities by disabled parents and their organizations, we had insufficient information about the extent to which there was appropriate support available to disabled parents and about the views of disabled parents on the barriers they faced in raising children. The aim therefore was to carry out a piece of research that allowed parents to share with us their experiences and views across a range of issues, including transport, employment, benefits, housing and education, as well as the traditional domains of health and social care service use. Second, in the first half of the 1990s disabled parents had come indirectly to the attention of academic, policy and lay audiences through the construction of some children as 'young carers'. The researchers on this study had questioned the political and methodological basis for this, arguing that parental support was the primary issue, and not the provision of support to children to enable them to carry on 'caring'. A further aim, therefore, was to explore the factors influencing children's involvement in 'caring' work.

THE SAMPLE

In total, 80 families took part in the research. Seven families were interviewed in a pilot stage, with 67 families taking part in stage one, and 12 in stage two (six of the stage two families had already taken part on stage one and were re-interviewed). In order to carry out meaningful statistical analysis, and in response to the predominance of parental physical and mental health impairments as key variables in the 'young carer' literature, we did not include parents with learning difficulties. Parents had a wide range of physical and mental health impairments and were recruited mainly through voluntary sector groups and word of mouth. This sampling strategy resulted in an under-representation of parents experiencing mental distress, and therefore a small number were recruited through general practices. This meant that it was not a sample of service users, which – importantly – opens a window on the 'normative' experience of disabled parents, and does not merely reflect on them as a group defined as 'service users' (indeed, many were not).

In stage one, interviews were carried out with the disabled parent, their partner (if in a dual-parent family) and one child between 7 and 18 chosen (usually) at random. Interviews with the parent involved a detailed structured questionnaire that included questions that enabled statistical analysis (especially around 'caring' issues) as well as more open questions which provided more qualitative data. Questionnaires for partners (a small number of whom were also disabled) and children were shorter and concentrated, respectively, on parenting, domestic and 'caring' roles in the family, and use of free time and involvement in self-care, domestic and 'care' activities.

In stage two, in-depth interviews were carried out with families either where a parent was newly impaired, or where the parent had long standing impairments but where the family was experiencing important changes, whether in terms of the severity of impairments, or in terms of broader issues such as the birth of a new child. The aim of this part of the study was to capture the significance of change in the lives of disabled parents.

Findings

Support

Parents talked about the support they needed in order to parent successfully. They talked about being able to access their own house and garden, about needing to get out and about with children, about needing access to and contact with schools and teachers, and they talked about needing practical and emotional support with parenting and the opportunity to have a break from parenting. In other words, they described entirely mainstream parenting support needs; however, they often faced barriers in accessing these forms of support, whether in terms of inaccessible schools and houses (several had been sleeping on the sofa for months or years while waiting for adaptations to be made), the absence of transport, or the negative attitudes of others (which, for some, had cut them off from sources of informal support).

Those parents who had been service users talked about the scope for both disempowering and empowering support from professionals. Whilst some pointed to the way in which professionals had effectively closed doors to support through their attitudes, and particularly the limited horizons they had for the way in which support could be offered (for instance, simply telling partners that they had to give up work), others pointed to the effective support that could result when an alliance of key professionals and advocates were seen to be working towards a common goal. We argue, therefore, that it is inappropriate to talk about disabled parents having a special set of support needs; rather, the focus should remain on addressing barriers to obtaining support. We highlight the ways in which disability intersects with other forms of structural disadvantage, based particularly on socio-economic status and gender. We also argue that the role of statutory services in supporting disabled parents is one of promoting control and choice on the part of parents, and of recognizing the importance people attach to maintaining roles and relationships such as husband/wife, mother/father or son/daughter rather than 'carer', 'cared-for person', and so on.

'Young carers'

We asked detailed questions of parents and children with regard to children's involvement in 'caring' and other domestic work. Although children consistently reported slightly higher levels of involvement in a range of 'caring' activity, the overall picture is of low and irregular involvement. The parents we interviewed talked about the strategies they adopted, and the trade-offs they often had to make, to ensure their children did not become 'young carers'. We found, consistent with other work on 'young carers', that children of single parents are reported as doing more domestic and 'caring' work, and are more likely to be thought of as 'young carers' by their parents. This alerts us to the extra support that single disabled parents may require in order to prevent their children becoming 'young carers'. The interviews also threw new light on existing debates about the nature of 'young caring'. In particular, the role of children in actively seeking and/or resisting such a role was apparent in a number of families, yet had received little previous attention in the literature. We argue that a more sophisticated understanding of children's involvement in domestic and 'caring' work is required; in particular, one which sees these activities as the product of far more than parental impairment and service receipt (for instance, encompassing the place of such work alongside opportunities for paid work outside the home and the link between domestic work and pocket money).

Change

Change permeated the experience of disabled parents, and an ability to respond flexibly to changing circumstances in the family lives of disabled parents is a central challenge for professionals and agencies working to support them. The sources of changing circumstances were sometimes impairment related, but often changing relationships (with partners, schools, friends and family) and changing demands (e.g. of the parenting role) impacted on parents' experience of disability. For example, even where to a degree impairments pre-existed having children, for some these could be exacerbated and/or experienced as creating day-to-day difficulties for the first time after becoming a parent. The research has highlighted that for some disabled parents there can be long-term (physical and emotional) implications for impairments from the demands of parenting young children with little or no support.

An important area in which parents reported change as particularly significant was the passage of their children through the education system (a service, unlike social services, that all families had contact with). Parents tended to view primary schools as more accessible in a whole range of ways: the fact that they were closer to home, were often smaller, one-storey buildings, and seemed more geared up for wheelchair users (through what one parent called 'a pushchair mentality'). Importantly, they also involved a relationship with a single form teacher, which several parents with mental health impairments described as important. The move to secondary school, however, typically involved moving to a school further away, with multi-storey buildings, and a fragmentation of contacts with teachers. We argue, therefore, that the particular difficulties faced by parents with secondary school-age children are of key importance.

Some parents discussed the impact of negative attitudes towards disabled parents, and indeed towards disabled people becoming parents in the first place. These attitudes were apparent in different relationships, from immediate family to health and care professionals. Whilst none of the parents taking part in this study were newly first-time parents, some of their experiences suggested that disabled people who seek advice or support on becoming parents may sometimes feel under-supported or indeed dissuaded. This highlights the value of a lifespan perspective when considering people's experience of impairment, disability and professional involvement.

PHYSICAL IMPAIRMENT, MENTAL DISTRESS AND DISABILITY

The social model of disability was central in informing the approach taken with this research. The experience of impairment in the context of disability was also key to the ways in which parents experienced the parenting role. Our inclusion of parents experiencing mental health impairments particularly required that explicit consideration be given to debates concerning the experience of disability (by individuals and their families) and the experience of impairment, as well as the origins of impairment and distress as experienced by the individual. Whether personal accounts or diagnostic 'fact', the development of impairments – for example, epilepsy or depression – was sometimes discussed in relation to the emotional stresses emerging from a wide range of factors, from inadequate medical care, through to partnership breakdown and the demands of parenting on low incomes. Mental distress in particular was sometimes less clearly identifiable as 'impairment' given the socio-economic, interpersonal and psychological (as well as biological) precursors identified. Some parents who had a physical impairment considered the mental distress (such as depression emerging from inadequate support) that they experienced to have had the most significant consequences for parenting and family life. And so whilst the research points to the value of a social model approach in both understanding and addressing the barriers faced by disabled parents, it also points to ways in which impairment (particularly though not solely mental distress) itself requires consideration in the context of disability and other forms of exclusion.

Publication list

The Policy Press published a book by Richard Olsen and Harriet Clarke, based on this research, entitled *Parenting and Disability: Disabled Parents' Experiences of Raising Children*, in April 2003.

Pregnancy and Parenthood: The Views and Experiences of Young People in Public Care

Judith Corlyon and Christine McGuire
National Children's Bureau

(Note: This study was not originally commissioned as part of the Supporting Parents initiative, but was added to it after commissioning because of the relevance of the study's content. This summary was edited from a published briefing paper.)

In the late 1990s teenage pregnancy and parenthood became a major focus of national policy, culminating in the Social Exclusion Unit being directed by the Prime Minister in 1998 to suggest strategies to reduce the rates of teenage parenthood and to minimize the risk of social exclusion for teenage parents. One of the objectives of Quality Protects, the government's initiative to improve local authority services for children, is to ensure that the number of pregnancies to girls under 16 in public care does not differ from that in the general population.

The study

This study began in 1995 and was carried out over a three-year period. Data were collected from local authority officers, social workers, carers, pregnant young women and young mothers who were being or had recently been looked after by a local authority (component 1), and from groups of 14- to 15-year-olds, half of whom were looked after, predominantly in residential care, and half of whom – referred to as the comparator sample – were not looked after (component 2).

Findings

Local authority policies on sex education and parenthood for looked-after young people

In interviews with officers we explored the extent to which the local authorities carried out their responsibilities for the sex education of the young people in their care, who often miss sex education in school. In practice compensatory sex and relationship education was not routinely provided by carers or social workers who are untrained in this and uncertain of their responsibilities and of parents' wishes. Most of the authorities did not have policies on this at the time of interview, social workers lacked guidance and accommodation for young parents and pregnant teenagers was arranged on an *ad hoc* basis. Indeed, the local authorities did not routinely collect data on the number of pregnancies or cases of parenthood occurring amongst the looked-after population.

Young people in public care are not routinely provided with education for parenthood and adult life, despite the fact that their own experiences of being parented often serve as inadequate models. Pregnancy and motherhood frequently mean that more schooling is missed as local authorities do not always provide alternative education or secure a return to mainstream education for young mothers in their care. Provision of and funding for child care to allow young mothers to return to education is discretionary and unevenly allocated. Though arrangements for the transition out of care and after care of young people have consistently been made since the implementation of the Children Act 1989, these seldom address the specific needs of those who leave the care system with a child or have a child soon after.

Young people's views and experiences of relationships

More than half of the looked-after young people had no contact with their father and more than a quarter had no contact with their mother. Relationships that did exist with parents were much worse than those experienced by the comparison group. Looked-after girls were more likely than the boys either to be out of touch with parents or to report that parents ignored and controlled them, did not encourage them to make their own decisions and were generally unsupportive.

Residential carers were seen as providing some compensation, especially to girls, but there was a body of looked-after young people who considered that both parents and carers disregarded their feelings while curbing their activities. Looked-after young people in both groups were critical of social workers, citing their disregard of the young people's views, and their unreliability, unhelpfulness and unavailability. They were more likely than the comparison groups to rely for support on brothers, sisters and friends. Nevertheless, the young mothers and pregnant teenagers had difficulty in maintaining friendships and tended to see friends as leisure companions rather than sources of emotional support.

The looked-after young people had similar attitudes on sex under 16 as the comparison sample, but boys as well as girls felt subject to more pressure from the opposite sex to form relationships. There was also a fear of being excluded from a group where sexual activity was the norm. Opportunities to behave as they liked were enhanced in residential care because the level of supervision associated with family life was not possible.

Information about relationships, sex and contraception

The looked-after young people were not especially disadvantaged compared with the comparison sample in respect of information on sex and relationships either at school or from parents/carers, although girls were far less likely to have been given information on some crucial topics: contraception, emergency contraception, pregnancy and pressure to have sex. The looked-after boys reported having been given information at the wrong time, or having received less information than their comparator sample peers about pressure to have sex, sexual feelings, sexual relationships and accessing local health services.

The young parents and pregnant young people said they had had poor sex education and carers and social workers were frequently uncertain of their position on contraception and sexual activity. Some gave help and information. Others effectively denied young people the means to obtain contraception, irrespective of the young person's wishes. However, pregnancy was not a result of ignorance but a failure to apply what they knew, a view endorsed by the other looked-after young people where a cavalier attitude and embarrassment in discussing contraception played a major part.

Aspirations

Looked-after young people had aspirations on education, training and employment similar to those not in public care but saw factors such as their background, their criminal activities, and being a parent as barriers specific to them. All young people aspired to steady relationships but significantly more of the looked-after sample – especially the boys – also wanted to be married or cohabiting and have a child by the time they were 20. The lone mothers did not wish to continue parenting without a partner but also looked towards employment that would support them and their child, although sometimes they had aspirations to education and employment that appeared unrealizable. Looked-after young people are unused to having a say in their lives and many, therefore, had difficulty discussing their plans for the future and appeared to be fatalistic about what would happen to them.

Pregnancy

All the young people who were not pregnant or parents agreed that carelessness and feelings of invulnerability played the key part in pregnancy, rather than lack of knowledge on contraception, but the looked-after young people were much more inclined to think it happened because teenagers wanted something to love, or girls wanted a baby, or to trap their boyfriends, or to get housing.

This view was strongly rejected by those who were pregnant or had children. They greeted their unintended pregnancies with fear, anxiety, dismay and distress. The vast majority received little guidance from those involved in their care. Unsupported and unsure of what to do, the young women typically did nothing. The tendency not to act and the inability to comprehend the implications of pregnancy are not surprising given the fatalistic acceptance of events and the philosophy of living for the day already noted among these young people.

Most of the young people, whether in public care or not, were opposed to abortion on moral grounds. However, those in the comparison group, unlike those in public care, were more inclined to state that they might consider a termination of pregnancy in certain circumstances.

Parenthood

Those who were young mothers talked about the lack of money and loss of freedom but some also thought they had become more responsible; that the small age gap between themselves and their children would help them understand their child, despite their own childhood experiences; and they believed that training, work and leisure had been postponed rather than lost.

All the young people, whether looked-after or not, thought parents should be responsible, trustworthy and understanding. Those in public care also stress the demonstration of affection, being good fun, giving praise and having the opportunity to do things differently following their own bad experiences. More than half of the looked-after group had experienced parental imprisonment, alcoholism, punitive parenting, and abuse and neglect. They did not intend to bring up their children in the way they had been brought up, but they had been given very little information or help about child care and family life, even those who had children.

Support

Pregnancy and parenthood sometimes effected a reconciliation between a young woman and her mother, but this sometimes did not help because their mother demanded support rather than giving it or gave the social workers concern because of the mother's own parenting history. Social workers were disliked and mistrusted by young mothers, because of their power to take the baby into care if there were any parenting problems.

After-care workers and former carers were most likely to be the main sources of support, but some young mothers were not referred to after-care services and not all could draw on the help of former carers, with the result that they often moved into the community unsupported in parenthood.

The great majority of young people, but especially the boys in public care, did not think that being a father these days was easy. Nevertheless, many girls in both samples had a very poor opinion of young men's sense of responsibility. Some young mothers were unsure about the role they wished the baby's father to play, many rejected him, preferring to struggle alone rather than accept inadequate help from an unreliable partner. We had little evidence of young mothers being actively encouraged to maintain the relationship with the baby's father. Furthermore, it was rare in our sample to find supported accommodation that encouraged fathers to be involved with their partner and child, and this only served to drive fathers further out of the picture.

Messages for policy and practice

- Many looked-after young people do not experience positive relationships with adults from which they might learn. Parents and social workers are prone to ignore them, disregard their feelings and opinions and make decisions on their behalf without consulting them.

- Young people not given the chance to learn about trust and respect and feeling unloved and uncared for are likely to enter into a sexual relationship without consideration of either the suitability of the partner or the implications of their actions. Unless they receive affection and learn to understand that it need not be contingent upon sex, they are likely to continue to search for love through sexual relationships and parenthood.

- Being in public care appears to place extra pressure on young women *and* young men to begin sexual relationships at an early age and, especially for those in residential care, provides them with enhanced opportunities for doing so.

- Many local authorities still do not have policies and guidelines on sex and relationship education for young people in their care. These are essential if young people are to get the information they deserve and those working with them are to be supported and trained to deliver it.

- Boys in public care appear to have more pressure from girls to have sex than do their counterparts not in public care. At the same time they are likely to be less concerned about pregnancy, to feel too embarrassed to discuss contraception with a new partner and to aspire to marriage and children at an early age. Yet little attention is paid to the sex education of young men who are looked after, and even less to their emotional needs. Programmes aimed at preventing unintended teenage pregnancy might profitably be addressed equally to both genders.

- Young women in public care do not receive adequate counselling and support when they become pregnant and lack awareness of the consequences. Being unused to making decisions for themselves and having developed a fatalistic acceptance of the future, they are liable to do nothing. In this case, failing to act means carrying the baby to term.

- Systematic recording of data on young people in public care who become pregnant or parents is not always undertaken by local authorities. It is, therefore, hard to envisage how they can gauge the scale of appropriate services and support for them.

- Accommodation, education and child care provision for young mothers who are in or have recently left public care is typically piecemeal, variable and frequently subject to either individual whim or the availability of resources. Greater cooperation between voluntary and statutory agencies and between local authority departments could ensure more effective systems of support.

- After-care workers reportedly play a valuable part in the lives of care leavers. It is important to ensure that all young mothers, often more vulnerable than their childless peers, can engage with their local after-care service and that leaving care policies and guidelines specifically address the needs of young mothers and pregnant young women.

Publication List

Corlyon, J. and McGuire, C. (1999) *Pregnancy and Parenthood: The Views and Experiences of Young People in Public Care.* London: National Children's Bureau Enterprises.

The Parenting Role of Imprisoned Fathers

Gwyneth Boswell, Professor of Criminology and Criminal Justice
De Montfort University
Peter Wedge, Emeritus Professor
School of Medicine, Health Policy and Practice, University of East Anglia

Enshrined in legislation (Children Act 1989, Section 2 (7)) is the notion of shared parental responsibility for children, whether partners are together or separated. Additionally, the UK has ratified the UN Convention on the Rights of the Child which states, inter alia, that children should be protected from any form of discrimination or punishment on the basis of their parents' status or activities (Article 2); further, it emphasizes children's right to maintain contact with a parent from whom they are separated (Article 9). In excess of an estimated 125,000 children were 'sentenced' to enforced separation from an imprisoned parent at the time of this study. There is no reason to suggest that these principles do not apply as much to them as to children who are otherwise separated from their parents.

The study

In terms of the central aims of the Department of Health's Supporting Parents initiative, this research into the parenting role of imprisoned fathers examined particular support measures, discovered parents' difficulties and the relevance of these measures for them and their children. It also explored views on possible alternatives which could enable parents to be better supported in fulfilling their parenting roles and commented on links between potentially supportive agencies, prisoner fathers and their families. Inevitably, this included some consideration of the notion of the prison itself as a support system.

THE SAMPLE

The study focused first on 181 men from 25 geographically spread prison establishments characterized by having:

1.   a parenthood/fatherhood course, or

2.   a specific children's/family visits scheme, or

3.   both a course and a scheme, or

4.   neither of these.

These establishments included six young offender institutions which, typically, contain a significant number of teenage fathers whose children may potentially endure particular adversity. Second, the study focused on 127 partners or other principal carers of inmates' children. Interviews with inmates and partners/children's carers investigated the father's role whilst in prison and (prospectively) on release, what might be done to aid this, the value of any fatherhood course or children's visit scheme experienced, possible improvements, known actual and preferred links between agencies (prison and community) and families, and believed impact on the child(ren). The proportion of black ethnic minority prisoners interviewed was 7 per cent in the adult sample and 14 per cent in the young offender sample; the overall proportion of black ethnic minority partners/carers was 6 per cent. A small number of interviews (25) with children of varied ages also directly elicited their views and feelings about contact with their imprisoned fathers. Additionally, 16 staff involved in running special courses and visiting schemes were interviewed and asked for facts and views about these provisions.

Findings

Fathers who return

Over three-quarters of the sample (both young and adult) were expecting to return to live with or near their children. Whilst over 20 per cent emphasized their 'play' role with children, the majority of prisoner fathers looked forward simply to 'being with' their children again on release. Most also wanted to repeat with their own children their positive experiences of being fathered and to avoid repeating their negative ones. This bears out research which has demonstrated the need to move on from characterization of fathers (often a 'deficit' model in the case of absent fathers) to the notion of 'generative' fathering – that is, caring for and contributing to the life of the next generation.[11]

---

11   Hawkins, A.J. and Dollalute, D.C. (1997) 'Beyond the Role-Inadequacy Perspective of Fathering.' In A.J. Hawkins and D.C. Dollalute (eds) *Generative Fathering: Beyond Deficit Perspectives.* Thousand Oaks, London and New Delhi: Sage Publications.

Healthy child–father relationships and the penal system

Other research has shown the potential importance to children of their fathers, both directly in interactive relationships and indirectly through support to and co-caring with a child's mother. This study provides evidence that, at an extreme, the criminal justice and penal systems constitute a damaging experience for children. In the cause of justice to victims, the protection of society and retribution for offenders, parents are forcibly separated from each other (often for long periods) and fathers are forcibly separated from their children (usually for periods which, to a young child, can seem almost eternal). Seeing their father in prison will often involve children in a lengthy, uncomfortable and boring journey which ends in one hour or so spent in an alien environment where, frequently, the child cannot touch or be touched by his or her father; on this visit, the child might find nothing 'provided' for his/her age group and might have been searched en route to the visits hall. For many children the reality of Ordinary Visits is depressing and frustrating. In very many ways the system damages the child–parent relationship rather than supports parents. There is, though, another side.

Relationship-enhancing prison visits

This study showed that there is a minority of prison establishments where children and parents feel valued and supported. Relationship-enhancing opportunities for children and other family members are provided through children's/family visit schemes, despite the institution's understandable concerns for security and the passing of drugs. There is recognition that children also have needs and that steps can be taken to assist them, in line with Prison Service Standing Order No. 5: '…one of the roles of the prison service [is] to ensure that the socially harmful effects of an inmate's removal from normal life are as far as possible minimized…contacts are, therefore, encouraged especially between an inmate and his family…' Children's and family visit schemes were found to be feasible and welcome, as well as motivating and humanizing of family and inmate. Contact with children in the home setting, via town visits or home leave, was the most ameliorating of visit types. Despite the relatively high proportion of children fathered by men in Young Offender Institutions, however, no children's or family visit scheme was operational in any of these establishments.

Involved fathers

In addition to visits, other contact was maintained between children and fathers through letters and telephone calls and, even for some, through audio/video tapes. Some inmates reported regular correspondence between their children and themselves, and many told of very frequent telephone contact. By these means, physically absent fathers were able to sustain a psychological presence in their children's lives – where finance and availability of telephones permitted. Almost all children and partners spoke positively of the beneficial effects.

Fatherhood/parenting courses

About 30 per cent of adult inmates and 80 per cent of the young offenders in this stratified sample had attended a fatherhood/parenting course; among these, 64 per cent of the adults and 80 per cent of the young offenders itemized what they had learned, particularly about baby-care skills and child development, and reported that the course had changed the way that they perceived the fathering role. It was not, however, within the remit of the study to test out whether these changes were implemented upon release.

Young offender fathers

Just over half of young offender fathers in this study received no visits from their children. Partly this related to geographical and travelling constraints, but for the most part was a product of fragmented relationships with the children's mothers. Some of the babies/small children had never seen their father; other children had been taken into local authority care; one had been adopted without his father's consent. On the positive side, however, around half of this group of young offenders attended parenthood classes, and many of them expressed a strong motivation to do well as fathers. Additionally, of those who were in contact with their children, some had overcome complex and adverse circumstances in order to put their children's interests first and ensure that the relationship continued.

The children's voice

All the children interviewed were in ongoing contact with their prisoner fathers and were positive about the continuation of these relationships during the prison sentence and beyond. Nevertheless, all of them also expressed sadness or distress of some kind. By way of indirect confirmation, the children of at least half of inmate and partner/carer respondents were reported to have presented more difficult behaviour at home following the father's imprisonment. Further, children's views suggest that parents underestimate the problems for children in coping with the knowledge of their father's imprisonment in the school setting.

Agency links

A striking feature of the study was that 64 per cent of partners/carers, 42 per cent of adult inmates and 30 per cent of young offenders reported no links with helping agencies, though, for a minority, this was from preference. Although 59 per cent of young offenders, 38 per cent of adult inmates and 18 per cent of partners had links with their home-based probation service (not infrequently described as unhelpful), it was clear that the majority of parent respondents did not receive, turn to or know about organizations which might support them during this critical period in their lives.

Messages for policy and practice

The study's key messages for the support of imprisoned fathers in their parenting role are as follows:

- Prisons themselves have a role to play in supporting parents in strengthening family ties whilst fathers are in prison. Since this is also in the interests of reducing recidivism, prisons could take some responsibility for this by appointing a supervisor to oversee this aspect of prison life. This is particularly important because the durability of existing children's and family visit schemes, and often of parenting/fatherhood courses, tends to depend on the enthusiasm and commitment of the leading personnel who, particularly in the case of visit schemes, tend to come from the voluntary/charitable sector. It could also afford the possibility of building external evaluation into schemes/courses to assess their value to children and to prisoner rehabilitation, a constituent which is frequently missing from these initiatives.

- The need for schools to develop clear strategies for the provision of support and trusted teacher-confidantes to children in this situation.

- The reality, during this study, was that most children and fathers were succeeding in maintaining contact (albeit often of a limited kind) via a combination of prison-based support systems and the good will of their closest informal support systems – that is, the family who, often at considerable personal and financial cost, travelled to prisons to interact with the formal support systems. In the other direction, the success of the parenting programmes also suggests a means by which learning from a formal support system might transfer to an informal one – that is, again the family. Thus the crucial nature of the partnership here is clear, in respect of the dual aims of prisoner rehabilitation and child/father relationship maintenance. Despite the range of voluntary support and self-help groups across the country, however, very few parents were aware of any of these resources. Yet, with further injection into the support network of these latter facilities, the kind of integrated support programme which runs in the US meeting the needs of prisoners, partners/carers and particularly children at different developmental stages[12] could well be in embryo here.

- Given no apparent reason for ethnic origin bias in this sample, the low percentage of black ethnic minority prisoners (7% and 14% YOIs) and partners (6%) proportionate to the prison population should be noted for investigation as to whether black parents are receiving equivalent and welcome access to formal support systems compared with white parents.

- The overall findings from this study of the parenting role of imprisoned fathers have highlighted one of society's important dilemmas – the punishment of lawbreakers versus the rights and needs of children to sustain meaningful contact with their incarcerated parent. Criminal justice policy could moderate the extent of this dilemma through greater use of community-based sentences for non-violent offenders and by extending the availability of home leave and the Home Detention Curfew system.

Parents who Reject One of their Children

Alan Rushton, Cherilyn Dance and Teresa O'Neill
Institute of Psychiatry, King's College, London

The study

Previous research has shown that children singled out for rejection by birth parents have particularly poor adjustment and difficulty forming attachments when subsequently placed in adoptive homes.[13] The focus of the current study was therefore on birth families in which there were parent–child relationship difficulties with just one child in a sibling group. The study was conducted in three phases, with the overall aim of gaining a better understanding of how such problems arise and to explore what professional interventions might help resolve these difficulties while ensuring protection of the singled-out child.

---

12   Johnson, T., Selber K. and Lauderdale M. (1998) 'Developing Quality Services for Offenders and Families: An Innovative Partnership.' *Child Welfare: Journal of Policy, Practice and Program*, special issue, LXXVII, Sept/Oct, 595–615.

13   Rushton, A., Dance C. and Quinton, D. (2000) 'Findings from a UK Based Study of Late Permanent Placements.' *Adoption Quarterly 3*, 2, 51–71; Dance, C., Rushton, A. and Quinton, D. (2002) 'Emotional Abuse in Early Childhood: Relationships with Progress in Subsequent Family Placement.' *Journal of Child Psychology and Psychiatry 43*, 3, 395–407.

Phase I (Health Visitor Survey) aimed to establish how easily families with these problems could be identified, health visitors' views on the probable cause of the difficulty and their response to them. Data came from 107 health visitors in two county areas (88% participation rate).

Phase II (CAMHS Study) explored the ways in which child mental health service professionals understood the difficulty, the approaches they used to intervene and their experience of the families' reactions to offers of therapeutic help. Data came from 53 child mental health professionals (65% participation rate) based in one inner city and one rural area.

Phase III (Social Services Study) sought to establish social service responses when a referral for possible emotional abuse concerned just one child or all the children in the family. Data came from the case records for all referrals to four social services area offices in two local authorities (a total of 649 families).

In phases I and II, information was collected by means of structured face-to-face interviews with professionals on their experiences with singling-out families. Phase III compared social work records in cases of suspected emotional abuse targeted on one child.

Findings

PHASE I (HEALTH VISITOR SURVEY)

- Over two-thirds of health visitors (68%) identified at least one family from their current case load for whom there were concerns.

- Nearly half of these families (46%) had both biological parents but reconstituted families were over-represented in the sample (34%).

- Reconstituted families, and to a lesser extent lone parents, were frequently lacking support from family and friends.

- The identified children were described as receiving much more criticism, blame, punishment, high expectations and hostility than their siblings and much less comfort, or praise.

- Most of these children were described as anxious and withdrawn. The remainder exhibited attention seeking, over-activity, behavioural problems and developmental difficulties.

- Over a third (39%) of the mothers were described by health visitors as suffering from significant mental health problems.

- Of the reconstituted families, the most common reason for singling out was that the index child was born of a previous partner, often where the relationship was characterized by abuse or unhappiness.

PHASE II (CAMHS STUDY)

Fifty-three child mental health professionals with expertise in family and parenting problems were interviewed. They expressed a great deal of concern for the enduring consequences of negative parental relationships with the children.

- Practitioners highlighted the dilemmas of working with families where trust was hard to establish and where the problems were difficult for the families to discuss.

- All the practitioners emphasized the need for extreme sensitivity in the initial stage of the encounter with the family. If parents presented a highly critical view of the child, the practitioner had to be careful not to be seen by the child to accept the parents' negative view. On the other hand, to challenge the parents' view too abruptly ran the risk of alienating them and provoking them to end cooperation.

- The practitioners formulated the family problems in different ways, although it was harder for them to be sure what lay behind singling-out-for-rejection specifically. They tended to favour explanations involving parenting problems first rather than child problems leading to negative parental attitudes.

- Where families did not engage with the service they were usually referred back to the original referrer. This approach did not appear to be sufficiently child-centred as the child's welfare was not closely monitored or depended upon a re-referral at a later stage.

PART III (SOCIAL SERVICES STUDY)

- Examining the social services' responses to allegations of emotional abuse showed that half of their assessments were brief and superficial. Responses were largely incident-based and did not lead to an assessment of relationship difficulties.

- Insufficient information was gathered to allow complex relationship problems to be identified and their possible origins understood; to assess the likely consequences of emotional abuse; or to explore the extent of risk and to devise an appropriate response.

- Referrals of single children were significantly less likely to be accorded high priority and much less likely to receive thorough and structured assessments.

Messages for policy and practice

Successful interventions with families where a child is singled out for negative treatment will always present a severe challenge to child welfare and mental health services. The root causes of such relationship problems are often hard to explore and it is difficult to gauge whether or when negative parental attitudes are likely to lead to significant harm.

These cases are often referred on to specialist resources but the families do not become fully engaged with them. For this reason the child's service contact history and developmental progress needs to be systematically recorded and tracked. This should guard against constant re-referral and re-assessment over an extended period. The implementation of the Integrated Children's System should help with tracking, especially by means of standardized recording and electronically held data.

Health visitors provide an essential screening service for families in difficulty but will only be in a position able to detect relationship problems if they have the time to get to know the families well. Better training is needed for health visitors to re-enforce their role in assessment, identification and referral.

If social service assessments of alleged emotional abuse are cursory, as they often were in the agencies investigated here, senior managers need to be aware of such deficiencies and to provide supervision and organize skills training to guarantee high standards of assessment.

It is important, given the frequent occurrence of mental health problems (mostly depression), noted in the rejecting mothers, for better links to be forged between child and adult mental health services. The specific causes of maternal psychological problems in these cases need to be explored and possible connections with differential negative parenting examined.

The provision of more easily accessible, non-stigmatizing, community-based parenting programmes is recommended to increase the choice of type and location of services for these families. As these cases can easily fail to be connected with services, all agencies need a specially devised plan to help engage the families and maintain protective surveillance of the children. Finally, high levels of professional skill will be required from all the relevant agencies to detect these problems, to help parents to acknowledge the difficulties and to offer effective therapeutic help while operating within a child protection framework.

Family Support at the Centre: Family Centres, Services and Networks

Jane Tunstill and Marilyn Hughes
Department of Health and Social Care, Royal Holloway College
Jane Aldgate
The Open University

In many ways, the story of family centres in the last quarter of the twentieth century is a microcosm of the tensions surrounding the development of child care policy and practice. It is a story of a highly regarded form of provision being overtaken by the intended as well as unintended consequences of national policy. The history of family centres has been well documented and shown the range of styles of family centre provision,[14] but there has been very little attempt to evaluate outcomes systematically. Some questions that need to be answered include:

- Do centres help to keep families together?
- Do they help prevent children coming into the care system?
- Are they a cost-effective way of delivering family support services?
- Can they sustain multi-disciplinary work?
- How are they rated by service users?

In reality, previous research on family centres had addressed only one of these themes in any depth: the views of service users. The Children Act 1989 significantly changed the relationship between *family support* and *child protection*. Some of the studies commissioned to the implementation of the Act focused on family support,[15] but one or two crossed the traditional boundary between *need* and *risk*. These showed that children at risk of significant harm could be protected by supportive services in the community, of which family centres were an important element.[16] Indeed, in 1994, the Audit Commission had suggested that family centres could provide a 'one stop shop' for family support services, albeit one which did not preclude access to a social worker if appropriate.[17] In short, the future was looking good for family centres.

14   Holman, R. (1998) *Putting Families First.* Basingstoke: Macmillan Education; Warren, C. (1993) *Family Centres: A Training and Development Handbook.* Arundel: DoH/Tarrant Publishing.

15   For example, Tunstill, J. and Aldgate, J. (2000) *Services for Children in Need: From Policy to Practice.* London: The Stationery Office; see also Department of Health (2001) *The Children Act Now: Messages from Research.* London: The Stationery Office.

16   Brandon, M., Thoburn, J., Lewis, A., and Way, A. (1999) *Safeguarding Children Within the Children Act 1989.* London: The Stationery Office.; Thoburn, J., Wilding J., and Watson, J. (2000) *Family Support in Cases of Emotional Maltreatment and Neglect.* London: The Stationery Office.

17   Audit Commission (1994) *Seen But Not Heard: Co-ordinating Community Child Health and Social Services for Children in Need.* London: HMSO.

Thus, by the end of 1997 there was widespread acknowledgement of the value of family support services, encouraged by policy thrust to shift the balance between compulsory and voluntary support services for children at risk, which became known as the 'refocusing' debate.[18] The New Labour government came into power in 1997 committed to tackling child poverty and social exclusion and greatly to expand the provision of early years services as part of this. A range of community-based initiatives were introduced to this end, of which the most widely publicized has been Sure Start. The study reported here coincided with this new policy direction. There was a certain irony in a study being commissioned to explore the networking and coordinating functions of family centres, when the ground was shifting beneath their feet.

The study

The aims of this study, which were set out in the context of the refocusing policy, were as follows:

1.   To examine the potential of family centres as a gateway to family support services.

2.   To explore the extent to which family centres facilitate or develop links with informal support networks within the community.

3.   To explore the potential for family centres to act as coordinators of family support services.

The study used a number of quantitative and qualitative methods:

- a postal survey of over 400 family centres in England

- in-depth semi-structured interviews with managers of 40 family centres

- structured interviews with 100+ family centre users

- postal questionnaires to over 60 professionals with links with family centres.

The data collected provides a fascinating picture of the organization, provision and networking of family centres between 1998 and 2001. In other words, the study was in a strong position to identify the impact of New Labour policy for children and families, and its impact on the working of family centres.

Messages for policy and practice

A GATEWAY TO SERVICES

The study found that family centres *did* act as a gateway to services both within and outside the centre. Centres succeeded in this task in three main ways:

1.   by providing a range of services within the centre

2.   by joint working with other agencies

3.   by consolidating links with formal and informal sources of support in the community.

SERVICES ON THE GROUND

Family centres had a key role in the development of parenting skills from low key, informal modelling and advice to intensive assessment, analysis and remedial work. Although the welfare of

18   Department of Health (1995) *Child Protection: Messages from Research.* London: HMSO.

children was central to family centre work, the majority of services were focused on parents, often in situations where there were few or no other sources of parenting advice or support.

Direct work

There were examples of family centres working with parents to help meet parents' expressed needs, increasing their confidence and self-esteem, and enhancing their understanding of child development, play and behaviour management. The most productive approach involved helping families facing particular challenges *without* singling them out from other centre users. This focused, supportive approach offered a positive alternative to more traditional one-to-one social work interventions.

Networking and multi-agency working

Multi-agency working and networking were important in helping families get access to a broad range of external services. As well as undertaking collaborative work with other agencies – for example, health and education – family centres participated in local strategic meetings about planning social services. They also participated in planning meetings with other family centres in their locality. This networking activity was vulnerable to restrictive pressures on staff and resources.

Coordinating family support services

The majority of family centres also had an important role in the coordination of services for families. Coordinating activities ranged from meeting the specific demands of referrers to the delivery of their own services in collaboration or in parallel with other services (for example, from health or education). Sometimes, social workers and family centres coordinated services together. Sometimes family centres were the predominant service providers. At other times they added to the provision of other agencies, such as Home-Start, Women's Refuges and hostels for homeless women.

Staffing

Centres contained staff with a range of experience and qualifications, especially in social care and social work. This gave users access to perspectives that combined child development expertise with a casework approach. This effective but delicate balance was at risk from external pressures from those who had the power to commission services. In spite of this, family centres had proved extremely adaptable to the changing demands of external funders through developing the skills of existing staff rather than relying on recruitment.

NARROWING THE GATEWAY

Although the philosophy was to provide positive services that families liked, there were considerable pressures to narrow or even close their gateways and to reduce the range and accessibility of their services. This arose because the majority of family centres in the study were dependent, to some extent, on local authority funding. A key finding was that the range of services provided by all family centres, whether they were statutory or voluntary sector, were affected by pressures on local authorities to meet their new and existing statutory obligations in the context of:

1. local authority restructuring and pressures on them, particularly social services departments, through the new responsibilities created by increased need and new priorities, such as Quality Protects

2. pressures on and within voluntary sector organizations

3. tensions between social services and other service providers, especially in relation to family centres, in terms of:

   a) the sharing and/or delegation of responsibilities

   b) devising a collective approach to services for children and families

4. tensions around service priorities on the timing of interventions, i.e. earlier or later

5. the impact of government and other initiatives on family support and associated priorities, relating to areas, age groups of children, and types of intervention

6. problems associated with the recruitment and retention of social workers.

These pressures had various impacts on centres. Because of these external pressures, decision making was more likely to take place outside the family centres. This outside control meant that they became vulnerable to restrictions in terms of who could use their services and what those services should be, especially when they were part of or heavily dependent on social service funding. In these cases they could be told to provide the 'core services' of rapid assessment and remedial interventions to assess parenting and minimize risk to children and discouraged from providing 'subsidiary' services designed to enhance parents' and children's personal and social development.

When this happened families had to depend on support from other sources, if this was available. Because the needs of and services for people who came to family centres were changing, staff team profiles were also changing. In some cases social services' restructuring resulted in plans to transfer, without replacement, family centre staff to social work duties. Reductions in services were the likely consequences of reductions in staff. The demands on local authorities of Quality Protects could work to restrict family centre work too, in a climate of scarce resources, where the major focus was on work with children in the care system. Finally, pressures also came when Ofsted regulations changed nursery and pre-school services or when other government initiatives took work and resources away from, or directed specific work to, family centres.

There was evidence of counter 'campaigns' by many centres to preserve their broad gateway role. They strove to continue to provide personal development activities for families alongside services associated with a child protection role. Sometimes imaginative ways of working the system through liberal interpretation of definitions of services were devised or 'unofficial' measures were taken to meet needs, while still providing core services to specified client groups. Family centres also increased their efforts to coordinate external, community-based services for families but, where staffing levels were being reduced, there was less likelihood of having the time for this sort of activity.

THE FUNDING GAME

The factor that had most negative impact on family centres was the nature of the funding. The impact of funding from social services has been discussed but there was also increasing involvement of other local authority departments, such as community education or housing. Funding from organizations other than local authorities was almost non-existent. Health services were likely to fund only occasional, short-term, specific projects and were reluctant to acknowledge health outcomes from family centre work, even though health visitors had been a regular source of referrals to family centres concerning children's developmental needs and mental and physical health problems of their parents. Non-statutory organizations rarely provided funding. Children's organizations were more likely to supply management, staff and buildings than funding. Overall, funding was likely:

- to be short term, i.e. lacking predictability and continuity
- to involve bids to a diversity of sources
- to be given for closely specified purposes.

These problems restricted forward planning and caused insecurities among staff and families. One major charity withdrew support for projects completely and suddenly. This immediately de-creased the staff, the range of services and the number of users.

Centres also bid for time-limited and targeted money from funders such as the Lottery or Children in Need and government initiatives such as Single Regeneration or the Deal for Commu-nities. Multiple funding could give centres more independence but funding was usually only avail-able for specific pieces of work and applying for it was very time consuming and took staff time away from clients and services. There is a need to streamline and standardize application proce-dures, which would help the development and/or sustainability of family centres. It would also help if other agencies, such as schools, could share their resources with family centres.

FAMILY CENTRES WORK IN THE HERE AND NOW

The study showed that family centres are well placed to provide community-based services for children and families. They have the capacity to meet the needs of both children and their parents without sacrificing one to the other. Most centres work with parenting difficulties whilst avoiding a model of wilful or pathological neglect. Rather, they see problems as stemming from the parents' own lack of experience of good parenting or family life and see change as achievable in the here and now.

Centres tried to change the context of parenting by meeting parents' needs, building on their strengths, increasing their confidence and filling gaps in their skills and knowledge of child devel-opment, play and behaviour. They also worked on the parents' own personal development, in areas such as improved literacy and self-image.

CONCLUSION

The main conclusion is that whilst there has been a widespread development in family centre services over the past decade there has also been a process of reduction of the range of services through diversion towards a specialized role. This is especially unfortunate because the strengths centres possess are at the heart of government policy to support families and enhance the develop-mental welfare of children. Through their holistic approach to families, centres can balance indi-vidual family members' needs and wants with the needs of children and young people and take a long-term view of service provision. Family centres represent a valuable resource for local authori-ties and other public sector service providers to continue to implement one of the fundamental principles of the Children's Act 1989, that children should have the opportunity to grow up in their own families.

List of Readers

Project	Readers
Enabling Parents (the SPOKES project)	Dr Julia Hardy, Principal Educational Psychologist, Education Directorate
Effective Strategies for Parents with Young Children with Behaviour Problems	Dr Jacqueline Barnes, Leopold Muller Centre Medical School; Dr Francis Gardner, Lecturer and Clinical Psychologist
Supporting Parents Caring for a Technology-Dependent Child	Peter Limbrick, Chair, Handsel Trust; Jeanette McGrogan, Community Children's Nurse
Parenting and Disability	Michele Wates, Disabled Parents Network; Gill Keep, Head of Policy, National Family and Parenting Institute
Supporting South Asian Families with a Child with Severe Disabilities	Christine Lenehan, Council for Disabled Children
The Fostering Task with Adolescents	Hilary Corrick, Policy and Development Officer for Children and Families, SSD Southampton; Sonia Heywood, Regional Development Worker, Quality Protects, SSI
Supporting Foster Placements	Mick Upsall, Planning and Project Manager, SSD Derbyshire; Sue Gourvish, National Foster Care Association; Francis Dallyn, Team Manager, Fostering Teams, SSD Leicester
Pregnancy and Parenthood	Helen Armstrong, Service Development Manager, SSD Darlington; Rosie Brown, North Derbyshire Health Promotion
The Parenting Role of Imprisoned Fathers	Liza Catan, Trust for the Study of Adolescence
Parenting in Poor Environments	Dorit Braun, Chief Executive, ParentLine Plus; Lucy Draper, Coordinator, Thomas Coram Parents' Centre
A Study of Stepchildren and Step-parenting	Dorit Braun, Chief Executive, ParentLine Plus; Jane Batchelor, Social and Policy Sciences, University of Bath
Parenting Different Children	No comments received
The Role and Potential of Family Centres in Coordinating Formal and Informal Family Support Services	No comments received
A Normative Study of Children's Injuries	No comments received

Appendix C

Members of the Overview Group

The affiliations of members of the group were those current at the time the overview group was meeting.

Carolyn Davies	Research and Development Division, DOH (DOH Coordinator)
David Quinton	University of Bristol (Academic Coordinator)
Pat Lees	University of Bristol (Assistant to the Coordinators)
Virginia Burton[1]	Family Policy Unit, Home Office
Bruce Clark	Children's Social Care Division, DOH
Erica De'Ath	Chief Executive, NCVCCO
Sue Gourvish	National Foster Care Association
Bob Jezzard	Health Services Division, DOH
Helen Jones	Children's Services, Social Services Inspectorate, DOH
Marion Lowe	Chief Executive, Family Fund Trust
Mary McLeod	Chief Executive, National Family and Parenting Institute
Peter Smith	Social Care Group, SSI
Kevin Woods[2]	Children's Social Care Division, DOH

1   Virginia Burton was replaced by Clare Roskill, Family Policy Unit.
2   Kevin Woods was replaced by Tessa Ing, Children's Social Care Division, DOH.

Subject Index

A & E, injuries presenting at 68
abortion, and unwanted teenage
  pregnancy 137–8
absent parents, contact 65, 66,
  213
abuse 149
  see also emotional abuse
access
  to family centres 161–2
  to services 210–11
    for disabled parents 126–7
accidents, leading to injury 67,
  216–17
accommodation
  for pregnant teenagers 140
  see also housing
activities
  constructive in behaviour
    intervention 75
  in local area 210
  organising in foster care 94
Adolescent Fostering study *see The
  Fostering Task with Adolescents*
adolescents
  boundary setting 87–8, 93,
    203
  future aspirations 136, 245
  ideas of family 134–6, 245
  relationships
    with foster carers 89
    with parents 138, 244, 246
    with social workers 139,
      244, 246
  sexual activity 88, 136, 246
  status of pregnancy 137
  teenage pregnancy 134–41,
    170, 245
  see also children; young people
adoption
  review and changes 35, 47
  and unwanted teenage
    pregnancy 137–8
Adoption and Children Act 2002
  47
Adoption and Permanency Task
  Force 34, 47
advice
  lack of for pregnant teenagers
    138
  as support 24
  see also information
advocacy services 159
affection, expression, parenting
  task 26

after-care workers 140, 189, 246,
  247
age, in disruption prediction 91
aggression, of parents, and injury
  68
aloofness 91
anti-social behaviour 220–1, 223
  see also behavioural problems
anxiety 59, 60, 63, 66, 122, 237
assessment
  of emotional abuse by social
    services 155
  of needs 159, 197, 238
    by family centres 167
    of disabled parents 128
    ICS 52
    right of carers 49
    in service provision 35, 36
  of parenting capacity in
    pregnant teenagers 139
  of support in parenting 25
attachment behaviour 91
attitudes
  of birth children to fostering 97
  of children towards step families
    64–5, 66
  towards disabled parents 242
  towards sex 136, 141, 244
  towards support by parents 62
  towards teenage fathers 246
awareness, of support services 209

babies, injuries 67
baby bond 40
barriers, to support for disabled
  parents 241
basic needs, inability of families to
  provide 59, 208
behaviour
  and incident of injuries 68
  of parents 24–7, 27
    see also parenting; parenting
      styles
  youth offending 45
  see also behavioural problems
behaviour intervention programme
  71–6, 219–24
behaviour management services
  159
behaviour support plans 45
behavioural problems 59, 201,
  208, 221
  in foster care 90, 92
  intervention 74–6, 219–24
  studies 17, 71–6, 219–24
  see also behaviour
benefits 40, 58, 116, 124, 127,
  164, 194

'Best Value' in service provision
  38
birth children
  impact of fostering 95, 97
  influence on fostering success
    92
body, injuries to 67
boundaries
  setting
    in foster care 87–8, 93, 203
    in inter-agency working 194
    parental task 16
boys
  sex education of looked after
    teenagers 247
  see also adolescents; children;
    young people
bruising 67
burns 67

CAMHS *see* Child and Adolescent
  Mental Health Services
car ownership, by disabled parents
  124
career choices, of teenagers 136
carers *see* foster carers
Carers and Disabled Children Act
  2000 49
*Caring about Carers: A National
  Strategy for Carers* 49
casualty, injuries presenting at 68
challenging behaviour *see*
  behavioural problems
change
  experience of children 212,
    214
  impact on disabled parents 242
Child and Adolescent Mental
  Health Services 51, 150,
  151, 152, 156, 194, 199,
  223
child benefit 40
Child and Mental Health Services,
  grants 51
child poverty 43
  see also poverty
child protection 223
Child Safety Orders 45
Child Support Agency 40–1
Child Support and Pensions and
  Social Security Act 2000 41
Child Trust Fund 40
child-centredness 87, 203
childcare
  provision 42, 159, 210
  support for 24, 60
childish attachment 91

263

children
   activities for 210
   attitudes *see* children, views
   in care 134–41, 243–7
      Quality Protects programme
         46
   as carers 49, 124–5, 129, 242
   contact with absent parents 65,
      66, 213
   disabled *see* disabled children
   experience of life changes 212,
      214
   injuries 67–70
   needs when fostered 224–5
   rejection 149–57
   transition of disabled children to
      adulthood 237, 240
   views
      of fostering 88–9
      of imprisoned fathers 250
      of step-families 64–5, 66,
         213
      taking account of in service
         provision 34, 36, 47
      visits to imprisoned fathers
         142, 143, 144–5, 146,
         200, 249
   see also adolescents; young
      people
Children and Families Directorate
   34, 38
Children and Young People's Unit
   34, 37, 43
children's centres, for integrated
   care 43
Children's Fund 43
Children's Social Services Core
   Information Requirements
   52
Children's Taskforce: An Introduction
   38
children's tax credit 40
children's visiting schemes (prison)
   143, 144, 249
Choice Protects programme 35,
   46–7
circumstances 58–9, 62
   improvement 238
clinical nursing, of disabled
   children 108–10, 233
cliques, in family centres 160,
   165
cognitive development, aiding,
   parental task 26
commitment, in foster care 90
Community Children's Nursing
   teams 108
community groups 185
   links with family centres 162

community support 79–80, 211
community-based programmes
   42, 74–6, 156, 171, 201
   see also family centres
conciliation services for SEN
   disputes 50
conduct, improvement 75, 76
Confident Parents, Confident Children:
   Policy and Practice in Parent
   Education and Support 26
consensual parenting 71, 72, 73
constructive activities, in behaviour
   programme 75
consumption, of support 79, 120,
   130, 187
contact
   with absent parents 65, 66,
      213
   of children in care with parents
      244
   of fostered children with family
      230–1, 232
   with imprisoned fathers 142,
      143, 144–5, 200, 249
contact work 159
contraception 137
control, parents' need for when
   using support services 78,
   82, 190–1, 210, 239
coordination
   role of family centres 164–6,
      256
   of support 157, 192
'coping' with parenting 80–1,
   208–9
crime policies, on youth offending
   45
crime prevention 223
criticism, of services 188, 210
cultural difficulties and needs
   119, 122, 238
cuts 67
CYPU (Children and Young
   People's Unit) 34, 37, 43

data collection, ICS exemplars 52
data sources 31
depression 59, 60, 63–4, 66,
   122, 212, 237
   maternal and problem behaviour
      72, 73
diagnoses, of disability 117, 122,
   125
diaries, cultural/socio-economic
   effects of recording injuries
   data 68
direct payment, for carers of
   disabled people 49, 50

direction of effects 80
disability, definition 107
Disability Rights Commission 48
Disability Rights Task Force 48
disabled children
   learning disabled ethnic group
      114–22, 234–40
   needs of parents 197
   Quality Protects programme 46
   technology dependent 18,
      108–14, 181–2, 184, 190,
      191, 192, 194, 232–5
disabled parents 47–50, 240–3
Disabled Parents study *see Parenting*
   and Disability: The Role of
   Formal and Informal Networks
disadvantage 58–9
   government initiatives 43
disclosure, of diagnosis of
   disability 117, 122, 125,
   236
disengaged parenting 71
domestic violence 44
drug misuse, action on 45

e-records 52
Early Excellence 34, 163
   centres 43
Early Years Development and
   Childcare Partnerships 42,
   163
ecology, of parenting 27–9, 180
Ecology of Human Development
   27
education
   of disabled parents 124
   improving life chances for
      disabled 49
   links with family centres 163
   of parents about safety 218
   of pregnant and young mothers
      140, 244
   special educational needs 50
   teenage hopes for 136
   see also schools; special schools
education maintenance allowance
   40
educational psychologists, effect
   on fostered children 104
EECs (Early Excellence centres)
   43
Effective Strategies for Parents with
   Young Children with Behaviour
   Problems 17, 71–3, 178,
   183, 187, 188, 202,
   218–19
emotional abuse 154–6, 172,
   200, 253

rejection 152–4, 170, 182
emotional age, responsiveness of foster carer 87, 94, 203
emotional problems, in foster care 92
emotional security, provision, parental task 26
emotional support 24, 72, 130, 131, 187
employment
    of disabled parents 124
    European Union directives 48
    schemes for disabled people 49
    see also unemployment
Enabling Parents: A Community Intervention to Address Behaviour Difficulties 17, 74–6, 80, 82, 178, 193, 201, 203, 219–24
engaged parenting 71
engagement, with children in foster care 87
environment, impact of poverty in 58, 208
equipment, supply for disabled child 112, 234
ethnic minorities
    difference in injury rate 70
    informal and formal support 118–19, 122
    support for prison population 251
    see also minority groups
European Union employment directive 48
evaluation, of support in parenting 25
evidence base 35
EWGs (External Working Groups) 51
Excellence for All: Meeting Special Educational Needs: A Programme for Action 50
expertise, of parent in management of disability 111, 191
External Working Groups 51
EYDCP (Early Years Development and Childcare Partnerships) 42

families
    difficult to help 170–2, 173, 199–200
    links with family centres 162
    stresses 82, 204
    support from 60, 98, 120, 127–8, 130, 145, 182–4
    teenage ideas of 134–6

family centres 133–4, 157–69, 170, 172, 201–2, 254–8
    see also community-based programmes
Family Centres study see Family Support at the Centre: Family Centres, Services and Networks
family circumstances, studies 16–17
family income 24, 58, 62, 115, 164, 208, 235
family learning schemes (prison literacy support) 144
family life, with disabled child 109–10, 233, 237
family policy, and general policy making 33
Family Policy Unit 34, 36–7, 40
Family Support at the Centre: Family Centres, Services and Networks 19–20, 157–69, 189, 254–8
family support grants 40
family visiting schemes 143, 144, 193, 199, 249
fatalism, of looked-after teenagers 136
fatherhood
    views
        of imprisoned fathers 143, 248
        of teenagers 134–6
fathers
    aggression and injuries 68
    in prison 133, 142–8, 170, 248
    teenage, attitude towards 246
final warnings 45
financial responsibilities 40–1
financial support 39–41
firm parenting 71, 72
'fit' of children in foster care 87, 90, 204
follow-up
    in research 31
    studies 178, 203, 204
formal support 22, 24, 60–1, 179
    community-based services 42–4
    for disabled children 111–14, 118–19, 120, 236–7
    for disabled parents 124–7, 129
    as part of ecology of parenting 29, 180
    for emotional abuse cases 155
    for ethnic minorities 118–19
    failures 131

links with family centres 162–3, 164
image 210
link workers in fostering 99–100, 101–2
national agencies 41–2
parents' requirements 78, 81
parents' views 81–2, 178
for prisoners and families 146, 147, 148
for rejecting families 150–1, 156
relationship with informal support 29, 120, 129–30, 186–7
as a relationship with parents 78, 192
responsiveness of services 132
for serious problems 44–5
sex education 138–9
in step families 65
foster care 17–18, 46–7, 84–106, 224–32
    differences from parenting 89–90
    duration of placements 90–3, 224–6, 228, 230
    support 95, 97–104, 105, 106, 228–9, 231–2
foster carers 84–6, 182
    effects of circumstances on success 92
    qualities 226–7
    training 231
    views 86–7
foster carers' groups 98–9, 228
The Fostering Task with Adolescents 18, 84–106, 178, 182, 183, 184, 184–6, 186, 188, 190, 191, 195, 203, 204, 228–32
Friends and Family Care 47
From Exclusion to Inclusion 48
funding
    of child care 42
    of Children's Fund 43–4
    of family centres 160
    New Opportunities Fund 42
    Parenting Fund 41, 44
    for Quality Protects schemes 46
    of short-term care for disabled children 113
    see also grants

gateway, role of family centres 164–6, 169, 255, 256–7
general population studies 16–17, 57–83

generalizability, in research 30
girls
    and teenage pregnancy
        134–41, 245, 247
    see also adolescents; children;
        young people
give and take, in informal support
    77
God Bless the Child 187
Government and Parenting: Is There a
    Case for a Policy Review and
    Parent's Code? 33
government policy 33–53, 163
grants
    for mental health care 51
    see also funding

head injuries 67
health care
    for children, policy 51
    improving life chances for
        disabled 49
health problems see disabled
    children; mental health
    problems; physical illness, of
    parents
health visitors
    links with family centres 163
    and rejecting parents 149–50,
        253
    role in support 73, 188
    use of service 61
holistic support 29, 158, 196,
    201–2
home carers, professional, use 110
home-based care
    for disabled children 112, 234
        nursing 109–10
home-school agreements 45
Homelessness Directorate 37
hostile/disengaged parenting 71,
    72, 73, 203
household income 24, 58, 62,
    115, 164, 208, 235
housing 62, 124, 164, 208235
    see also accommodation
hyperactivity, improvement 75, 76

ICS (integrated children's system)
    52, 197
illness see disabled children; mental
    health problems; physical
    illness, of parents
impairment 107
    see also disability; disabled
Implementation Support
    Team/Fund 50

Imprisoned Fathers study see The
    Parenting Role of Imprisoned
    Fathers
imprisonment, impact of 147
incidents (accidents) 67, 216–17
income 24, 58, 62, 115, 164,
    208, 235
independence, and support 77–8,
    182, 183
informal networks 22, 179
    for disabled parents 127–8
    see also informal support; social
        networks
informal support 22, 23–4,
    59–60, 77–9, 179, 182–4
    in difficult to help families 170
    for disabled child 111, 119,
        236
    for disabled parents 127–8
    in emotional abuse cases 155
    in ethnic minority groups
        119–20
    in fostering 95, 97, 101
    from family and friends 60, 98,
        120, 127–8, 130, 145,
        182–4
    lack of
        by users of family centres
            164
        from parents of pregnant
            teenagers 138, 170
        in rejection of children
            151–2
    limitations 131
    links with family centres 162
    mobilization 22–3
    for prison visits 145
    relationship with formal support
        29, 120, 129–30, 186–7
information 194–6, 209–10
    between services 196, 197
    for disabled parent 125
    improvements 41–2
    lack of on cases 171
    for parents of disabled child
        111–12, 117–18, 122,
        236, 238
    provision by family centres
        159, 165
    for service provision 39
    on young people in placements
        231
    see also advice
injuries 66–70, 214–18
    types 67
Injuries study see A Normative Study
    of Children's Injuries
integrated children's system 52,
    197

integration, of services 52–3
inter-agency working 53,
    112–13, 151, 169, 181,
    194, 201, 234
    see also joined-up thinking;
        multi-agency working
inter-connectedness of needs 81,
    118–19
interpreters 119, 122
intervention
    ICS 52
    in problem behaviour 74–6,
        219–24
inverse targeting effect, use of
    services 79, 120, 130, 187
invulnerability, belief of, and
    pregnancy 137

joined-up thinking
    in service provision 34, 36, 53
    see also inter-agency working

key workers 113, 119, 122, 126
    parents as 29, 81, 198, 199
    see also link workers

language, difficulties and needs
    117, 118, 119, 196, 238
learning disability
    policy 49–50
    see also learning disabled
        children
Learning Disability Awards
    Framework 50
Learning Disability Partnership
    Boards 50
Learning Disability Task Force 50
learning disabled children
    114–28, 232–5
    see also learning disability
Learning to Listen: Core Principles for
    the Involvement of Children and
    Young People 34
LEAs (local education authorities)
    45, 50
leg injuries 67
life changes 212, 214, 242
life skills 230
link workers 198–9
    parents as 29, 81
    supporting foster care 99–100,
        101–2, 188, 190
    see also key workers
Listening, Hearing and
    Responding 34
literacy, development in behaviour
    intervention 75, 221
local activities, for children 210

local authorities
   accountability of Youth
      Offending Teams 45
   childcare provision 42
   family centres 158–9
      funding 160
      influence on role 256–7
   improvement of fostering 46–7
   parental partnership in
      education 45
   Quality Protects programme 46
   lack of sex education policy
      139, 244
   support for carers 49
   teenage pregnancy strategy 38
   see also local education
      authorities
Local Child Curfews 45
local consultation, in funding
   allocation 43–4
local education authorities 45, 50
   see also local authorities
lone parents 59, 62, 208, 230
   New Deal 40–1
   support 73
looked-after children 134–41,
   243–7
loss of independence, fear of 62
love, in fostering 87

'malaise' scores 59, 116, 208
management action plans 46
mapping, of family services 53
MAPs (management action plans)
   46
maternity grant 40
medication, supply for disabled
   child 112, 234
mental health problems 59, 73,
   78, 116, 208, 243
   and rejection of children 150,
      253
mental health services 51
Minister for Children, Young
   People and Families 34
Ministerial Group on the Family
   35
Ministerial Sub-Committee on
   Active Communities and
   Family 35
minor injuries 66–7, 214–17
minority groups
   services 160
   see also ethnic minorities
mobilization, of informal and
   semi-formal support 79,
   186–7

models, of disability 107, 126,
   243
mothers, aggression and injuries
   68
Moving On: Young People and
   Leaving Care Schemes 134
multi-agency working 75, 76,
   256
   see also inter-agency working;
      joined-up thinking

National Child Care Strategy 42
National Citizen Advocacy
   network 50
National Family and Parenting
   Institute 39, 40, 41
National Health Service Plan,
   application to children 51
National Learning Disability
   Information Centre/Helpline
   50
National Parenting Helpline 39,
   41–2
National Service Framework for
   Children 51, 52
National Stepfamily Association
   39
NDDP (New Deal for Disabled
   People) 48–9
NDLP (New Deal for Lone
   Parents) 40–1
needs
   associated with disability 49,
      131, 239
   of fostered children 224–5
   inter-connectedness 81,
      118–19
   of parents 209, 239
      control 78, 82, 190–1, 210,
         239
   of prisoners and their families
      147
   of step-families 65, 213, 214
   see also assessment, of needs;
      basic needs
neglect 149
Neighbourhood Nurseries
   Initiative 42
Neighbourhood Renewal Unit 37
neighbourhoods, manifestations of
   poverty 58, 208, 210
neighbours
   support 98
   see also families
networking 166, 256
networks, for support 22, 127–8,
   179

New Deal for Disabled People
   48–9
New Deal for Lone Parents 40–1
New Forest study see Effective
   Strategies for Parents with Young
   Children with Behaviour
   Problems
New Labour, policies 33–4, 40
New Opportunities Fund 42
NFPI (National Family and
   Parenting Institute) 39, 41
NHS Plan, application to children
   51
non-stigmatising delivery of
   services 159, 168, 169,
   171, 200
Normal Injuries study see A
   Normative Study of Children's
   Injuries
A Normative Study of Children's
   Injuries 66–70, 214–18,
   216–17
nurseries, childcare provision 42
nursing care, for chronically
   disabled children 108–10,
   233

offending behaviour 45
open access, in family centres
   158–9, 161
outcomes
   in behaviour intervention
      221–2
   effect of parenting 202–3
   in fostering 91–2, 94–5,
      100–4, 228–30
   importance in support 210
   for learning disabled children
      from ethnic communities
      237–8
   for step-families 213

Parent Network 39
parent partnership schemes 45,
   50
parenthood, views of 134–6,
   136, 143, 244–6, 248
parenthood courses, for prisoners
   145, 147, 249
parenting
   academic debate 15
   concept of 181
   description 26–9, 180
   disabled children 109–10, 114
   ecology of 27–9
   facilities at family centres 159
   in foster care 84–6, 89–90
   influences on 27, 28, 180

legacy of problems in 219
effect on outcomes 202–3
parenthood courses for prisoners
145
Parenting Orders, for setting
behaviour standards 45
professionalization 109–10,
111
rejecting behaviour 133
in step families 64, 213
effect of support 25, 30,
203–4, 204–5
for disabled parents 127,
128, 129
tasks 26
see also parenthood; parenting
styles; parents
Parenting Difficult Children 149
Parenting and Disability: The Role of
Formal and Informal Networks
18, 123–32, 183, 194,
240–3, 283
Parenting Fund 41, 44
Parenting Orders 45
Parenting in Poor Environments 16,
58–63, 77–81, 82, 182,
183, 185, 186, 187, 189,
190–1, 192, 195, 198, 203,
207–11, 216
The Parenting Role of Imprisoned
Fathers 19, 142–8, 170, 183,
189, 193, 196, 199, 200,
247–51
parenting styles 71–3, 201,
202–3
in foster care 89, 93–5, 96
in step families 64
see also parenthood; parenting;
parents
Parentline 39
Parentline Plus 39, 41–2
parents
criticism of services 188–9
disabled 47–50, 240–3
education in prisons 45
expertise managing disability
111
family centre use 164, 169
financial responsibilities 40–1
in most need of support 209
nursing of disabled child
108–10, 233
partnership with 34, 36
requirements from services
189–90, 209–10
responsibilities, emphasis in
service provision 35, 40–1
views
on family centres 164

on formal support 61, 62,
81–2, 83, 178
see also parenthood; parenting;
parenting styles
Parents who Reject One of their
Children 19, 149–57, 170,
183, 184, 193, 194, 196,
199, 200, 201–2, 251–4
partners, support from 95, 97,
146, 208
partnership
with parents 34, 35, 53, 78,
82, 169
family centres 158
schemes 45
peer pressure in teenage sexual
relationships 136–7
personal development services
159
physical abuse 149
physical care, parental task 26
physical illness, of parents 116,
122, 208, 237, 243
physical punishment 68, 72
planning, ICS 52
policy
changes in, during Supporting
Parents initiative 14–15
impacting on families 33–53
involvement of family centres
163
lack of commitment to families
in prison 142
on teenage pregnancy 134
Poor Environments study see Parenting
in Poor Environments
positive parenting 93–4
positive regard, parenting task 26
potent parenting 71
poverty 58, 62, 82, 208, 210
see also child poverty
Practical Implications of the Emerging
NSF for Children 51
predictors
of disruption 91–3
of problems in coping 208–9
of success in fostering 96
Pregnancy and Parenthood: The Views
and Experiences of Young People
in Public Care 19, 134–41,
183, 184, 188, 192–3, 195,
196, 199, 243–7
pregnant teenagers 134–41, 170,
245
lack of advice and support 138
Prison study see The Parenting Role of
Imprisoned Fathers
prison visits 142, 143, 144–5,
146, 200, 249

prisons, role of support for family
250, 251
private nurseries, childcare
provision 42
professionalism, in fostering 87,
90, 100, 191
professionals, relationships with
78, 90, 105, 110–13, 118,
233–4
psychological inputs, fostering
103–4
punishment 68, 72, 218
in step families 64

Quality Protects 35, 46, 48, 49,
163, 243
relationships with foster carers
89

randomized control trials 74
reading, improvement during
behaviour intervention 75,
76
realizing potential, in service
support 35, 36
reasoning, to control behaviour
72
reciprocity 77, 182
reconstituted families, and
rejection of children 252
referrals, to family centres 161–2
Rejecting Parents study see Parents
who Reject One of their Children
rejection of children 149–57,
252–4
assessment 197
causes 153
incidence 150
relationships
with ex-partners and family 65
in formal support 78, 192
in foster care 90, 105
of foster carers with partners
95, 97
between influences in parenting
180
in informal support 78, 79
between looked-after teenagers
and parents 138, 244
effect of negativity on children
252
between parents, and correlation
of injuries 68
of parents with professionals
78, 90, 105, 110–13, 118,
233–4
quality of, in parenting 27
in step families 64, 66, 212

of teenagers
with foster carer 89
with parents 138, 244
with social workers 139,
244
*Report into Prison Disturbances April
1990 by the Right Honourable
Lord Woolf and His Honour
Judge Stephen Tumin* 142
reporting bias 68, 69
representativeness 31
research methods 30–2
research proposals, for Supporting
Parents initiative 13–14
resources
link from family centres 165
for parenting 27
in support 24
respect, for parents by support
services 78, 192
respite care 103, 118, 195, 237
responsibilities
financial 40–1
of parents 26–7, 44–5
responsiveness
of foster carers 87, 94, 203
of link workers in fostering
100, 190
of services 132, 190, 194
review
of adoption 35, 47
of fostering 46–7
ICS 52
risk assessment, of emotional
abuse 155

safety, in the home 69, 217, 218
safety equipment, and injuries
68–9
*Safety and Justice: The Government's
Proposals on Domestic Violence*
44
sampling 31
Schools: Building on Success (Green
Paper) 43
schools
disclosure of parent's disability
126
sex education 138–9
support
for children with imprisoned
fathers 250
in fostering 103
for learning disabled children
119, 122
see also education; special schools
SCIE (Social Care Institute for
Excellence) 39, 41, 42, 47

secure base, in fostering 87
self-referral 61
semi-formal support 23, 24, 61,
62, 179, 184–6, 210
for disabled child 111, 119
in fostering 98–9
SEN (special educational needs)
50
sensitive parenting 71, 72, 93–4,
203
serious difficulties, support for
families 44–5
serious injuries 68, 216–17
services *see* formal support
setting boundaries *see* boundaries,
setting
SEU (Social Exclusion Unit) 37,
44–5
sex, attitude towards 136, 141,
244
sex education 134–5, 138–9,
141, 196, 245, 246
sexual abuse 149
sexual activity, of teenagers 88,
136, 246
short breaks 195
for carers 103
see also respite care
short-term care, for disabled
children 112–13, 118, 194
shouting, as punishment 72
single parents *see* lone parents
skill development, parental task
26
sleep disturbance, of parents with
disabled child 233
smacking 68, 72
Social Care Institute for Excellence
39, 41, 42, 47
social contact, facilitation, parental
task 26
social exclusion
reducing truancy and behaviour
problems 45, 223
Sure Start initiative 43
Social Exclusion Unit 37, 44–5,
134
social model of disability 107,
126, 243
social needs, of disabled children
49
social networks 60
see also informal networks;
informal support
social services
for children 46
relationship with family centres
161, 162–3, 167–8

response to difficult families
199–200
response to emotional abuse
154–5
use 61
Social Services Inspectorate
Performance Assessment 46
social workers
relationships with 139, 189,
204
support
for fostering 99–100,
101–2, 105, 188, 190
for pregnant teenagers 199
views of fostering 88
socialization, parental task 26
sources
of data in research 31
of support 23
South Asian study *see Supporting
South Asian Families with a
Child with Severe Disabilities*
Southampton study *see Effective
Strategies for Parents with Young
Children with Behaviour
Problems*
special educational needs 50
special needs
in foster care 91–2
and informal support 182–3
special schools 237, 239
specialist groups 184–6
specialist support 24, 203–4,
204–5, 227
speech therapy, use 61
SPOKES project/study *see Enabling
Parents: A Community
Intervention to Address
Behaviour Difficulties*
staffing, of family centres 161,
256
step-families 63–6, 211–14
Step-family study *see A Study of
Stepchildren and Step-parenting*
step-fathers 65, 66, 212
stresses
on families 82, 204
on foster carers 92–3, 95,
97–8, 101
from family and friends 183
relationship with injury and
punishment 218
strict parenting 71
studies, of Supporting Parents
initiative, design 178
*A Study of Stepchildren and
Step-parenting* 16, 63–6, 188,
211–14, 216

supervision, of teenagers in foster
care 88, 94, 203, 230
support 83, 181
and ability to cope 80–1
attitude of parents 62
barriers for disabled parents
241
for change 214
content 23, 24–5, 83
coordination 157, 192
failure of services 170–1
for families with serious
problems 44–5, 170–2,
173, 199–200
from family and friends 60, 98,
120, 127–8, 130, 145,
182–4
for fostering 95, 97–104, 105,
106, 231–2
identifying needs 22
image of services 210
key points 28
and level of problems 60, 62
effect on parenting 25, 30,
127, 128, 129, 203–4
for parents of children with
problem behaviours 72–3
parents as coordinators 27, 28,
83
parents/carers' views 29, 61,
62, 81–2, 83, 178
from partners of prisoners 146
preference for practical services
61
for pregnant teenagers 138–41
prisons' role 250, 251
as a process 192–3
sources 23–4, 219
step-families' needs 65, 213,
214
terminology 21–2, 179
types 23–5, 209
see also formal support; informal
support; semi-formal
support
Support Foster Care 47
support groups 186
support networks 22
Supporting Families: A Consultation
Document 35, 41
Supporting Foster Placements 17,
84–106, 178, 182, 183,
184, 184–6, 187, 188,
189–90, 195, 203, 204,
224–7
Supporting Fostering study see
Supporting Foster Placements

Supporting Parents Caring for a
Technology-Dependent Child
18, 108–14, 184, 190, 191,
192, 194, 232–5
Supporting Parents initiative
limitations 15, 178
overview procedure 9–10
structure 13–14, 178
Supporting South Asian Families with a
Child with Severe Disabilities
18, 114–23, 182–3, 186,
187, 188, 195, 197,
234–40
Sure Start 34, 40, 43, 163, 172
Sure Start Unit 37

target setting, in service provision
38–9
task forces, implementing policy
38, 39
tasks, of parenting 26, 27
teamwork, in fostering 191
technology dependent children
18, 108–14, 181–2, 184,
190, 191, 192, 194, 232–5
Technology Dependent study see
Supporting Parents Caring for a
Technology-Dependent Child
Teenage Pregnancy study see
Pregnancy and Parenthood: The
Views and Experiences of Young
People in Public Care
Teenage Pregnancy Unit 34, 38
teenagers see adolescents; pregnant
teenagers; young people
telling, of disability 117, 122,
125, 236
therapeutic intervention, in
rejection 153–4
threats, as behaviour control 72
Towards Inclusion 48
TPU (Teenage Pregnancy Unit)
34, 38
trading, of informal support 77,
182
transition, to adulthood of
disabled children 237, 240
Treatment Foster Care 47
truancy 44–5

unemployment 58, 62, 208, 235
see also employment
units, for implementation of
government policy 36–8, 39
use of services by deprived families
61
users groups 184–6

Valuing People 49–50
violence, in step families 64
visiting schemes, in prison 143,
144, 147, 193, 199, 249

Woolf Report 142
work ethic
encouraging 34, 41
schemes for disabled people 49
work/life balance 36
working families tax credit 40

YOTs (Youth Offending Teams)
45
young offenders 45
fathers 250
parenthood courses 145, 250
young people
as carers 49, 124–5, 129, 242
views of fostering 88–9
see also adolescents; children
Youth Action Groups 45
youth offending see young
offenders
Youth Offending Teams 45, 51

Author Index

Akram, Y. 115–23, 235–40
Aldgate, J. 157–69, 254–8
Audit Commission 254
Aynsley-Green, A. 51

Belsky, J. 27
Biehal, N. 134
Boddy, J. 66–70, 215–18
Boswell, G. 142–8, 247–51
Brandon, M. 254
Bronfenbrenner, U. 27
Brown, G. 41

Children and Young People's Unit 34
Clarke, H. 123–32, 240–3
Colton, M. 254
Cornah, D. 71–3, 218–19
Corylon, J. 134–41, 243–7

Dance, C. 149–57, 251–4
De'Ath, E. 26
Department for Education and Skills 43, 50
Department of Health 34, 38, 49, 49–50, 243, 254
Dixon, J. 63–6, 211–14

Emerson, E. 115–23, 235–40

Farmer, E. 85–104, 228–32

Ghate, D. 58–63, 207–11
Gibbs, I. 85–104, 224–7
Glendinning, C. 108–14, 232–5

Hall, S. 66–70, 215–18
Hatton, C. 115–23, 235–40
Hazel, N. 58–63, 207–11
Henricson, C. 33
Herzog Jr, A. 187
Holiday, B. 187
Holman, R. 254
Home Office 35, 41, 44, 142
Hughes, M. 157–69, 254–8

Johnson, T. 251

Kirk, S. 108–14, 232–5

Lauderdale, M. 251
Lipscombe, J. 85–104, 228–32

McGuire, C. 134–41, 243–7
Morse, C. 66–70, 215–18
Moyers, S. 85–104, 228–32

Olsen, R. 123–32, 240–3
O'Neill, T. 149–57

Pitt, C. 66–70, 215–18
Pugh, G. 26

Quigley, M. 63–6, 211–14
Quinton, D. 251

Rayner, A. 71–3, 218–19
Reid, M. 66–70, 215–18
Robertson, J. 63–6, 115–23, 211–14, 235–40
Robinson, M. 211
Rushton, A. 149–57, 251–4

Scott, S. 74–6
Selber, K. 251
Shah, R. 115–23, 235–40
Sinclair, I. 85–104, 224–7
Sizer, C. 71–3, 218–19
Sloper, P. 117
Smith M. 63–6, 66–70, 211–14, 215–18
Sonuga-Barke, E. 71–3, 218–19
Stevenson, J. 71–3, 218–19
Sylva, K. 74–6

Taylor, G. 71–3, 218–19
Thoburn, J. 254
Thompson, M. 71–3, 218–19
Tunstill, J. 157–69, 254–8
Turner, S. 117

Warren, C. 254
Wedge, P. 142–8, 247–51
Whitehead, E. 63–6, 211–14
Wilson, K. 85–104, 224–7